D0057007

AN AMERICAN MUSIC

AN American Music

THE SEARCH FOR AN AMERICAN MUSICAL IDENTITY

Barbara L. Tischler

New York Oxford
OXFORD UNIVERSITY PRESS
1986

Oxford University Press
Oxford New York Toronto
Delhi Bombay Calcutta Madras Karachi
Petaling Jaya Singapore Hong Kong Tokyo
Nairobi Dar es Salaam Cape Town
Melbourne Auckland

and associated companies in
Beirut Berlin Ibadan Nicosia

Published by Oxford University Press, Inc.,
200 Madison Avenue, New York, New York 10016

Library of Congress Cataloging-in-Publication Data
Tischler, Barbara L., 1949–
An American music.
Bibliography: p.
Includes index.
1. Music—United States—20th century—History and criticism. 2. Music and society. I. Title.
ML200.5.T55 1986 781.773'09'042 85-29882
ISBN 0-19-504023-6

9 8 7 6 5 4 3 2 1

Printed in the United States of America

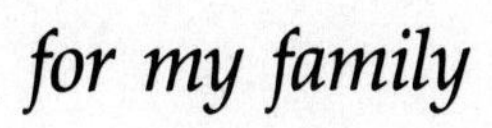

for my family

Acknowledgments

A number of institutions and individuals helped me to understand history and write this book. The Society of Fellows in the Humanities at Columbia University, under the chairmanship first of Richard Brilliant and then of Eugene Rice, was an exciting and challenging "home" during my two years as an Andrew Mellon Postdoctoral Fellow in the Humanities. I benefited from the critical ear of my colleagues and the never-flagging intellectual enthusiasm and personal friendship of the Society's director, Mrs. Loretta Nassar. In 1981–82, an American Association of University Women fellowship enabled me to spend a year writing when this project was still in its dissertation form, and a research grant from the Sinfonia Foundation also helped in this endeavor. The Department of History at Columbia University was generous in its financial and intellectual support of my work throughout my graduate career.

Studying history at Columbia for this former musician was made possible by more than institutional support, and several members of the department deserve special thanks for their critical enthusiasm for my work. Stuart Bruchey was a master's essay adviser whose pleasure in a well-written paragraph was matched only by his enthusiasm for a well-conceived idea, and my writing and thinking grew under his guidance. Sigmund Diamond brought his experience and insight to bear on the challenge of how to create a researchable project from an interesting idea. From Alden Vaughan, Nathan Huggins (now of Harvard University), and William Leuchtenburg (now of the University of North Carolina) I learned valuable lessons concerning the craft of historical analysis and the joy of reading and writing good history. All three of these scholars devoted considerable time and energy to my questions and speculations on this and other projects. Jack Beeson of Columbia's Music Department was an attentive and helpful dissertation reader who helped me to clarify some of my ideas about the complexity of music in America and American music. A major influence on the development of this project as a dissertation and as a book was the thoughtful commentary and lively interest of Walter Metzger. His remarks generally provoked more questions than answers, and he entertained enough ideas in our discussions for more than one book. Ultimately, he allowed me to design my own project and take responsibility for it. A good adviser cannot do more.

Sometimes friends and colleagues provide the right encouragement and substantive ideas at just the right time. Tom Bender of New York University read a draft of the manuscript and provided some organizational suggestions that helped me to highlight the strengths of this research on American cultural history. Jack Salzman, the director of the Center for American Culture Studies at Columbia, also offered valuable advice on the manuscript at an early stage. Neil Weil provided technical assistance that made it possible to make the transition from scissors and tape to a more sophisticated editing method.

Extremely helpful people at Oxford University Press deserve special thanks. Sheldon Meyer saw value in this project and offered important suggestions for improving it. Leona Capeless was a meticulous and thoughtful editor whose questions often sparked new ideas, and Pamela Nicely provided valuable assistance at the copy editing stage.

My best critic has always been my husband, Steven Tischler. His support transcends proofreading, child care, and much-valued support for my professional attainments to include even a toleration for the most experimental modern music. Because he has been willing to ask difficult questions and challenge my answers, the years of dissertation and manuscript writing have produced a better book. Because of his love and enthusiasm, those years have also been great fun!

B.L.T.

New York
January 1986

Contents

AN AMERICAN MUSIC

Introduction

The history of concert music in the United States has been punctuated by periodic calls for a compositional idiom that reflects the American experience. This history has also been characterized by an equally strong debate regarding the best methods and materials with which to create such a recognizably national style. The absence of much well-known nineteenth-century concert music that claims a particular American identity as compared with the significant body of works composed between 1935 and 1945 that seem to be "about" America (many of these by such important composers as Aaron Copland, Virgil Thomson, Roy Harris, and others) has encouraged an analysis that emphasizes a gradual separation from European influences and an awakening cultural consciousness on the part of American composers and audiences.

This book argues that the appearance of American composers as serious competitors for audience and critical recognition coincided not with a retreat from Europe but an increased involvement in the forging of modern music in cities like Rome, Vienna, and especially, Paris. If American composers have come of age in the twentieth century, as indeed they have, they have done so not as self-conscious Americanists who shunned the European musical models that had so long dominated the cultural *Welt* in this country but as activists in the international search for new music by the 1920s.

The importance of the modern movement to American musical development has been underestimated, as historians and musicologists have often looked for a continuous evolution of an American musical personality, especially by the beginning of the twentieth century. David Ewen wrote in 1942, for example, that the 1920s was a crucial decade for the maturation of the American composer's skills and talent, as it was then that he

> became more sure of himself, less inclined to look across the ocean for models, more confident than ever before in American potentialities and resources. This reorientation, a postwar phenomenon, was a most significant trend. Once the American composer no longer felt himself inferior to Europe, he could cultivate in his own way and achieve unrestricted fertility.[1]

Ewen was correct about the importance of the 1920s, but he cited the wrong reasons. As young Americans flocked to Europe to study after World War I, they replicated a pattern long-established by their predecessors. But it was *what* they studied that represented a change in direction as well as an opportunity to compare their creative efforts with those of their European counterparts on an almost equal footing. It was not the cultivation of a national music for the concert hall but the participation in an international quest for "new" music that gave the American composer the tools with which to achieve "unrestricted fertility" in the years following World War I. And in the midst of the enthusiasm for American scenes and popular and folk music between 1935 and 1945, it was the composer trained in the techniques of modern composition who achieved considerable success with his excursions into popular Americana.

It is hardly new to argue that American composers imitated their European teachers in the nineteenth century. In spite of calls for an American declaration of cultural independence, this society had other, more immediate problems. It was the resolution of such necessary matters as settlement and expansion as well as the emergence of middle and upper classes to support institutions of high culture that made it possible for concert music to establish itself, as least in this country's major cities, prior to the twentieth century. But before American composers could claim to have found the essence of national cultural identity in historical inspiration or rhetorical assertions of musical independence, they first had to grapple with Michel Guillaume Jean de Crèvecoeur's famous question of the 1780s, "What is an American?"

European composers in the mid-nineteenth century seldom had difficulty with the question of how to express a national identity in their music. For most writers of nonprogrammatic symphonies, concerti, and overtures, the issue was simply irrelevant. While the Romantic musical sound of this period is usually associated with German cultural identity, there is little that is identifiably "German" in a Schubert symphony or a Beethoven piano concerto. It was simply the case that composers who could call themselves culturally, if not yet nationally, German were those who were most active in advancing the approach to composition that dominated European music outside of the French and Italian opera houses. Interestingly, even where a homogeneous folk culture and nationalist political currents inspired composers to express patriotic sentiments in music (Smetana in Bohemia and Grieg in Norway come to mind in this context), they expressed these feelings, which were often explicitly anti-German, in music whose stylistic exemplars were German.

Most nineteenth-century American composers also gave little thought to the issue of cultural expressions of national pride. They followed in the footsteps of their European teachers by writing symphonic music without a nonmusical program or pieces with appropriately faraway and fantastic literary inspiration. Those few Americans who hoped to create a national music did not envision their goal outside of the context of the musical Romanticism in which they had been trained, and they could not have anticipated that the "liberation" of the American composer from his perceived European fetters would result not from a rejection of Europe but from an international re-evaluation of the question of what constitutes music. It is no wonder that most of the music of the self-consciously American composers of nineteenth-century concert music sounds as if it could have been written anywhere. Without its title, there is no way to determine the nationality of the patriotic intentions of a piece like *Tyler's Grand Veto Quick Step*, composed in 1844 by the immigrant and proudly American composer Anthony Philip Heinrich.

At the beginning of the twentieth century, a group of American Romantic composers attempted to place folk and popular music into symphonic works for the concert hall. These nationalists by quotation answered at least part of Crèvecoeur's question by asserting that America could find its musical identity in local versions of transplanted English folk ballads, Indian tribal melodies, and spirituals and work songs of Afro-American slaves. Such "exotic" material was musical seasoning intended to provide a dash of regional or national flavor to compositions that otherwise diverged hardly at all from accepted patterns of nineteenth-century Romantic orchestral writing.

Why did the nationalists by quotation fail to contribute significantly to the American musical repertoire, while Smetana, Grieg, Sibelius, and other European nationalists had succeeded before them in writing Romantic music that expressed a recognizable national identity? The issue here is not strictly one of musical quality, and the point here is not to argue whether Henry F. Gilbert's *Dance in the Place Congo* is any better or worse than, for example, Smetana's *Má Vlast*. Rather, it is important to understand that Smetana succeeded because we recognize his work as a statement of Bohemian or Czech nationalism that utilized folk tunes common to an entire nation, and we have to read program notes to realize that Gilbert intended to write American music by quoting some of the melodies and rhythmic patterns performed in Congo Square in New Orleans.

One explanation of the failure of American musical nationalism through the quotation of folk music lies in the absence of a homogeneous population with a peasant or folk culture that could provide music recognizable by an entire population as American. European concert music composers had a tradition of country dances and folk melodies from which to draw for their compositions. And the period from the end of the Napoleonic Wars to World War I was an age of nationalism for Germans and the peoples of the Austro-Hungarian Empire. Shared ethnic and cultural experiences that had prevailed for centuries preceded political movements for nationhood. Even though the absolutely homogeneous population and the purely recognizable musical idiom were probably abstractions at best, European populations with a common heritage could more closely approximate this ideal than could the United States at the beginning of the twentieth century, a time when its population was heterogeneous and its cultural patterns were strongly influenced by foreign currents.

At the heyday of American musical nationalism by quotation around World War I, musical Romanticism itself was experiencing a fundamental challenge to its continued vitality as a means for expression for composers throughout the Western world. As early as the 1880s, with the emergence of musical Impressionism in France, this challenge to the familiar brought forth a plethora of new and, to many, strange ideas about the nature and structure of music. For many American composers, the issue of cultural nationalism was abandoned for a time as irrelevant to the current debate over modernism in the 1920s. Later, the idea of "saying something about America" in concert music would be incorporated into these same composers' notions of modern music.

What united European and American modernist composers was a criticism within the profession of the purpose and intrinsic value of their art as well as a search for new technical means. Central to that search, and something that was stated explicitly by many modernist composers, painters, and other creative artists, was a dissatisfaction with the ideas and techniques of the immediate past. Of course, the creation of something new always suggests a rejection of at least some elements of the past. But the modernist, instead of abandoning recent forms while preserving the basic structure of his art, sought new art forms *and* new ideas of meaning in his creative work. For many, the tonal system in music and representation in painting, for example, had to yield to a new ordering of the relationship of musical pitches (as in the twelve-tone row) and the notion that such elements as color, shape, and line had meanings independent of the whole canvas that had to be experienced rather than seen in the traditional sense.[2]

Such new concepts formed for many artists a philosophical basis from which new art could be created, explained, and even justified. In music, the transition from the massive late Romantic orchestral sound to the minimalist perspective in chamber music, the so-called anarchy of the Futurist and Dadaist sight-and-sound productions, the rigor but not rigidity of serialist technique, and the incorporation of Baroque and Classical procedures and forms into modern works must have seemed more than dramatic to audiences that witnessed the results in curiosity, amazement, and often horror.

Early twentieth-century modern musical practice was diverse, if not scattered. For this reason, modern music remains an interesting phenomenon for study because, even though some of the "revolutionary" music of the avant-garde sounds tame today, the search for a music free of the limits of the tonal system and conventional rhythmic configurations continues. What was new in the early decades of the twentieth century was a rejection of Romanticism, and this rejection represented a more profound leap into the unknown of modernity than even those post-World War II technological changes that have made possible electronically generated sounds and computer-composed works. In our own decade, whether we compose with a synthesizer and a stop watch or write music that uses the orchestra of the nineteenth century to perform scores that composers of that century would not understand without considerable explanation, the goal is still to organize sound in interesting ways.[3]

The artistic changes of the early decades of the twentieth century were particularly important to the American concert music composer. Previously shunned in his own country unless his music had a recognizable "made in Europe" quality, he had generally eschewed national identification in his art. When he did begin to use folk music or historical and patriotic inspiration, he invited disapproval, even scorn, for bringing the vulgar music of poor southern white settlers, Indians, and slaves into the respectable concert hall. For the composer who considered himself a modernist, audience and critical responses to his experiments were no more positive, but he no longer agonized over whether his music was "American." It was simply modern music that, along with the new music of his European counterparts, displayed a novel approach to the craft of composition. If the path to success in the nineteenth century had lain in the imitation of the music of Europe, and if nationalism by quotation brought forth hybrid pieces that were neither particularly American nor particularly new and interesting, then the direction for many American composers by the 1920s was away from both Romantic musical convention and audible American references and national labels and toward the creation of international modern music. Ironically, it was the experience with modern compositional experimentation in the years around World War I that equipped some Americans by the mid-1930s to look to their own environment and compose music that touched familiar chords, even as it was characterized by modern sound and technique.

This book examines the interaction of European and American influences on this country's concert music, first in the context of the nineteenth century when most American music sounded as if it had been composed in Berlin or Vienna, and then as American composers joined the modern movement in the early twentieth century. The earlier century provides us with assertions of the need for musical independence as well as various celebrations of national power and accomplishment at which America's praises were sung to the strains of European and European-inspired compositions. The "100% Americanism" of the World War I period brought to the forefront the issue of American dependence on European, specifically German, music and serves as a period of transition for this study because after the War Americans resumed their study in Europe and came home well-versed in the new music. The modernist context allows for an examination of the various ways in which composers tried to reach a broad audience, sometimes even as regionalists or Americanists.

The early twentieth-century American composer did not achieve "unrestricted fertility" by tending his own garden. Instead, he found a stimulating, if less secure, environment in the realm of the new. His was one of a chorus of voices that sang the praises of experimental sounds and techniques. And when he looked homeward in the late 1920s to the jazz of the urban scene or in the late 1930s to populist visions of America, he found that the flexibility of his modern language even allowed him to be an Americanist if he chose. No longer writing with quotation marks around folk tunes, he could develop folk materials using techniques that revealed his commitment to one or more varieties of modern musical practice, thereby expressing an American identity in modern music for the concert hall. Many of his works are still performed today. The modern American composer of the first half of the twentieth century provided the first satisfactory answer to the question of how to create a concert music of his own.

1

Perceptions of Concert Music in the United States

Prior to the beginning of the twentieth century, American concert audiences almost always heard imported music, and arbiters of good taste whose opinions influenced what composers wrote and what performers sang or played offered judgments that transcended technical discussions of melodic contour and formal musical architecture. Clothed in the security of universal "truths" about art and society, these observers of music in America tended to denigrate this country's various folk traditions because of their persumed inapproriateness for the concert hall. At the same time, they were often skeptical of attempts to manufacture high culture in the European manner in their own country.

But in spite of critical disapprobation and audience inattention, there has been no shortage of American musical creativity, from the psalm singing of the early Puritan settlers to the efforts of immigrant and native-born American composers in the nineteenth and early twentieth centuries in this country's major urban areas. Throughout our national history, there have been periodic calls for the development of a unique American music that would derive its inspiration from the native environment and historical context and also withstand comparison with the "good" music imported from Europe. Various responses by music and social critics to this creative effort reveal a process of gradual acceptance of an American music of one genre or another into the European-dominated realm of high culture.

Whether or not writing about music can be reduced to "scientific" principles about art, such commentary reveals as much about the cultural context for art as it does about art itself. In the early twentieth century, such European critics as Sir William Hadow, Michel Dimitri

Calvocoressi, and Ernest Newman attempted to formulate precise theories about critical method and criteria for judging music for the concert hall. Writing in the *Edinburgh Review* in 1906, Hadow declined to define this critical standard precisely, but he did express fear of its abandonment. "Such abrogation," he wrote, "would reduce the republic of art to the level of Plato's democracy, where there is no government and no order, where Jack is as good as his master, and where the very beasts of burden contest your title to the roadway."[1] Such a call for a unified critical method and standards foundered because it emerged as Western music itself was experiencing profound challenges to its nineteenth-century presumptions, and it was no longer possible in the new century to agree on a universal foundation for musical aesthetics.

Even before Hadow's plea for high artistic and critical standards, George Bernard Shaw, who could claim the title of both cultural and social critic, recognized the impossibility of divorcing a critic from his background and prejudices. While he did not defend the completely subjective approach to criticism advocated by Anatole France and Claude Debussy, Shaw reminded his readers that they could not escape

> the critic's tempers, his impatiences, his sorenesses, his friendships, his spite, his enthusiasms (amatory and other), nay his very politics and religion if they are touched by what he criticizes. They are all there hard at work; and it should be his point of honor—as it certainly is his interest if he wishes to avoid being dull—not to attempt to conceal them or to offer their product as the dispassionate dictum of infallible omniscience.[2]

Shaw did not repeat Richard Wagner's declaration of the mid-nineteenth century that the "immoral" profession of musical criticism should be abolished, but he did advise readers to question judgments emanating from all critical pens, including his own.

But if musical commentary from critics and social commentators reflected only the idiosyncrasies of particular writers, it would be of little value to the cultural historian. Such commentary can and often does provide insights into views of culture and society that have resonance far beyond the context of a particular performance. In most historical periods, arbiters of musical taste have expressed strikingly similar views on the quality of music in this country as well as the nature and value of music whose composers claimed the designation "American."

It is worth noting that the critics of Hadow's opinion who claimed a degree of scientific objectivity in their evaluations of music and performances as well as those who, like Shaw, offered no such objective standard and forced their readers to accept their views at face value, contributed to a critical canon that remains in force in the twentieth century. Members of the educated audience read what the critics have to say, and composers and performers worry about the content of the same print, radio, or television reviews. The opinions expressed by arbiters of musical taste reveal as much about the critic and his political and cultural context as they do about the music itself.

Most cultural commentators and arbiters of good taste prior to World War I held to a vision of American culture founded on European models. In the context of their comments on music, these men expressed their opinions on issues as far-reaching as the nature and vitality of American democracy. As connoisseurs of fine music, educators, reformers, and, in many cases, spokesmen for established cultural institutions, they add to our understanding of critical and historical judgment in matters of culture as well as the world view of a particular class of cultural commentators. A representative sample of writings about music helps to enliven as well as clarify the narrative of American musical development to World War I.

Such revealing commentary often appears in unlikely places. In the earliest English settlements in America the production and consumption of high culture generally took a back seat to the establishment of a physical and spiritual community in the new land. The importance of art to the young society was questioned by a Bostonian in 1719 who asserted that a farmer who raises grain

> is more serviceable to Mankind, than the Painter who draws only to please the Eye. The hungry Man would count fine pictures but a mean Entertainment. The Carpenter who builds a good House to defend us from the Wind and Weather, is more serviceable than the curious Carver, who employs art to please his fancy. This condemns not Painting nor Carving but only shows that what's more serviceable to Mankind, is much preferable to what is less necessary.[3]

Curious carver and musician alike faced the fact that their talents would be more appreciated if they could be turned to practical, material uses. In colonial America we find useful objects decorated in a beautiful and original manner by artisans who exhibited the talents of artists. A few colonial composers turned their attention to the task of creating original and useful music for worship and entertainment. The tension between materialism and culture, between the physical and economic requirements of the many and the ability of the few to consume and of an even smaller few to create works of art, existed in this country's earliest settlements.

The Europeans who settled in the New World in the seventeenth century brought with them a musical heritage in addition to their religious beliefs and political traditions. English patterns exerted an important, if not the predominating, influence on culture in the colonies.[4] But almost as soon as the settlers began to make music, they began a process of adapting English models to suit their New World needs. The extent to which this process took place varied considerably from region to region. New Englanders, for example, were not content merely to use what they had brought from England. In contrast, the Virginian William Byrd, according to historian Thomas J. Werternbaker,

> took his Latin, Greek, and Hebrew authors or the sermons of the good parish minister, very much as he would take a bottle of wine, as something already prepared for the good of his mind and soul. But the Bostonians wanted to have a hand themselves in the fermenting of their intellectual wine, and though what they produced was often a bit sour, at least it was in part their own creation.[5]

This disparity was also reflected in the type of music and the purposes that it served in New England and the South. Southern gentlemen who could afford to import music and musicians were consumers of the finest products of Europe's secular culture. In contrast, the New England Puritans focused on religious music that they created themselves. The first tentative step toward the formation of an American musical culture emerged from their struggle to purify the practice of congregational worship, of which the singing of psalms was an important part.

Psalm singing, the chanting or melodic rendering of the poetry of the Old Testament Book of Psalms, was a collective activity in colonial New England. Worshipers sang psalms at the meetinghouse or at home in family gatherings, and there were no choirs or highly trained professional musicians to impose the standards of European court or high church on Puritan religious and musical expression. Indeed, the singing of psalms was regarded only as a means of highlighting the interpretation of the poetry. The compilers of *The Whole Booke of Psalmes Faithfully Translated into English Meter*, known commonly as the *Bay Psalm Book*, argued forcefully against elegant settings of these texts with the assertion, "God's altar needs not our polishings,"

> and so we have attended conscience rather than elegance, fidelity rather than poetry, in translating the Hebrew words into English language and David's poetry into English metre; that we may sing in Sion the Lord's songs of praise according to his own will.[6]

Because the Puritans put sincerity of worship before elegance of singing style, they placed little importance on the ability to read music. But over several generations, as worshipers sang their individual versions of the *Bay Psalm Book* tunes, some ministers and would-be musical reformers decried the cacophonous results of this collective fading of memory and inability to read musical notation. The practices of "lining out" the melody or "setting the key" by a member of the congregation who could remember the appropriate tune or choose a singable key often led to disastrous results. Judge Samuel Sewall wrote of one such experience in his diary for October 25, 1691: "After evening exercise, 2d part of 84th Ps. Litchfield; I knew not that [I] had the Tune till [I] got to the 2d line, being somewhat surprised . . . and the Tune I guess'd at, was in so high a Key that I could not reach it."[7]

By the 1720s many ministers in New England had joined a crusade for "Regular Singing," in which worshipers learned the rudiments of note reading in order to be able to sing approximately the same tune at the same time for any given psalm. Opponents of this innovation defended the practices of lining out a melody and setting the key by one confident member of the congregation as "Usual Singing," a traditional part of worship that could not be altered, no matter how the resulting cacophony assaulted the ear. But Cotton Mather, an astute observer of colonial life in Massachusetts and a staunch defender of the philosophy and standards of the founding Puritan settlers, was a partisan for the Regular Singing cause. His tract *The Accomplished Singer*, published in Boston in 1721, was a defense of the new musical practices in the interest of maintaining tonal order in the meetinghouse.[8] The title page of this pamphlet indicates that Mather considered the questions,

> First, how the Piety of *Singing* with a true DEVOTION may be obtained and expressed, the glorious GOD after an uncommon manner Glorified in it, and His People Edified. And then, how the MELODY of REGULAR SINGING, and the SKILL of doing it, according to the RULES of it may be easily arrived unto.[9]

In addition to defending Regular Singing, Mather sounded a theme in his writings on music that would become a preoccupation of many critics in the nineteenth century, the elevation of intellectual and aesthetic standards as well as religious expression. Such elevation could be achieved only through the appropriate use of the right music. Mather made it clear in *The Accomplished Singer* that just any tune would not do, nor would any haphazard variety of group singing suffice for singing God's praises. He favored "such a *Modulation* of *the Voice,* as will naturally express the *Satisfaction* and *Elevation* of the *Mind*, which a Grave SONG shall be expressive of."[10] Musical unity, at least in congregational singing, could best be achieved through the implementation of Regular Singing.

In a society in which church discipline was perceived as important to community discipline, it seemed appropriate for ministers to pass judgments on the music that was such an integral part of worship. Orderly singing and orderly activity in the meetinghouse were necessary to the maintenance of the covenants of the founding Puritan settlers. Ministers and others in the early eighteenth century looked with growing alarm at the rise and diversity in population, the limited land resources of many towns, and an increasing preoccupation with material rather than spiritual matters as signs of deterioration of the very fabric of society. Richard Bushman commented in his case study of Connecticut during this period that seventeenth-century society had been stable because

> it was relatively static. Society in 1690 was still clearly fashioned on the pattern that the first settlers envisioned. During the eighteenth century rapid expansion was to place greater strains on society than the agencies of government could bear. By 1765, after a series of disruptions, a new society would be in the making.[11]

Interestingly, while the ministers and musical reformers who perceived that their society and worship were in decline hoped to return to what they thought was the perfection of the previous century, they turned to new techniques to accomplish this end. But the reformers would find that the innovation of Regular Singing would not bring back the old fervor in worship. Instead, this development encouraged the founding of singing schools to teach the basic elements of note reading and of choirs to put the new technique into practice. The singing school gave rise to the singing master, a teacher who often was also a composer of the music that his pupils practiced and his choirs performed.

In the latter half of the eighteenth century, the Stoughton, Massachusetts, singing school was one locus of the creative activity of an original early American composer, William Billings. A tanner by trade, Billings had no training in the European musical styles of his day, and his music represents the tradition of the meetinghouse and singing school rather than the courts and churches of Europe. Just as Billings composed with little regard for the standard rules of composition, he encouraged other composers to do the same. In his *New-England Psalm Singer* (1770) he even suggested that future musical creators not even follow his models, asserting instead that "it is best for every composer to be his own Carver."[12]

Billings was both the subject and the author of some early and unusual musical commentary in Boston. *The New-England Psalm Singer,* comprised one hundred twenty-six canons, anthems, and other pieces composed in a style "as plain and simple as possible; and yet [I] have tried to the utmost of my power to preserve the modern Air and manner of singing."[13] By this, Billings meant that he had maintained the block harmony style of setting many of his melodies, while reserving a more florid, or "modern" compositional technique for others. But his critics took him to task for avoiding dissonance, claiming that the music in this collection sounded old-fashioned.[14]

In response to this criticism, Billings included in his next collection, *The Singing Master's Assistant* (1778), the tune *Jargon* that contains hardly a consonant sound. The piece was a joke and the words reveal Billings's mock seriousness:

> Let horrid Jargon split the air,
> And rive the nerves asunder;
> Let hateful discord greet the ear,
> As terrible as thunder![15]

Billings continued his response with an address to the Goddess of Discord. The manifesto begins:

> DREAD SOVEREIGN—I have been sagacious enough of late, to discover some evil-minded persons have insinuated to your highness, that I am utterly unmindful of your Ladyship's importance; and that my time, as well as my talents, was wholly taken up in paying my devotion to your most implacable enemy and strenuous opposer, viz. the GODDESS OF CONCORD; which representation is as false as it is ill-natured; for your ladyship may believe me without hesitation, when I assure you on the word of an honest man, that knowing your Ladyship to be of a very captious disposition, I have always been very careful of trespassing on your grounds for fear of incurring your displeasure, so far as to excite you to take vengeance (which is well known to be your darling attribute).[16]

Far from putting the criticism to rest, the address to the Goddess sparked yet another critical response. According to many accounts, soon after the publication of *The Singing Master's Assistant*, Billings found two screaming cats hanging by their tails from the door of his shop. This unusual cultural commentary did not prevent Billings from continuing to compose in his own style and contributing to the song literature of the American Revolution (as with his anthem *Chester*), in spite of the economic hardships attendant to pursuing a musical career in eighteenth-century New England.

While nineteenth-century critics often found Billings's music to be rough, unattractive, and not consistent with the rules that governed musical composition in his day, much of his music was popular with his contemporaries, not only in his native Boston and Philadelphia, but as far away as the frontier town of Marietta, Ohio.[17] One admiring critic called Billings' "the rival of Handel," whose music "will recommend itself to the judges of musical merit, in *Europe* as well as in *America*." In the immediate post-Revolutionary decade, it was common to find assertions of the value of anything American, particularly in comparison with the products of Europe. This critic made much of Billings's autodidacticism, and while he did not claim this as a particularly American trait, he did assert that the English, our rivals in almost all things but clearly still more advanced in musical matters, "will pay proper tribute to his merit, as soon as they are acquainted with his productions."[18] Billings, hailed as a self-taught American genius by some, ended his life in poverty and was practically ignored and certainly underrated by students of American music until the twentieth century.

The Revolutionary War generation contained a number of Americans with the means and talent to pursue their musical interests and contribute to the cultural life of the new nation. Francis Hopkinson, for example, was a prominent Philadelphia lawyer and signer of the Declaration of Independence who was an amateur composer and cultural connoisseur.[19] In 1788 he dedicated a collection of his songs to George Washington, and he was also an active collector and publisher of music by European composers, thereby helping to acquaint other musical amateurs in the colonies with cultural trends in Europe.

Thomas Jefferson and Benjamin Franklin were also talented amateur musicians who helped to elevate American cultural standards by bringing fine European music to the new United States. Jefferson was a moderately accomplished violinist who hoped to establish his own group of performing musicians at Monticello. He inquired of a Parisian correspondent in 1778 whether laborers might be found in France who could ply their trade here and also "perform on the French horn, clarinet or hautboy and bassoon." He would have implemented his plan to hire these workers "but for the bounds of an American fortune [that] will not admit the indulgence of a domestic band of musicians."[20]

Franklin played the guitar, harp, and a type of dulcimer called the sticcado pastorale, and he put his imagination to work on a process for improving the tone of the harpsichord. Although he was an aficionado of fine culture, Franklin was not always content to accept the European musical product uncritically. He argued against those popular musical artifices of his day that rendered a vocal line unintelligible, and he even attacked the ornate vocal writing of the renowned George Frederick Handel. He likened such "unnatural" musical devices as trills and ornaments to wigs, which had first been used "to imitate a good natural head of hair; but when they became fashionable, though in unnatural forms, we have seen natural hair dressed to look like wigs."[21]

Recognizing that creative musical personalities were beginning to emerge on this side of the Atlantic, Franklin noted in 1763 that, as the necessities of settlement had been taken care of, it was now possible to think about the development of culture and cultural institutions in the new nation. "Already," he observed, "some of our young geniuses begin to lisp attempts at Painting, Poetry, and Musick." He boasted to Mary Stevenson of "a young Painter [Benjamin West] now studying at Rome," and he sent her some recent American poetry and musical compositions by "a young friend of mine" (presumably Francis Hopkinson) who was "a great admirer of Mr. [John] Stanley's musical Compositions, and has adapted this Piece to an Air in the 6th Concerto of that Gentleman."[22] Miss Stevenson forwarded the piece by the young American to the English organist for his comments and suggestions, which the latter provided.

Hopkinson, Jefferson, Franklin, and others for whom music was important, albeit an embellishment, helped to enliven the cultural life of the Revolutionary period by acquainting themselves with the best work that European and American artists, writers, and musicians could create. They contributed to the development of an American cultural consciousness which, in turn, further encouraged creativity here.

But even the stirrings of American political and cultural consciousness did not inhibit the acceptance, even the predominance in the cities, of European culture and an interaction between European immigrant composers and their new environment. The 1790s saw a flowering of interest in imported music in urban areas where audiences were already familiar with a variety of entertainments from Europe. English theatrical troupes had performed in the colonies from the construction of the first theater in Williamsburg in 1716, and Lewis Hallam's company of English players performed in New York from 1753. Other popular amusements included Punch and Judy shows, trapeze artists, a clown named "Pickle Herring," and scientific exhibitions.[23] In addition, urban audiences attended concerts and dramatic productions that featured the music of European composers, some of whom had recently settled in the United States.

The professional musicians who migrated to this country after the Revolution settled primarily in Philadelphia, New York, and Boston, cities that grew in size and importance and soon replaced the smaller southern cities of Charleston and Williamsburg that had been important during the colonial period. In order to earn a livelihood, they were simultaneously composers, performers, concert managers or theater directors, and teachers. While these musical jacks-of-all-trades struggled to survive economically, they generally were not called upon to teach drawing, languages, and dancing, as had some of their predecessors, nor did most of them die in poverty, as had William Billings.

Alexander Reinagle in Philadelphia, Benjamin Carr and James Hewitt in New York, and Johann Christian Gottlieb Graupner in Boston were well-schooled and enterprising immigrant composers whose success after the Revolution illustrated that there was indeed a place for the cultural entrepreneur in America's growing cities. Reinagle composed ballad operas on the English model; Carr edited a journal, published new compositions, and ran a music business; and Graupner helped to found Boston's Philharmonic Society and the famous Handel and Haydn Society. Hewitt ventured into the realm of American patriotic music with a keyboard piece, *The Battle of Trenton,* which quoted the popular *Yankee Doodle.*[24]

The music that middle- and upper-class audiences heard in urban theaters sometimes reflected the political passions of the post-Revolutionary period. Federalists and their opponents alike were not averse to using a familiar tune with new and timely lyrics to improve their popular standing at election time. Composers knew that they could draw larger audiences and increase the sales of their printed pieces by using popular tunes to support one, the other, or even both political points of view. Federalists and Jeffersonians both found musical references to approve in Benjamin Carr's *Federal Overture,* his most famous composition. Published in 1794, this work included nine familiar songs, including *Yankee Doodle,* the Federalist *Washington's March,* and *Ça Ira* and *The Marseilles Hymn,* both of which were identified with the anti-Federalist cause. Interestingly, Carr pleased both American political parties with English and French melodies. In music, as in politics in the early days of the republic, American attitudes and party loyalty were shaped in large part by allegiance or hostility to the major European powers.

Carr also contributed to the discovery of a new American patriotic song. In the first issue of *The Gentleman's Amusement,* he published the tune to Philip Phile's *President's March.* Phile's tune attracted the attention of the actor Gilbert Fox, who asked Joseph Hopkinson, son of the composer Francis Hopkinson, to fit patriotic words to the march. Fox sang the new song, *Hail Columbia,* at the New Theater in Philadelphia on April 25, 1798, and it soon became one of the country's most popular patriotic tunes, appealing to both Federalists and Jeffersonians. In this instance the European influence on American music was considerable, as the composer of the original *President's March* was very likely the German immigrant Philip Pfeil. We know little of his background, but his contribution to the music of his day has remained in the patriotic repertoire of the nation.

As art music established itself in urban theaters and concert halls, older traditions of hymn and psalm singing held fast in smaller communities and in the countryside. Unlike their professional counterparts in the cities who put American texts to European tunes, the psalm and hymn tune writers in rural areas tended to be amateur composers who did not necessarily follow the established stylistic principles of cultivated music. These spiritual descendants of William Billings, including Daniel Read, Timothy Swan, and Jeremiah Ingalls, represented a continuation of the eighteenth-century musical tradition that was soon relegated to a lesser position in mainstream American musical history. While these composers contributed to local worship, their work did not affect the continuing development of high culture in America's cities.[25]

The immediate post-Revolutionary period also saw an effort by some well-educated American composers to incorporate the styles of European music into church music here. Andrew Law, Samuel Holyoke, and Oliver Holden advocated dignity rather than chaos in religious music. In the name of musical and spiritual reform, they used the melodies of Handel, Haydn, and Mozart for the setting of devotional texts rather than original melodies by American self-taught composers. Books such as the *Massachusetts Compiler of Theoretical and Practical Elements of Sacred Vocal Music* included what its editors, all of whom were cultivated American composers who favored "good" music for religious purposes, regarded as the best examples of European compositional style and technique.[26]

Andrew Law even went so far as to attack native musical compositions as "faulty."[27] Law, who early in his career had included some pieces by American composers in his collections, ceased to do so by the close of the eighteenth century. For him as for others who denigrated the attempts at American culture that Franklin had lauded only a few years before, religious and cultural purity could be achieved only with the proper musical settings. This music came from recognized European masters and their American imitators. This position was supported by critics such as John Hubbard, a professor of Mathematics and Moral Philosophy at Dartmouth College. Although he was not a musician, Hubbard was an active observer of the New England musical scene who had little praise for the fuguing tunes and psalm settings of Billings's generation, arguing that

> to catch any idea from such a chaos of words, uttered at the same instant of time, a hearer must be furnished with ears as numerous as the eyes of Argus. Such fuges [*sic*] must be a perversion. They cannot affect the heart, nor inform the understanding.[28]

Hubbard compiled his own collection of Thirty Anthems (1814) for use at Harvard College that contained music by Handel, Henry Purcell,

Jeremiah Clark, and William Byrd as a corrective to the current situation and as a contribution to the elevation of American musical taste.

In the early nineteenth century, many American concert music composers asserted the value of their own work as they attempted to create acceptable and recognizably American music of high quality. As if in response to the Rev. Sydney Smith's indictment of American culture,[29] American composers, both immigrant and native-born, set out to prove the worth of their contributions to art. But they faced a contradiction of which, perhaps, they were not aware: while their writings and speeches stressed the unique nature and high quality of American music, their compositions were stylistic imitations of the works of the European masters. However much they claimed that national character could be expressed in a musical portrait of the Kentucky landscape or in an opera based on a story by a writer from New York, these apologists for American music contributed little to the development of a recognizable style.

The careers of Anthony Philip Heinrich, William Henry Fry, and George F. Bristow illustrate the problem of the American composer caught between the desire to express a distinctive national identity and the demand that his compositions meet standards of "good taste." Heinrich was born in Bohemia and came to the United States in 1816. Having barely escaped economic ruin as a merchant in Europe, he suffered further reverses in this country in the depression of 1819. With no means of earning a living, he transported a love for his new country and his amateur violin-playing skills to the wilds of Kentucky. There he taught himself to compose in the manner of the European symphonic music with which he was already familiar and presented concerts of the works of Haydn, Mozart, and Beethoven, as well as his own compositions, in Louisville, Lexington, and Frankfort.

Unlike the immigrant composers of the post-Revolutionary generation who paid little attention to the question of national identity, Heinrich called himself an "American composer" within a few years of his arrival here. He attempted to portray the vastness of the American land and the greatness of its history. In the preface to *The Dawning of Music in Kentucky*, he wrote that

> the many and severe animadversions, so long and repeatedly cast on the talent for Music in this Country, has been one of the chief motives of the Author, in his exercise of his abilities; and should he be able, by this effort to create but one single *Star* in the *West*, no one would ever be more proud than himself, to be called an *American Musician*.[30]

Heinrich thought that using American scenery and national history as inspiration would rectify what he saw as an absence of specific national character in this nation's concert music. Looking at the sources of Romantic inspiration for European music, he found nature (as in a Schubert song cycle), exotic and faraway places (as in Mendelssohn's *Fingal's Cave* overture), and the realm of fantasy (as in Berlioz's *Symphonie fantastique*). Could the spirit of the country in which he now resided not also be reflected in Romantic music? Heinrich answered this question for himself with compositions like the *Texas and Oregon Grand March* and *Tyler's Grand Veto Quick Step*, both composed for piano in 1844. Among his orchestral works with specific American programs were *Pushmataha, a Venerable Chief of a Western Tribe of Indians* and *National Memories, An Heroic Overture for Full Orchestra*. Despite Heinrich's claim that these were uniquely American compositions, they sounded like European Romantic music.

Although William Henry Fry did not compose about the frontier, he too was a pioneer on behalf of America's music and composers, and he was sensitive to the difficulties faced by composers here who hoped to have their music performed by major orchestras. Audiences and concert managers assumed that good music was European music and that American composers, if any existed at all, had little to say. The presence of talented immigrants, refugees from Europe's revolutionary upheavals around 1848, only made the situation worse. Fry believed that American composers had to create their own opportunities for public exposure, and that is precisely what he did. He gave a series of lectures in New York in 1852–53, some of which included his own compositions. Fry criticized audiences for their worship of European composers, expressing his dissatisfaction that "the American public are too fond of quoting Handel, Mozart, and Beethoven, and European artists generally, and decrying whatever is not modeled after their rules." And composers were also to blame for their plight, in Fry's estimation, as he advised them to "stop imitating European models, and cut loose from foreign leading-strings in Art, as our fathers did in politics and government." In language that foreshadowed that of Charles Ives and Henry F. Gilbert, Fry asserted that the American composer should not allow the names of acknowledged European masters

> to prove an eternal bugbear to him, nor should he pay them any reverance; he should only reverance his *Art*, and strike out manfully and independently into untrodden realms, just as his nature and inspirations may incite him, else he can never achieve lasting renown.[31]

Fry insisted that the American public had to abandon its uncritical loyalty to European music or risk the prospect of never having a music of its own. He proposed that it was time for an American Declaration of Independence in the arts that would lay the foundation for

> an American School in Painting, Sculpture, and Music. Until this Declaration of Independence in Art shall be made—until American composers shall discard their foreign liveries and found an American School—and until the American public shall learn to support American artists, Art will not become indigenous to this country, but will only exist as a feeble exotic, and we shall continue to be provincial in Art.[32]

Fry saw the path to national creativity and greater artistic sophistication in the cultivation of originality, but his call for an American school of musical composition met with little enthusiasm. In the mid-nineteenth century, American composers generally studied abroad (as had Fry himself), and it is no wonder that they returned home steeped in the prevailing cultural ideas of the Continent, both in terms of their musical training and the sources of programmatic inspiration that they regarded as "appropriate" for concert music. Fry's own music bears little American national influence, as titles such as the *Santa Claus* and *Childe Harold* symphonies and *Leonora,* an opera based on a play by the English writer Edward Bulwer-Litton, indicate. Fry's music was often difficult and original, but it cannot be considered "American" in sound, as even this most ardent cultural nationalist was hard-pressed to say exactly *how* concert music in the United States should diverge from its European models. Fry offered a battle cry in his lectures, but he produced no models that other composers could imitate.

George F. Bristow, who composed an opera based on Washington Irving's story of Rip Van Winkle in 1855, was a violinist and choral director as well as a composer. He did not attempt to paint musical pictures with a distinctly national character in his music, but the choice of an American story and setting for his opera is noteworthy. Bristow was noted for refinement rather than originality, and there was little in the first production of this four-hour opera to evoke early America except a portrait of George Washington that formed part of the scenery. The music of *Rip Van Winkle* was correct, according to the standards of its time, but one reviewer noted that it was so bland that "Rip Van Winkle himself, that humorous old Dutchman, loses, by the music he has to sing, all his primitive character and in a musical sense, almost nothing but Dutch phlegm remains."[33] For most American Romantic composers of the early and mid-nineteenth century, it was easier to talk about the need for an American musical idiom than to create one. Bristow's music was appreciated, not for its "American" qualities but for its resemblance to the contemporary concert music of Europe.

The creative activity of the midcentury American Romantics was often eclipsed by that of a new generation of immigrant musicians (including Carl Bergmann, Theodore Thomas, Otto Singer, Bernard Mollenhauer,

Carl Zerrahn, and Theodore Ritter), most of whom came here from Germany. Like their English predecessors in the 1790s, these men contributed actively to the musical life of America's large cities, but they did not always find it possible to duplicate the cultural conditions they had left. Many complained of the materialism of concert promoters, the lack of sophistication of the American audience, and popular enthusiasm for the type of spectacle for which P. T. Barnum was famous. Although most of these musicians adapted to the American cultural environment even as they helped to improve it, some remained critical. Joseph Gungl, a German composer who came to the United States in the 1840s but returned to Europe within a few years, was bitter at the absence of good taste here. He commented that, however much the American may surpass the European as a businessman,

> just so much, perhaps, in all departments of the fine arts—but especially in music—is he behind all, and is therefore not capable of enjoying instrumental music. It is a matter of course, that only the so-called anti-classical can, in any degree, suit the taste of the American public: such as waltzes, galops, quadrilles—above all, polkas. That there are exceptions I cannot deny: but only a few—a very few.[34]

Perhaps the staunchest upholder of those standards of musical taste that Gungl articulated was John Sullivan Dwight. Dwight belonged to the generation of Boston reformers who identified with Transcendentalism, Fourierism, or such social causes as temperance, prison and institutional reform, the abolition of slavery, and labor reform, all of which were intended to improve the individual and society as a whole. A conservative, even reactionary, proponent of high culture, Dwight believed that the right music could civilize and elevate Americans to the status of good citizens, if only they would listen to it. As Boston's most influential musical spokesman, Dwight espoused notions of cultural improvement that were consistent with ideas of social control offered by reformers in other contemporary movements, especially in his insistence that a familiarity with European concert music could inspire order in a disordered American society.

To many middle-class native Bostonians, the growth and diversity of popular culture was indicative of a society in flux. The life of this society on the move in economic and social terms diverged sharply from the nostalgic vision of those who compared the apparent confusion of the midcentury present unfavorably with the presumed stability of the past. It also provided grist for the mill of reformers, among them Associationists like Dwight, who saw much that was in need of correction. This reform vision was one in which temperance replaced demon rum, work discipline reformed criminals and the insane, and American society would rid itself at once of the evil of slavery. Such a vision was orderly in its conception and naive in its expectations, and it is not surprising that one of its proponents should focus on culture as an aspect of American life that was also in need of improvement. Dwight sought order in America's musical life, just as he looked for clarity and understanding in society as a whole. His notion of musical reform for Americans was based almost entirely on the models of cultural propriety he knew best, those of the European concert hall and opera house.

Although Dwight was trained for the ministry, he was never permanently settled in a pulpit. He was more comfortable sermonizing in *The Dial* and in the Associationist phalanx at George Ripley's Brook Farm, where he supervised the musical life of the community and wrote and edited articles on a broad range of topics for *The Harbinger*, Brook Farm's official journal dedicated "to Social and Political Progress."

The language of Dwight's musical reviews was often that of the cultural crusader. He expressed faith in the "ministry of music" that would "prepare many minds for that great day of Humanity" in which man would achieve a true understanding of himself and his world.[35] And his enthusiasm for Handel's oratorio, *Messiah*, was expressed in phrases familiar to the members of Brook Farm:

> Associationists! Pioneers of the first humble phalanxes! Ye that can sing, learn Handel's Hallelujah chorus; it will be a grand unitary act of worship; in it may you consecrate yourselves to your sublime idea and feel your unity with one another and with the Race; for there exists no clearer prophecy of that than in such music, giving voice to the inmost spirit of the recorded prophecies of old.[36]

In 1846 Dwight commented on a series of concerts in Boston presented by Anthony Philip Heinrich. Where twenty-four years earlier, John Rowe Parker, editor of the *Euterpiad*, had proclaimed the Bohemian composer to be "the Beethoven of America,"[37] Dwight took issue with Heinrich's tendency to compose descriptive pieces portraying American places and events. "Imitation and description," he wrote,

> are not the true end of music. A series of historical events may have unity enough in themselves to make a very good story; but it does not follow that just that series of subjects, translated into so many musical themes, will still have unity as music.[38]

Dwight's other writings indicate a preference for absolute music over program pieces by composers of any nationality. Where Heinrich believed that it was possible to forge a national music with national inspiration, Dwight argued that an American scene or event did not necessarily inspire good American music.

On April 10, 1852, with the support of friends in the Harvard Musical Association, Dwight began to publish his own journal in which he promoted the Associationist idea that a better society would emerge from the improvement of the individual. Such an improvement would be facilitated by exposure to the best models of European musical propriety. "Music," he asserted in the first editorial in *Dwight's Journal of Music*, "must have some most intimate connection with the social destiny of man; and that, if we but know it, concerns us all." That social destiny would not, he felt, be the end product of the "very confused, heterogeneous" musical activity of his fellow Americans. "A thousand specious fashions," he claimed, "too successfully dispute the place of true art in the favor of each little public. It needs a faithful, severe, friendly voice to point out steadfastly the models of the True, the ever Beautiful, the Divine."[39] For nearly thirty years, until its final issue on September 3, 1881, *Dwight's Journal of Music* carried on a crusade for those musical models that its editor was certain would help Americans to achieve the unity and order he valued so highly. The *Journal* attracted many important contributors who added their voices to a small but growing number of writers on music in this country, including music education reformer Lowell Mason and Alexander Wheelock Thayer, the famous biographer of Beethoven. Dwight felt that even if good music reached only a small audience, a fact of cultural life that he was forced to concede, it nevertheless had the capacity to change society. He had written in 1846 that music

> is a great reformer, it is the voice of the inmost heart of wronged humanity chanting the great day of its redemption, the day when universal unity shall reign and Society and Industry and Life in all its spheres be music. If this be not true, Beethoven, Handel, and Mozart have lived for nothing.[40]

Dwight hoped that the salutary effects of good music would reach the masses of Americans who would then abandon their popular entertainments in favor of the more elevating offerings of the concert hall that the middle and upper classes regarded as "art."

Dwight disliked popular music because he assumed it was bad music that stirred man's worst passion. During the Mexican War he was one of the Boston Transcendentalists who opposed the fighting on moral grounds, and he added to his condemnation of senseless fighting an attack on the music that roused men to rush to the battlefield. Commenting on a concert by the Boston Academy of Music that contained several marches and pieces with military programs, he noted,

> in times like these, when a nation has gone mad with the old fever of conquest, and the demoralizing process has begun of attuning the popular sentiment to false and barbarous excitement, and blunting the sensibilities to tales and scenes of blood and horror; when there is no good thing to be hoped from government or the press, it certainly is desirable that music should not prostitute its divine faculties to the same base uses.[41]

For Dwight, music was meant for higher things than war, and those pieces labeled "military" only damaged men who fell prey to their influence. Military and patriotic music in peacetime also fell under Dwight's scrutiny, and he expressed considerable disappointment in the artistic tastes of Bostonians on the 1856 celebration of America's independence. He decried the Fourth of July's "ringing of bells, the thunder of big cannons, the petulant plague of petty fire-crackers, the blare of numberless brass bands, and all the confusing patriotic noises that make up a celebration of the nation's birth-day."[42]

Dwight was certain that most Americans had no appreciation of the true and the beautiful in art and that they were easily swayed by appeals to simple patriotism. He had little hope for the future of Americans as a musical people when he wrote that

> we take to noise, to *sounding* demonstrations, as a duck takes to water. Stunned with all this glory, with breast full of patriotism, and ears full of "Yankee Doodle" and "Hail Columbia," what can we have to say, or what report of music as Art? And verily it is a bad time with us, in respect of music. There may be much good silent planting going on, but there is little open fruit-bearing or reaping. Concerts and operas are scattering and comparatively insignificant.[43]

In the context of his denigration of popular music, Dwight also disapproved of composers who pandered to popular tastes by incorporating familiar tunes into their concert pieces. He had no good words for variations on *Yankee Doodle* trilled at the keyboard or for the sentimentality of quotations from sad spirituals or slave songs. He did not even consider that there was an indigenous American musical tradition that might find its way into works for the concert hall. Dwight believed that Americans needed not their own music but inspiring European music, arguing as early as 1840 that

> the Psalmody of the country choir and the dancing master's fiddle, the waltzes and variations of the music shop, Russell's songs and "Jim Crow" and "Harrison Melodies," are not apt to visit the popular mind with deep emotions of true music. Handel should be heard more, and Haydn, and Mozart, and Beethoven. The works of true genius cannot be too familiar, since they are always new like nature. [They] should salute our ears until the nobler chords within our souls respond.[44]

Unlike his friend and colleague in the Transcendental Club, Ralph Waldo Emerson, Dwight did not have confidence in Americans' ability to create their own cultural models. Where Emerson had optimistically declared in his "American Scholar" address of 1837 that "our day of dependence, our long apprenticeship to the learning of other lands draws to a close. . . . We will walk on our own feet; we will work with our own hands; we will speak our own minds."[45] Dwight knew that there could be no American cultural independence until our composers mastered the art of writing good European music. In reviewing some new American pieces that he described as "not very remarkable except as contrasted with the common run of popular music," Dwight argued that the publication of even such unimpressive American music could be credited to the presence of European composers, performers, and conductors in our midst. The appearance of the works under review demonstrated that

> the visits of European artists have not been without a quickening influence among us, and in spite of our utilitarian education there is something in the divinest of the arts of the Beautiful most congenial with the inner life of the people.[46]

Dwight also railed against critics who were taken in by popular composers whose music he regarded as facile but not truly artistic. For example, the concerts of the pianist and composer Louis Moreau Gottschalk, best known for his sentimental crowd-pleasing melodies, his quotations of popular and patriotic melodies, and his evocation of the tropics with the melodic and rhythmic patterns common to the Caribbean, met with critical enthusiasm everywhere but in Boston. Gottschalk's remarkable pianistic technique and quick pen conveyed images of the Caribbean in such pieces as *Le Bananier* and *Souvenir de Puerto Rico* and replicated the melodies of the plantation and New Orleans in *Le Banjo* and *Bamboula*. When the *New York Tribune* compared Gottschalk's piano music favorably to the sonatas of Beethoven, Dwight responded that he thought it paradoxical that Beethoven's great piano works could be "surpassed by a young man, an American, chiefly noted for his brilliant play and for the composition of 'Bananiers' and 'Bamboulas.' "[47]

Dwight was confident of his musical taste, but he, like all critics, could be fooled by his prejudices. At one of his Boston performances, Gottschalk programmed an unfamiliar piece by Beethoven, attaching his own name to it. He also listed Beethoven as the composer of a work that had come from his own pen. Dwight responded exactly as could have been expected—he praised the "Beethoven" composition for its plain virtues, and he criticized the "amateurish inanities of the brash American." After the appearance of Dwight's remarks, Gottschalk wrote to the critic to apologize for an unfortunate printing error in the program. According to music historian Irving Lowens, the composer thanked Dwight for "his generous praise and the ability to distinguish the genuine from the spurious."[48] Dwight had fallen victim to his own prejudice that, as a popular composer and performer who used American musical and pictorial resources, Gottschalk necessarily had nothing to say.

Dwight believed that the right music was a positive force that would tame Americans' wilder instincts and help them steer a true and orderly path toward democracy. He wrote in the *Atlantic Monthly* in 1870 that, as a democratic people, Americans "need music more than others." The right music could be that positive influence on our national character that would "tone down our self-asserting and aggressive manners, round off the sharp, offensive angularity of character, subdue and harmonize the free and ceaseless conflict of opinions." He argued that this country's rampant liberty would

> bring its own ruin unless there shall be found some gentler, harmonizing culture, such as may pervade whole masses with a fine enthusiasm, a sweet sense of reverance for something far above us, beautiful and pure; awakening some ideality in every soul, and often lifting us out of the hard hopeless prose of daily life. We need this beautiful corrective to our crudities.[49]

Dwight went on to argue that Americans could learn much from the German reverence for Bach, Mozart, and Beethoven, composers whose music would point us away from materialism and toward higher ideals.

What Dwight never explained was *how* music, even the music of Beethoven, could achieve such lofty goals, and he was never able to understand why his prescription for curing the ills of man and American society was not more popular. Like many reformers of his day, he was an idealist, less interested in the process of reform than in its ultimate product. Dwight assumed that the art music of the educated few would inculcate the masses with the values of an ideal society. He was decidedly conservative, describing his cultural tastes as "ultra-classical, pendantic, transcendental."[50] His reform vision did not allow for individual American efforts that diverged from accepted and familiar European models.

With the gradual improvement in the quality of orchestral programs and in the performance level of American orchestras, American composers who had studied in Europe began to have a medium through which they could reach the increasingly sophisticated concert audience. Coming of age after the Civil War, these composers generally felt little need to express a uniquely American character in their music. Self-assured in their individual identities (some could trace their American lineage back several generations) and well educated at American universities in Europe, they composed symphonies, tone poems, choral works, and overtures in the musical language that brought favorable recognition from conductors, audiences, and critics. The best way to be an American composer in the last decades of the nineteenth century was to write European-inspired music of high quality.

In 1900 musicologist Rupert Hughes noted that before John Knowles Paine "there had never been an American music writer worthy of serious consideration in the larger forms,"[51] a statement that reveals Paine's high standing as a symphonist at the turn of the century. Paine's reputation was further enhanced by his position as the nation's first professor of music at Harvard University. A Romantic by inclination and training, Paine's program pieces rarely portrayed America and were instead based on such sources as the legend of Poseidon and Aphrodite and Shakespeare's *As You Like It* and *The Tempest*. While he was not given to quoting popular or patriotic melodies, Paine nevertheless responded to requests for special works, such as the *Centennial Hymn*, composed for the Philadelphia Exhibition in 1876. His *Columbus March and Hymn* was commissioned for the opening of the World's Columbian Exposition in Chicago in 1893, and his *Hymn to the West* received its first performance at the St. Louis World's Fair in 1904. In spite of their "American" titles, none of these pieces contains specific musical references that can be identified with this country. Paine's popularity was based in large part on his ability to give the concert audience exactly what it expected—an orchestral sound that could have come from the pen of a German Romantic composer.

Paine was joined at the end of the nineteenth century by a number of other American Romantic composers whose music rarely bore a noticeable national label. Slightly younger than Paine, Arthur Foote, George Whitefield Chadwick, Edgar Stillman Kelley, and Horatio Parker were among those who composed symphonic and chamber music based on literary classics rather than their American environment, if they composed with a program in mind at all. Their works were accepted as models of "good" music.[52]

Although writers on American music tend to praise the compositions of Amy Marcy Cheny (Mrs. H. H. A.) Beach as also representing the correct style of Paine's followers, they cannot help drawing attention to her sex as if it were a handicap not only to achieving success and acceptance as a composer, but also to the very act of setting down melody in musical notation. Women composers were hardly taken seriously at the end of the nineteenth century, particularly if they ventured into the man's world of the symphony or piano concerto. In 1917 the *Musical Observer* offered articles by Dr. Heinrich Möller under the title, "Can Women Compose?" (The answer was a qualified yes. Women, according to Möller, could write art songs and simple piano pieces, although more complex works were clearly beyond their intellectual and musical ability.)[53] But Mrs. Beach took her activities as a pianist and composer very seriously indeed, and her symphonic works reveal her European training and ability as a composer in the Romantic style. Like her contemporaries, she did not consider that it was either possible or desirable to attempt to create an American musical idiom, as she already expressed herself so effectively in her songs, violin and piano sonatas, and the *Gaelic* Symphony, among many other Romantic works.

The approach to composition and the musical style of Edward MacDowell were consistent with his time and with the ideas of his contemporaries, and he drew inspiration from his native land only infrequently. His second suite for orchestra, the *Indian Suite*, quoted Iowa, Kiowa, and Chippewa melodies gleaned, ironically, not from visits to tribal villages but from a German dissertation on American Indian music, Theodor Baker's "Uber die Musik der nordamerikanischen Wilden."[54] Musically, this is a Romantic symphonic work in which the composer intended to express something of American nationality by portraying Indian village life. But after the opening horn call, there is little except the titles of the various movements to evoke tribal life or American culture.

MacDowell expressed the attitudes of most of his contemporaries when he decried propagandistic attempts to promote the American composer. Instead, he argued, music written in this country should be judged on its craftsmanship and beauty, not on the national origin of its composer. When the conductor Felix Mottl announced a special program devoted to the music of American composers, MacDowell voiced his protest at such special pleading in a letter that was reprinted in the *Musical Courier*:

> I have for years taken a strong stand against such affairs, and although I have not seen the program, fearing that there may be something of mine on it, I write to protest earnestly and strongly against this lumping together of American composers. Unless we are worthy of being put on programs with other composers to stand or fall, leave us alone. By giving such a concert you tacitly admit that we are too inferior to stand comparison with the composers of Europe.[55]

The concert was held, and MacDowell's piece was replaced by a Berlioz march. The editor of the *Musical Courier* agreed with MacDowell that American composers should be judged on the merits of their music, noting that "there are no American composers except those who write ragtime and the coon songs; therefore there should be no distinction between those who attempt to write classical music in America and those who are doing it in Europe."[56] For this editor, as for MacDowell and his contemporaries, the best way to achieve recognition for American concert music was to do a good job of imitating the style of contemporary "good" music.

The American Romantics of the late nineteenth century did not create an American musical style because they did not see that task as important. They forged their own styles after the models of conservative European teachers. At the very time when Wagner's chromaticism was causing controversy and laying the groundwork for future challenges to the certainty of the tonal system, most of the Americans who had studied abroad were attracted to earlier models that were Classical in form and Romantic in thematic development. The success of Paine, MacDowell, and their contemporaries in contributing symphonic and chamber music to the late nineteenth-century repertoire demonstrated clearly that there *was* high culture on this side of the Atlantic. That culture was not unique to America but was derivative of Europe, and it was the European standard against which all things musical in the United States were measured. If William Henry Fry did not live to see the promise of his Declaration of Independence from the art of Europe fulfilled, he certainly would have recognized the musical forms and style in which the Romantic Americans of Paine's and MacDowell's generations composed, for it was similar to his own.

By the end of the nineteenth century, many writers on American music assumed that good taste had finally triumphed in the concert hall. They used their columns to observe the progress of high musical culture in American cities and devoted much of their attention to European symphonies and operas performed by European conductors and singers. Philip Hale was such a critic. A practicing lawyer before he journeyed to Germany to study piano, organ, and composition, Hale wrote music criticism for the *Boston Home Journal* from 1889 to 1903 and for the *Boston Herald* from 1903 to 1933, a period during which he also provided the program notes for the Boston Symphony Orchestra. Hale reviewed concerts and recitals and often wrote about the professional and private lives of famous musicians in Boston. Rarely did the topic of American music inspire him to put pen to paper. But in a column in the *Boston Home Journal*, Hale commented on the prevailing distrust in this country of American musical accomplishment and the extent to which German culture had come to dominate music here. Hale asked whether it was likely that

> we shall ever have a national music or music of strong national characteristics. It seems doubtful; we are without a musical past, nor were we a musical nation. We have many composers of talent who study here and abroad and write much that is admirable; but so far as nationality goes, the music might as well be signed with a foreign name. There is a tendency with us to imitate other nations in dress and ideas; and individuality is almost wholly disregarded. Our audiences are too apt to admire and applaud at dictation; and a foreign name or the mysterious fiat of a society leader often awes the crowd. It looks as though for some years to come we should blindly submit ourselves to the Germans. It is here at least the musical language. German is spoken at rehearsals of orchestras composed of men of various nationalities, and supported by Americans. And when the chief supporter and patron of the Boston Symphony Orchestra wished the other day to express to the orchestra his personal gratification at the work of the past year, it is said that he composed with care a letter in the German language which was read aloud in German by an imported German.[57]

Although Hale raised the issue of the domination of German music in America, especially in Boston, most late nineteenth-century critics did not advocate the presence of more music by Americans on concert music programs. Indeed, the critics generally agreed on the positive value of the German contribution to music in America, if not to the development of American music. Writers on music also generally agreed that it took a year or more of study at a European conservatory or with a private teacher to make a performer of an accomplished technician or a composer of a talented American music writer. When John Knowles Paine returned from study in Berlin and performed a recital in his home town of Portland, Maine, the local newspaper declared that "the result of his years of study abroad was quite apparent. The clever boy who went forth from among us has returned a thoroughly educated and accomplished musician."[58] And a reviewer in the *Atlantic Monthly* compared Paine's First Symphony favorably to works by popular European composers when he wrote in 1876,

> in this work Mr. Paine has shown himself strong in all the qualities which one expects to find in a great composer. In his easy mastery of the minutest details of counterpoint we recognize the devoted student of Bach. His work is distinguished by a clearness and conciseness of form which Mendelssohn has hardly surpassed, while it has much of the virile strength in which Mendelssohn fell short of Schumann.[59]

And even as late as the 1930s, Paine's consistency in his approach to composition that has often been called "academic" or "correct" was praised as a virtue. Critic Richard Aldrich noted that Paine's style did not exhibit

> "American" characteristics; Paine's musicianship was purely a product of European influences, as indeed was inevitable in his day and for a good while thereafter. But whatever may be the present validity of Paine's music, it made history; it held up a high standard—it rather produced and established a high standard—of American art, and served a valuable purpose in keeping American music in the minds and affection of American music lovers.[60]

The American Romantics of Paine's generation were evaluated somewhat less favorably by critics who valued twentieth-century excursions into the realm of modern music. Paul Rosenfeld, a writer on musical and cultural issues in the 1920s and 1930s, commented that when this music emerged in the last third of the nineteenth century,

> it had neither the freshness and the power of the great mid-century prose and poetry, nor the intensity of the new American painting. It was "winter on earth" and the impulse was weak or convalescent. The music of Edward MacDowell, the first American to deserve the name of composer, amounts more to an assimilation of European motives, figures, and ideas than to original expression.[61]

But Rosenfeld did not expect late nineteenth-century American composers to be modernists before their time. Instead, he criticized particularly MacDowell's tendency to succumb to "nice" and "respectable" feelings in his thoroughly respectable music:

> It is shocking to see how full of vague poesy he is. Where his great Romantic brethren Brahms, Wagner, and Debussy, are all direct and sensitive, clearly and tellingly expressive, MacDowell minces and simpers, maidenly, and ruffled. He is nothing if not a daughter of the American Revolution. He hymns "America" thinking of the Mayflower and its lovely load. His mind fondly dwells on old-fashioned New England gardens, old lavender, smoldering logs, sunsets. . . . This sentimentality is not only a matter of titles and mottoes, the music is drenched of it.[62]

If anything, Rosenfeld would have had Paine, MacDowell, and their contemporaries be more adventurous Romantics.

Around the turn into the twentieth century, a number of American Romantic composers began to take some risks with the propriety of their works in the interest of creating music that would be recognizably American. Anti-European in rhetoric but not anti-Romantic in musical style, these men quoted the melodies of Indians, slaves, and white Anglo-Saxon settlers. This "Americanness by quotation" captured the attention of the musical public for a short time prior to World War I, as the technique seemed to synthesize the familiar Romantic orchestral sound with native musical materials. The effort to forge a national music from regional folk sources was sincere, but the resulting pieces were neither paradigms of nineteenth-century Romanticism nor examples of a new American musical idiom.

These turn-of-the-century musical nationalists, like their early nineteenth-century counterparts, departed from conventional wisdom by looking for musical materials in their own country. They hoped to chart a new course and create a vital American musical art founded on the life around them. As Gilbert attempted to create a national music based on folk sources, critic Olin Downes recognized three distinct periods in the development of a national musical culture. Writing in the *Musical Quarterly*, Downes said that the first stage was one in which composers copied foreign models and achieved success in writing in familiar and popularly accepted styles, much as Paine and others had done at the end of the nineteenth century. The second stage involved the "revolt against imitation, and the equally necessary cultivation of folk-melody, in order to formulate an authentic idiom and get back into touch with the spirit of the composer's people." It was this stage in which American concert music now found itself. But, Downes argued, the mere revolt against imitation of foreign models would not create a national music. He described a third stage of this process in which "the spiritual consciousness of the people and the musical idioms transmuted and developed from the original folk-songs, rather than the material, are responsible for the highly specialized expression of a leading composer, who remains a true prophet of his people."[63] Downes foretold the contribution of a group of modernist composers in the development of folk sources in the context of the new music after about 1935.

A composer whose works expressed the ideals of Downes's second stage of national musical development was Henry Franklin Belknap Gilbert. Called the "Mark Twain of American Music" by one admiring critic, Gilbert saw folk music as the true source of a national music.[64] He wrote in 1915 that it was necessary for American composers to "kick over the traces of European tradition, and to treat American subjects, to use fragments of melody having an American origin as the basis of musical structure." With regard to foreign influences on American music, Gilbert wrote that "as long as we run after foreign gods with too great assiduity we shall never have a god of our own really worthy of our respect and worship." Recognizing that his folk sources might be considered crude by listeners unaccustomed to hearing the music of the plantation or tribal feast in the concert hall but optimistic about the future of American music, Gilbert said that he and other American composers "*have* hitched our wagon to a star, the star of youth which shall indeed eventually drag us out of the slough of vulgarity."[65] Two years later he decried the fact that most of the American music performed by this country's major orchestras was "imitative of European traditions wherein the spirit of folk music has been deadened by generations of art music imitation."[66]

Gilbert argued that the domination of American music by European styles and techniques muted "the spirit of America" so that "the great potential which is the birthright of the American composer . . . has been thoughtlessly bartered away for a mess of clever European pottage."[67] But he was too steeped in the European art music tradition himself to look beyond the simple quotation of folk melodies in his orchestral compositions. Gilbert also decried modern musical developments as "decadent," perhaps because they were outside the scope of his training as a student of Edward MacDowell. He was a Romantic whose American national vision was an outgrowth of the fundamental belief that "the greatest, the most significant, and the most characteristic art of the world is always the flower of a particular national consciousness."[68] Recognizing that some of the works of his pioneering generation of American musical nationalists were "crude attempts indeed, and of no particular artistic worth," he nevertheless emphasized that the true achievement of his colleagues lay in their quest for something uniquely American in music. "A broad national consciousness," he wrote in 1913, "has caught our composers in its grasp and whispered to them in no uncertain manner that if one wishes to build strong and sturdy structures one has to build at the foundation—and—that imitative art can never be great art."[69]

Gilbert and his colleagues, like American composers before them, faced what they perceived as a lack of interest in their work. Arthur Farwell commented that works like Gilbert's *Comedy Overture on Negro Themes* exhibited sufficient mastery in their thematic development of folk materials "to warrant their place on our first-class orchestral programmes throughout the country." But Farwell knew that it would take time for American nationalist music of this type to gain just recognition because "the cultured society which supports our symphony orchestras also supports an unwritten law that music is of Europe, and the orchestral conductor shall not forget himself with impunity, whatever his regard for certain American works may be."[70] Like Gilbert, Farwell was critical of the direction that American composers had taken in the late nineteenth century. Commenting in 1900 that "only German music [had] sounded natural" in this country, he expressed his frustration at the difficulty in gaining acceptance for American concert music and advised composers and audiences that the first correction we must bring to our musical vision is to cease to see everything through German spectacles, however wonderful, however sublime those spectacles may be in themselves.[71]

Farwell believed that the path to national music could be found by rejecting European influences and discovering American identity in the music of the Indian and the Negro. He declared that "America will never retain what is not true to herself, and Europe will forever reject what is merely imitative of her." Of course, it was naive to expect that the musical language common throughout the Western world could be supplanted by the melodic and rhythmic patterns of the tribal village or plantation, and Farwell ignored the fact that European concert music composers had long utilized the folk materials of their own countries when he asserted that the American composer "must stoop to conquer; he must come down from the clouds of European refinement-imitation and understand the crude but inexhaustibly vital realities of his people which, for him, are their music and their independence."[72] Farwell was joined in his particular enthusiasm for the music of the American Indian by Charles Wakefield Cadman, Charles Stanford Skilman, and Arthur Nevin, among others. These men used American folk materials in their symphonic and operatic works (Cadman's *Shanewis* received its premiere at the Metropolitan Opera House in 1918), but they did not stray far from the musical Romanticism of their predecessors.

Sometimes the traditional elements of the musical language in which a piece was composed could obscure what were intended to be quotations of familiar patriotic or folk melodies. Leo Schultz's *American Festival Overture*, for example, quoted a phrase from *Yankee Doodle*, but the composer "so metamorphosed the theme that it [had] none of the triviality of that well-known tune," according to William Henry Humiston, the program annotator for the New York Philharmonic Society, which first performed the piece.[73] Whatever the validity of Humiston's judgment on the musical quality of *Yankee Doodle*, it is clear that the process of thematic development obscured the original folk character of the tune. When A. Walter Kramer composed the *Chant Nègre*, one of his *Two Sketches for Orchestra*, he attempted "To enunciate a melody in the idiom of the Negro—the pentatonic scale is used—and clothe it in an orchestral garb that shall enhance it."[74] Charles Wakefield Cadman justified the mixture of native American melodies and Romantic harmony and orchestration, noting that the beginnings of an American school of music "must tie us to a *tangible something*, and the trail-blazers have utilized the means at hand for their 'infant' expression of a music expressing the land which they call home." But Cadman was not willing to sacrifice the sound he knew best in order to create a national musical expression. He counseled American composers to write "*good* music, whether it smacks of a European conservatory or of the broad free reaches of the Far West."[75]

In marked contrast to the opinions of composers who were actively seeking an American musical language, *Musical America*'s writers and editors generally took a dim view of the notion that such a music could be created by combining folk materials and the standard symphony orchestra. They declared that such folk sources "might be useful for a time," but they could not "serve as the basis of the American music of the future, but only as occasional spices."[76] One writer, Angelo Read, revealed a commonly held bias in favor of European culture when he took issue with Dvořák and MacDowell for attempting to create an "American" atmosphere in some of their compositions by quoting Afro-American or Indian musical sources. He argued that the music of the Negro was particularly inappropriate for evoking an American national character. American music, he wrote, would have to "come from the people. In order therefore to make it National, the Negro and the white must become one race, which thing is absurd."[77] A month later, Read said that Negro music could not "be inherited by the American people, for they have no part in it. Consequently it can never be used as a foundation for national purposes."[78] Read and other critics raised an issue that many American nationalist composers prior to World War I had failed to consider fully, namely, whether the spirituals, folk songs, and Indian melodies that they quoted so freely could be representative of all of America. To be sure, a piece that was supposed to portray the frontier and that featured an authentic Indian tribal melody might touch the imagination of the city dweller and inspire romantic ideas about the American past, but could it reflect the totality of the American experience? Further, Read and other contemporary observers maintained that what they called "aboriginal music" had little to offer the cosmopolitan audience for concert music that was more accustomed to Beethoven and Wagner. And it was to this audience alone that critics addressed their remarks about "culture."

Daniel Gregory Mason was among the more ascerbic critics who recognized the limited contribution of national music based on folk themes. He expressed disdain for both folklorism and modernism to such an extent that he referred to American music between 1914 and 1928 as the "Music of Indigestion." He complained of America's lack of a musical tradition and the confusion that he saw around him among composers who had created what he called a "modern day Babel." He singled out for special mention

> Henry F. Gilbert's negroes in his "Comedy Overture on Negro Themes": not full-blooded, you will observe but half-breeds—quadroons—octroons—descended by some repellent miscegenation from Beethoven and Mendelssohn. Notice Charles Wakefield Cadman's Indians whose only arrows are collars from Troy, and who wear derby hats. Even John Powell, the most gifted of all our "folk" composers, apparently does not recoil when, in his *"Rhapsodie Nègre"* (French titles have appealed to American composers ever since the days of Gottschalk) the swarthy faces of his protagonists suddenly assume the Jesuitical smile of Liszt.[79]

Mason called the American nationalist composers "polyglot parrots," and he despaired of ever finding a representative and appropriately elevating American musical idiom. (We should note, however, that Mason himself was not above occasionally quoting a folk melody in his own compositions.) Mason used his critical pen to lobby for a more traditional approach to American musical composition.

While *Musical America* was reluctant to announce the dawning of a new era in American national music inspired by the "discovery" of folk music by European-trained Romantic composers, the editors did point to signs of improving quality in American concert music in general. A 1907 editorial noted that such non-national and often nonprogrammatic music was finally receiving more recognition and that

> after years of assuming an attitude of what appeared to be just rather good-natured contempt for the music of America, the older world is beginning to lend a more appreciative ear, and a number of American composers are now really admitted to have created things which possess the promise of immortality.[80]

The critical identification with European music and nineteenth-century standards was further illustrated in a remark by *Musical America*'s editor, John C. Freund, that "high class" audiences for opera and symphonic music were "the same everywhere."[81] Freund saw no reason to think that an American concert audience would need or want an American music. He was correct to criticize the nationalist composers of the first decades of the twentieth century for claiming to have found a representative musical idiom, but he also denigrated this attempt at cultural nationalism because of his oft-stated preference for traditional Romantic music that claimed no particular national identification.

Gilbert and his colleagues were joined in the search for characteristic American music by Charles Edward Ives. In his use of the symphony orchestra, voice, piano, and chamber ensemble as vehicles for painting musical pictures and evoking a nineteenth-century vision of small-town America, Ives deserves to be called a Romantic. But in his efforts to portray the images and spirit of an older New England, Ives used many of the techniques that belong to the language of modern music, including polytonality and polyrhythms, quarter tones, and difficult and disjointed melodic lines. In many of his compositions, Ives extended the boundaries of what could be considered music and not simply noise. He was awarded the Pultizer Prize in 1947, by which time he was a 73-year-old recluse who had composed no music at all for more than twenty-five years. The Third Symphony, for which the Prize was awarded, had been composed between 1901 and 1904.

The music of Charles Ives reflected his own national pride, a strong identification with New England, and an interest in the everyday popular music of his region. Ives developed his own compositional techniques that make parts of his music sound "modern" in an attempt to re-create the music he heard around him. He heard polytonality and polyrhythms in the amateur church choir of the small New England town in which the fervency of religious expression counted for more than a professionally trained voice; he heard tone clusters in the sounds of the church bells, the slightly out-of-tune country fiddlers, and the sound of a train whistle; and he heard the clash of keys in the meeting of two marching bands in the small-town Fourth of July celebration. The hymns, dance tunes, and patriotic songs he quoted and developed were all American, and he was unique in the extent to which he transcended simple quotation of familiar materials in an attempt to use familiar songs as material for thematic and rhythmic development.

Ives's Second Pianoforte Sonata, *Concord, Mass., 1840–1860*, was a piece in which the composer intended to portray New England and reflect the influence of American Transcendentalist philosophers. Composed between 1908 and 1915, this work, whose four movements are entitled "Emerson," "Hawthorne," "The Alcotts," and "Thoreau," was accompanied a few years later by a prose work, *Essays Before a Sonata*. Ives wrote extensively about the piece itself and the philosophical ideas that had inspired its creation. Of Emerson, he wrote:

> Though a great poet and prophet, he is greater, possibly, as an invader of the unknown—America's deepest explorer of the spiritual immensities—a seer painting his discoveries in masses and with any color that may lie at hand—cosmic, religious, human, even sensuous.

Ives admired and attempted to emulate Emerson's searching of the unknown realm of spiritual possibility as well as Thoreau's ability to "express profound truth and deep sentiment."[82]

Ives thought himself to be consistent with Emerson's philosophy in his belief that the mental and spiritual inspiration out of which his music developed was as important as the notes themselves. For those who failed to comprehend his often free and rambling style, he noted that "apparent confusion, if lived with long enough, may become orderly" and "vagueness is at times an indication of nearness to perfect truth."[83] For this reason, Ives refused to alter or "correct" in his compositions the sounds of the hymn tunes raggedly sung in his hometown church or the clashing of tunes and keys on Independence Day.

Ives's career further exemplified Transcendentalist values in his interest in the constant change and growth of music outside the potentially restricting bonds of any particular compositional school. In this respect his musical philosophy was fundamentally different from that of Arnold Schoenberg and other members of the Vienna School, for example, who replaced one set of conventions with a compositional framework of their own. Ives discarded elements of existing styles that he didn't like, used what he did like from older traditions, and sometimes even used techniques that were quite modern for their time.

In addition, Ives often combined seemingly contradictory ideas and images in his music. For example, in the second movement of the Fourth Violin Sonata, he juxtaposed the sacred (represented by a quotation from the hymn, *Jesus Loves Me*) and the secular (expressed in a musical portrait of nature on a summer day, with the sounds of forest animals and boys throwing rocks in a brook). Eclecticism and an independent, experimental spirit were characteristics of the Transcendentalist thinker *and*, in an important sense, of the modern composer. Ives's private printing of the *Concord* Sonata, the *Essays Before a Sonata*, and a volume of 114 Songs was a practical expression of the composer's independence and willingness to go his own musical way. Even though these works met with virtually no response on their appearance in 1920, Ives was proven correct in the long run—within thirty years, his music was known and almost appreciated.

Ives never expressed a fondness for music critics, and that assessment was generally mutual during the most active and creative part of his life. He often referred to critics as "weak men in silk skirts," and he addressed many unfavorable remarks to his imaginary critic Rollo, who preferred Romantic, predictable, non-American music.[84] Interestingly, in music as in politics and his insurance business, Ives placed his faith in the judgment of the majority of Americans. He offered an amendment to the Constitution in a paper called *The Majority*, in which he proposed that all important questions be put to a popular vote. This represented an extension of the New England town meeting to the realm of national politics. Once again Ives revealed his Transcendentalist faith in man's (and, therefore, the majority's) capacity to do good, although he clearly had more faith in the processes of government than most of the nineteenth-century Transcendentalists did. Where Ives's analysis fell short was in his faith in the "average man" to understand his music, even though at the end of the twentieth century his is an important, if sometimes enigmatic, name in the history of concert music in the United States.

Prior to this country's participation in World War I, music in the concert hall seemed generally to follow a linear pattern of increasing sophistication, as the United States attracted better musical interpreters from abroad and as American musicians and composers honed their skills and developed their talents by studying abroad. Calls for an American national music fell on increasingly more receptive ears, as the men of Henry F. Gilbert's generation attempted to create such a music with folk materials. But the public and orchestra managers persisted in regarding the American composer and the music he created as an inferior product to be offered only on Independence Day and on Washington's or Lincoln's birthdays. As long as critics lauded music that was "correct" in the context of the standards of nineteenth-century European Romanticism and as long as few composers forged their own independent paths, concert music in general was destined to improve while music that claimed to be "American" was held suspect and rarely performed. Even the late nineteenth- and early twentieth-century celebrations of national power, peace, and achievement, and the experience of World War I failed to inspire lasting and meaningful attempts to make an important American contribution to the world's concert music. The emergence of American music for the concert hall would have to wait for the challenges to the nineteenth-century aesthetic provided by the modern movement of the early twentieth century.

2

Celebrations of National Power: American Ideals Set to European Music

In the last third of the nineteenth century, the United States became a world power in many important respects. The development of industrial potential, transportation facilities, and military might, along with increases in land area and population and the exercise of influence in the Western Hemisphere, made it possible by 1900 to assert American ascendancy with confidence. Americans looking forward to the new century, in the words of historian Jack Cameron Dierks,

> were continually conscious of the growth, of the burgeoning farms and factories around them, of the proved success of audacious enterprise. It galled them to think that to many Europeans the great Republic was considered as far removed from the power-roiled inner sanctums of world affairs as Walden forest might have been. Everybody knew America was a force to be reckoned with; it was time for the strapping youth to take his place as a man among men, and a bit of traditional suspender snapping to announce the transition would not be out of order.[1]

But to what extent did such accomplishment and confidence pervade the realm of American culture? While American orators intoned intricate rhetorical flourishes asserting the uniqueness of their country's experience in the world and the supremacy of its democratic institutions, few argued that high culture here, specifically the American music composed for the concert hall, could rival that of Europe.

During the period of musical deference to European styles prior to World War I, there were a number of celebrations of American pride and power that provided a potential forum for the American composer to be heard on his own terms. The restoration of peace after the Civil War inspired a major spectacle in 1869, the Great National Peace Jubilee and Music Festival, which was followed in 1872 by another Jubilee to celebrate world peace. These events, along with the Philadelphia Centennial Exhibition of 1876, the World's Columbian Exposition of 1893, and other world's fairs and international exhibitions held in the United States, all aroused considerable patriotic feeling and interest in all things American. Many well-known and highly respected composers were invited to contribute to these celebrations, and the music they created reveals the state of American musical art in the concert hall.

As the United States approached its first century of independence, there seemed, in spite of the recent devastation of the Civil War years, to be many reasons for national pride. The experiment in democracy, many believed, had succeeded and showed no signs of giving way to the worst features of European monarchies. Further, the expansion of the country had proven the truth of James Madison's assertion that an extended republic was viable. Although the Civil War had been a difficult test of strength for the North, a source of military and societal agony for the South, and an apparent contradiction of the notion of a united America, it was possible by the end of Reconstruction to see the War as a trial from which the country had emerged stronger than ever.

In succeeding years, veterans would meet on the sites of old battles to commemorate in speeches and well-publicized photographs past victories and defeats, to dedicate elaborate war monuments, and to share reminiscences. Veterans in the blue and the gray uniforms seemed to share more in the experience of having fought than in the causes that had divided and brought them to the battlefields in the first place. Indeed, by the time the United States went to war with Spain in 1898, Union and Confederate soldiers had been reunited by the composers of popular sheet music. For example, *Columbia's Flag*, a song and chorus respectfully dedicated to the Blue and the Gray and composed by a "volunteer," warns foreign foes of "the readiness of the Blue and the Gray to follow and die for the emblem they love." And in a musical resolution of Civil War issues, E. Witzman Publishing Company in Memphis released *Dixie Doodle* in 1898. This piano piece was a medley of *Dixie, Hail Columbia, Massa's in the Cold, Cold Ground, Columbia, Gem of the Ocean*, and a finale of *Dixie* and *Yankee Doodle* played in counterpoint.[2] The Civil War had torn the country apart, but the theme of survival, no matter how tainted it may have been by the abuses of Reconstruction and its ignominious end, was common among those who sought to mute the horrors of the past in visions of future glory for the American republic. If the orators of the postwar period could be believed, the eyes of Americans were firmly "fixed on the future."[3]

One such visionary who had grand plans for music in Boston that would represent the nation as a whole was Patrick Sarsfield Gilmore, a bandmaster who conceived, planned, and supervised the Great National Peace Jubilee and Music Festival "In Honor of the Restoration of Peace and Union Throughout the Land," which was held on June 15-19, 1869. Boston had never before seen a musical event on such a grand scale. Gilmore's personal efforts to attract private and business sponsors raised enough money to erect a coliseum seating fifty thousand, in which spectators could witness the performance of a chorus of as many as twenty thousand voices accompanied by one thousand orchestral musicians. One special concert even included "One Hundred Members of the Boston Fire Department who [were] thoroughly rehearsed in their part of the performance of the 'Anvil Chorus' from Verdi's 'Il Trovatore.' "[4] The performing forces for regular concerts were imposing in themselves, including a chorus of 504 singers and 590 orchestral players drawn from New York, Philadelphia, Baltimore, Cincinnati, Chicago, and St. Louis, in addition to the players already on hand in Boston.[5]

The enterprising Gilmore saw in his festival the potential for a grand patriotic event. The Peace Jubilee attracted President Grant, several governors, cabinet members, and army officers. The scheduling could not have been more carefully planned, short of playing a grand patriotic concert on the Fourth of July itself. June 17 was the anniversary of the Battle of Bunker Hill, and this allowed the citizens of Boston to celebrate the important role that Massachusetts played in the American Revolution as they rejoiced in the restoration of peace after the Civil War. Gilmore solicited and received testimonials from state and local officials that lent the aura of official sanction to this event, which was financed for the public's musical enjoyment and celebration of peace by private subscriptions and the sale of advertising space. Governor William Claflin sounded patriotic and musical themes:

> . . . inasmuch as music inspired our soldiers in the late war, in their weary marches and on hard fought battlefields, and was withal a valuable auxiliary in securing our victories, I think "the restoration of peace and union" could be celebrated in no more appropriate manner, and I very willingly add my name to the list of subscribers.[6]

The opening of the festival seemed to promise a grand patriotic spectacle, if not refined musical entertainment. The first concert featured the aforementioned chorus of twenty thousand and a one thousand-member orchestra, "with the additional accompanying effects of artillery and infantry firing, the chiming of bells, etc," performing the *Star Spangled Banner* and *Hail, Columbia* as well as "several pieces upon the Programme, Including the National Airs of England, France, Russia, Prussia, Austria, and other nations." The nation's technological advances contributed to the noise level of the concert, as the program announced that "The Bells will be rung, and the Cannon fired, by electricity from the Music Stand."[7]

The theme of the second day's concert was peace, although the programs were anything but tranquil. Massive choral forces performed excerpts from oratorios by Handel, Haydn, and Mendelssohn as well as Beethoven's Ninth Symphony. To close the day's musical events, Carl Zerrahn, a German immigrant who had achieved considerable success in Boston, conducted an orchestra of one thousand in Rossini's *William Tell* overture. The celebration of the anniversary of the battle of Bunker Hill also included the overture to *Fra Diavolo* by Auber with fifty trumpeters playing the solo part, the *Anvil Chorus* assisted by the Boston Fire Department, and an *American Hymn*, whose text and music had been composed by Matthias Keller, a German bandmaster who had settled in Boston.

As Gilmore surveyed the state of music in America, he found its citizens ripe for large-scale patriotic entertainments, but he did not find among his countrymen any composer eminent enough to merit inclusion in his programs.[8] His attitude toward the appropriateness of European music at an American celebration of national unity is clear from the assertion that

> the music which will be rendered at the festival is not light and trifling; the sublimest strains of Handel, Haydn, Mendelssohn, Mozart, Rossini, and Beethoven will be heard. The occasion is one of peace. Peace is the ally of religion. Peace and good will is the theme of the angels' song. The music selected is most appropriate for the occasion.[9]

Gilmore did not look for music for the Festival's programs in the works of Heinrich, Fry, Bristow, or the young John Knowles Paine, who had recently returned from study in Europe to teach at Harvard University. If his eyes were fixed on America's future, his ears were turned toward the European music of the past and present.

In spite of the obvious difficulties of performing with such massive forces, audiences responded positively to the Festival's concerts with their attendance and their cheers, even if some of the performances tended to drag a bit under the weight of numbers. For example, the *Springfield* [*Mass.*] *Republican* reported that the chorus, "Thanks be to God," from Mendelssohn's *Elijah* was applauded "with a spontaneous heartiness which shows how classical music is beginning to be appreciated, and that the masters are gaining on the ground of the earticklers."[10] The article went on to assess the value of Gilmore's efforts to the advancement of American culture:

> So we congratulate Mr. Gilmore and his ten thousand coadjutors. In spite of hindrances and obstacles, the Jubilee must be set down as a success, meriting in sober truth very much of the enthusiastic praise which has been bestowed upon it, and taking rank as the greatest event in the musical annals of our country.[11]

The *New York Sun* also praised the musical activities in Boston, claiming that the United States could now assume a leadership role in world music:

> Heretofore America has not had standing in the musical art-world. England has looked down on us. Germany has supposed that no festival could be given here except by her Sangerbunds. Italy and France have recognized us for no higher possibilities than the production of their operas. At one step, without any preliminaries, without more special preparation than could be crowded into a few weeks, we have lifted ourselves, so far as great musical art gatherings are concerned, to an artistic level with these nations. Hereafter, when the noted music festivals of the world are enumerated, not only will it not be possible to ignore America, but she must head the list.[12]

Confidence in American musical accomplishment and assertions that this country is no longer culturally inferior to the nations of Europe are familiar themes here. In addition, the *Sun* writer seemed to single out for special praise the absence of long years of practice and months of preparation for the Jubilee, as if to say that American enthusiasm played as important a role as time spent in the rehearsal hall. John Sullivan Dwight, editor of the journal that reprinted much of the favorable commentary about the Jubilee, remained silent on the impact of the event. Instead, he reprinted two critical letters to the *New York Tribune* that expressed his own skepticism about the wisdom of the project "so unblushingly heralded after the manner of things as uncongenial as possible to the whole sphere of Art."[13] Conceding the success of the event, he consigned it to the realm of popular entertainment and was thus able to avoid expressing an aesthetic judgment on the quality of the performances themselves.

Gilmore's second grand festival, this one on the theme of world peace, occurred in June and July of 1872 and was offered to the public as a commemoration of the end of the Franco-Prussian War. The event lent prestige to Boston as the host city to a variety of international ensembles, including the Band of the Grenadier Guards of London and those of the Republican Guard of Paris and the Kaiser Franz Grenadier Regiment. With at least one concert a day between June 17 and July 5, audiences were treated to a wide selection of European marches, overtures, battle pieces, operatic scenes, and symphonies, albeit with considerably less artillery fire and anvil accompaniment than in the 1869 Jubilee. Nevertheless, Dwight described with obvious relief the end of the occasion in terms that made clear his preference for more modest entertainments:

> The great, usurping, tyrannizing, noisy and pretentious thing is over, and there is a general feeling of relief, as if a heavy, brooding nightmare had been lifted from us all. Verily the Gilmore dog-star *has* raged, as we anticipated, through a "heated term" of three long, weary, crowded weeks, during which one saw nothing, heard nothing, read nothing, ate and drank and breathed nothing but jubilee, jubilee, jubilee, and everybody suffered from an oppressive sense of *over-much-ness* in the very atmosphere, while all newspaperdom kept up such a multitudinous ringing chorus in praise of our dear old Athens, that no one would be surprised to hear her name pronounced, *Boast-town*. God forbid! A little modest dignity and self-possession . . . [and] a little less ambition for the display of enterprise on an unprecedented scale, will win the world's respect in the long run more surely than "jubilees."[14]

More American composers were represented on the 1872 Peace Jubilee's programs. In addition to the novelty pieces, national airs, and seemingly endless band concerts, Gilmore chose hymns by Lowell Mason for the audience to sing, Dudley Buck's *Peace and Music, Homage to Columbia* by Ermina Rudersdorff, and a chorus from *St. Peter*, a new oratorio by John Knowles Paine. Indeed, it was a sign of progress in the realm of high culture for music by an American composer to appear on the same program as works by Wagner, Liszt, Rossini, and Donizetti.

For Americans after the Civil War, the notion of continued and unending progress in the areas of commerce, industry, political democracy, and, to a lesser extent, high culture was an attractive one. The nation's first one hundred years seemed to reaffirm the validity of the separation from the old and "decadent" cultures of Europe. In his address for the Fourth of July celebration at the Philadelphia Centennial Exhibition, New York lawyer and orator William J. Evarts recognized the superior achievements of European nations in some areas but still found words enough to praise the young and powerful America. In view of the accomplishments of the Europeans, he noted that

> we may well confess how much we fall short, how much we have to make up, in the emulative competitions of the times. Yet, even in this presence, and with a just deference to the age, the power, the greatness of the other nations of the earth, we do not fear to appeal to the opinion of mankind whether, as we point to our land, our people, and our laws, the contemplation should not inspire us with a lover's enthusiasm for our country.[15]

The religion of progress and the faith in America's supremacy as a democratic nation considered neither the cost of that progress nor the areas in which democracy had failed to work for all Americans. But the rhetoric of national celebration tended to be congratulatory rather than critical. In this context it is not surprising that the speechmakers of 1876 should have looked to the past only with pride and that they viewed the future only with optimism.

Orators in 1876 took considerable pride in the statistics that illustrated increases in America's land area, population, and life expectancy (at least for white citizens).[16] And it did not require the skills of a demographer to realize that America was becoming more urbanized and that the five major cities of the 1870 census, New York, Philadelphia, Brooklyn, Chicago, and St. Louis, all with populations of between 250,000 and 500,000, were emerging as cultural as well as population and industrial centers. Even the disastrous Chicago fire of 1871 was seen as providential, as it afforded the opportunity to rebuild and create the "city of the future."[17]

Optimism was an important component of the intellectual climate in which the United States celebrated its one hundredth birthday. The event was planned as an educational and uplifting experience for the citizens of a democracy. Set in the 340-acre Fairmount Park, the Philadelphia Centennial Exhibition was carefully designed as a place of enlightenment and culture rather than as an open space that would allow for any improvised recreational activity. In this respect it was like many other American urban parks of the period, designed to provide a pleasant and controlled respite from the commerical world of the urban space. In Fairmount Park, visitors to the exhibition could stroll from one building to another along properly landscaped promenades and visit one exhibit after another that lauded American commercial, industrial, and political achievement.

Although this was to be a commemorative exhibition for the United States, it featured extensive participation by foreign governments. Thirty-six countries participated in some way in the six-minth-long fair, and fifteen nations erected buildings on the exhibition grounds.[18] Perhaps even more important than the extent of foreign participation in the Centennial Exhibition was the degree of foreign influence on an event whose oratory made few apologies for American accomplishment. The architect-in-chief of the project was Hermann Joseph Schwartzmann, who designed a permanent art gallery and horticulture hall in addition to numerous temporary buildings to house the exhibits.[19] Schwartzmann, who had arrived in the United States from Munich in 1868, made little attempt to connect the structural needs of the Exhibition with its avowed purpose, the celebration of one hundred years of

American independence. This was also true in most of the exhibits outside the realm of American technology. Except for one small replica of a "New England Log House," in which a few antique objects from the Revolutionary period were displayed, visitors had few opportunities to experience the centennial celebration in surroundings that reflected the American experience. Historian of the Exhibition John Brinckerhoff Jackson has noted that

> the absence of any attempt to recall American history or the evolution of American civilization was one of the remarkable features of the Centennial Exhibition. There had been a proposal for a demonstration of Colonial farming techniques, contrasting them with those of 1876, but nothing came of it. As can be imagined, there was no lack of full-blown oratory, both at the opening and at the closing of the fair; yet references to history were perfunctory or few. The past was prologue; interesting enough, but not to be compared with the marvels of the present and the promise of the future.[20]

The foreign influence on the Exhibition was also apparent in the decision of Philadelphia's civic leaders to dispatch a commission to several European cities to study the impact of previous large fairs on their host urban environments. Perhaps because the legislation authorizing the celebration, passed by Congress on March 3, 1871, stated clearly that "the United States shall not be liable for any expenses attending such exhibition, or by any reason of the same," the Centennial Board of Finance and the city administration felt obliged to learn as much as they could from the experiences of other cities. The commissioners who returned from Vienna and London emphasized the strain that such an event would place on existing city services and made a strong argument that it was only sensible to make some significant municipal improvements in order to secure long-term benefits for Philadelphia from the Centennial. The result was the construction of a new city hall in Penn Square and the expansion of horsecar lines to parts of the city that had previously had no form of mass transportation. In 1876 Philadelphia could boast the most extensive municipal transportation system of any city in the country.[21]

It was not art but the 5000 horsepower Corliss Engine and a display of Alexander Graham Bell's telephone that attracted most visitors to the Ehibition.[22] On opening day, May 10, President Grant's remarks as he started the Engine illustrated the theme of progress and the importance of technology, not the aesthetic dimension of American culture. "One hundred years ago," stated Grant,

> our country was new and but partially settled. Our necessities have compelled us chiefly to expend our means and time in felling forests, subduing prairies, building dwellings, factories, ships, docks, warehouses, roads,

> canals, machinery, etc. Most of our schools, churches, libraries, and asylums have been established within a hundred years. Burdened by these great primal works of necessity, which could not be delayed, we have yet done what this Exhibition will show in the direction of rivaling older and more advanced nations in law, medicine, and theology, in science, literature, philosophy and the fine arts. Whilst proud of what we have done, we regret that we have not done more. Our achievements have been great enough, however, to make it easy for our people to acknowledge superior merit wherever found.[23]

While the United States at its hundredth birthday had blazed new trails in conquering a continent, establishing industrial capitalism, and extending many of the benefits of democracy to its white male citizens, in matters of art and culture, America was still Europe's stepchild.

The reliance on a European-born conductor and the predominance of European music at this American celebration illustrate the prevailing ambivalence regarding the worth of concert music created in this country. Theodore Thomas, a German-born conductor whose efforts to improve the aesthetic tastes of American audiences as well as the performance standards of his orchestras were well known, was engaged by the Woman's Centennial Committees to select and conduct music at the opening ceremonies of the Exhibition and to conduct a series of concerts at the Edwin Forrest Mansion, which the Women's Committees had converted into a concert hall for the summer season. Thomas was the logical choice for this assignment. Even if the Centennial organizers had thought it was important to choose a native-born American conductor, they would not have found a man of Thomas's ability and reputation. Many American musicians did conduct local bands and community orchestras and they dominated the ranks of church choir directors, but no nonimmigrant American conducted a major symphony orchestra in this country on a regular basis before the close of the nineteenth century.

Thomas's personal artistic crusade took the form of programming and conducting only what he considered to be the best music and hiring only the most capable musicians to play it. Midcentury American orchestras were held in less than high repute for their lax discipline and lack of inspiration. According to music historian W. S. B. Matthews, players were

> largely without ambition, and hopelessly fast in ruts. There was a large repertoire that was gone over season after season. The expense of new music and the impossibility of getting it properly interpreted without a number of rehearsals beyond the resources of the conductor, kept affairs stationary.[24]

Thomas overcame these difficulties by drilling his players in the necessary musical mechanics until each piece sounded correct according to his standards. He often paid for the extra rehearsal time out of his own pocket.

Thomas began his American career as a performer, having been hailed as a child prodigy violinist in Germany. Leon Stein has written that there is "something of the Lincoln legend" in Thomas's early musical experiences in this country. As a young traveling performer he had to use all of his talents to gain a hearing in America's small cities and towns. He posted his own concert announcements, sold tickets, acted as his own usher, and after a quick change of clothing appeared on stage as the featured performer of the evening. Years later Thomas continued to play many parts, as tour manager, fund raiser, and artistic director of his various orchestras. Resourcefulness and determination enabled this German immigrant musician to exert a profound influence on the development of late nineteenth-century orchestral music in his adopted country.[25] Beginning in 1855 Thomas joined pianist William Mason and such famous immigrant musicians as Carl Bergmann and J. Mosenthal in presenting chamber music concerts in New York. For fourteen years the Mason-Thomas concerts presented excellent performances of standard works and also brought many new pieces to the United States, including works by Schumann and Brahms.

Thomas organized his own professional orchestra in New York in December of 1864. As a pioneer in the art of building an entire program in which each piece bore some relationship to the others on the concert, Thomas was very successful. His summer concerts in Central Park were called "a college where one could hear works, representing every part of orchestral literature, given frequently, and in proper co-ordination with other works congenial, or artistically contrasting with them."[26] Thomas tried to achieve a balance between giving the public popular music and introducing new and difficult works. He was not averse to programming light music, such as the waltzes of Johann Strauss, as he believed that if audiences could hear these pieces played well, they would develop a greater appreciation for a good orchestral sound. Thomas also introduced excerpts from the operas of Richard Wagner at a time when that composer was virtually unknown in this country. For example, in 1870, Thomas's orchestra performed the *Ride of the Valkyries* for the first time in the United States. Soon, the *Magic Fire Scene* (also from *Die Valkyrie) and Sigfried's Funeral March* from *Gotterdammerung* also found their way onto the programs of the orchestra. The artistic and popular success of the Theodore Thomas Orchestra in

New York and on tour would be a major factor in the founding of the Chicago Symphony Orchestra under Thomas's direction in 1891.

Support for Thomas as the Centennial Exhibition's music director increased as the time for the decision by the Women's Committees approached. A columnist in the *New York Daily Tribune* wrote that Thomas's orchestra was

> so far before all others in America that comparisons with others are out of the question. It is not only the best in America, but there are probably only two that seriously rival it in the entire world. It is therefore something that we shall take great pride in showing to our friends from abroad . . . we ought to exhibit it therefore as one of the most interesting products of our aesthetic culture and a triumph of American enterprise.[27]

The voices in opposition to Thomas's appointment were few indeed, especially as there seemed to be no logical alternative candidate. Nevertheless, one anonymous citizen did ask the *New York Daily Tribune,*

> What has Mr. Thomas done for native art? . . . Works have come from the brains of American composers, and have been offered to Theodore Thomas for his consideration, and while he acknowledged their merit, he refused them because they were American.[28]

It was true that Thomas programmed only those pieces by American composers which, he felt, conformed to the standards established by the best composers of Europe. But in 1875 the *Tribune* hardly considered the issue of programming music by Americans worthy of consideration. To the accusation that Thomas did not give the music of Americans its due consideration, the editors replied that "the great work of the musical leader in this country just now is not to encourage composers so much as to educate audiences. Fostering native art is the business of a Conservatory."[29]

Once Thomas's selection was approved, the Women's Centennial Committees, headed by Mrs. E. D. Gillespie of Philadelphia, set about the task of providing appropriate music for the Inaugural Ceremonies. American music and poetry were not neglected here. Thomas asked John Knowles Paine to compose the music for a *Centennial Hymn* to a text by John Greenleaf Whittier, and he also requested that Dudley Buck, a noted church music composer, write the music for Sidney Lanier's cantata, *Centennial Meditation of Columbia*. These two works were performed on opening day and at the first evening concert in the Edwin Forrest Mansion, renamed Women's Centennial Music Hall for the Centennial season. But neither piece received much attention during the remainder of the summer nor thereafter in the American concert hall.

The musical showpiece of the Centennial's inauguration was to be a march that would represent the festive and celebratory spirit of the event and also be of sufficiently high quality to remain in the concert repertoire. Mrs. Gillespie wrote to Thomas that her committees would "pay an honorarium for the composing of an inaugural march" if he could find "some famous European composer" to write it.[30] Thomas, long a champion of the music of Richard Wagner, contacted the composer in Bayreuth and suggested that he compose the inaugural. At first, Wagner declined, claiming that the pressures of a busy production schedule would preclude his writing something new, but eventually, he acceded to Thomas's request.

Wagner had no pretensions regarding the artistic merit of his march. The American music critic and biographer Henry T. Finck quoted him as having remarked that "the best thing about the composition was the money I got for it."[31] Nevertheless, Thomas had committed himself to a work that would receive several performances during the summer of 1876 and then would virtually disappear from American concert programs. Not only is there no attempt to create an "American" image or feeling in this work, it seemed to be a throw-away piece that not even Thomas's best efforts at cutting or rearranging could improve. As for the pictorial elements of the *Grand Inaugural March* the composer wrote to Thomas that

> a few soft and tender passages in the March are meant to depict the beautiful and talented women of North America, as they take part in the cortège. I am glad to say that it was my intention to have these noble-hearted women take the first place in the procession, rather than the men, because they were the chief promoters and most energetic workers for my composition.[32]

But, in spite of the dedication of the march to the Women's Centennial Committees, Wagner did not treat his chief supporters with either respect or consideration, particularly with regard to the honorarium for his efforts. The composer demanded $5000 deposited with his banker, before he would even begin working on the piece. Then, although he had promised full copyright control to the Committees, he refused to relinquish the copyright, saying that it was his impression that the ladies wanted only the glory that a piece from his pen would bring to their celebration. He could not imagine that they had any idea of publishing the march or of selling copies for a profit. This, of course, was exactly what Mrs. Gillespie and her committee women had in mind. Wagner also reneged on his promise to delay the European publication of the march until six months after it had been published in the United

States. In addition, he allowed an arrangement of the march, prepared by Anton Rubinstein, to be shipped to this country for sale even before he had sent the original manuscript to Thomas. Thus, the beleaguered conductor was able to learn in any music store in New York, Chicago, Boston, or Philadelphia that the march was "so poor that it was practically worthless" even before he had examined the score himself.[33] These events caused Thomas considerable disillusionment with Wagner (but not with his music, which he continued to conduct) and embarrassment at the situation. Charles Edward Russell, in his book on Thomas and the development of orchestral music in America, noted that Thomas's pride in his adopted country and its national celebration was hurt when

> he saw plainly that Wagner had viewed not only the occasion but the country with contempt. Anything was good enough for Americans. A final and gratuitous smart was the thought that he had been the means of putting on the program of a great and solemn national festival a composition beneath the dignity of its day and its significance.[34]

The Wagner march formed the centerpiece of the Centennial's Inaugural Ceremonies, amid many speeches, the starting of the Corliss Engine, and a variety of other musical works. Critic John Sullivan Dwight reserved comment on the Wagner march, although he conveyed skepticism about the immediate critical praise that it inspired from some of the more rhapsodic pens in Philadelphia. Dwight commented that these writers "bade us believe that Music stood upon its highest pinnacle that day, side by side with proud Columbia on her 'hundred terraced height.' " Dwight's journal reprinted a column on the Centennial's opening ceremonies from the Philadelphia *Transcript* that included the following assessment of Wagner's contribution to the festivities:

> No praise which has been lavished upon this noble compostion overstates its merit, and we are greatly disappointed in the taste of our countrymen if it does not soon become one of Thomas's most popular concert pieces. . . . it is a purely original work—perhaps one of the most original things Wagner has written since "Tristan." It goes without saying that the instrumentation is of the most gorgeous description, for in the use of the materials of his orchestra, Wagner is by general consent one of the greatest masters who ever lived.[35]

In response to his Philadelphia colleague, Dwight was moved to question the validity of procuring a march for this American celebration from Richard Wagner when it was possible that there were American composers who could have contributed such a centerpiece. Or, as Dwight asked, if a suitable work by an American composer could not be found, why not perform the finale of Beethoven's Fifth Symphony or a movement by Handel? The critic wondered,

> *Was* the music altogether a piece of "national good fortune"? Was its direction (by which we suppose is meant its selection) guided from the first by "liberality and good sense"? Liberality to be sure; it was indeed liberal and more than liberal to pay $5,000. for one noisy March,—more probably than Beethoven got for all the Nine Symphonies! But as to the good sense of making such account of any March at all, especially of sending for it to the most partisan composer of the age, . . . common sense forbid! We can assure this enthusiastic writer, that many a "serious musician" *does* hold it to have been "unworthy of the occasion." "No attempt at the sensational?" When the Centennial was captured from the outset by the Wagnerites, when the musical side of it was Wagnerized, was it not most effectively sensationalized?[36]

Although Dwight was moving a bit closer to recognizing the talent of American composers, he continued to crusade against the popular and the sensational in concert music in this country. In the case of Wagner's *Inaugural Grand March* his questions were well placed, as the spirit of the event might better have been served by the music of Beethoven, Handel, or even an American composer.

The musical portion of the May 10 ceremonies was repeated in its entirety at the first concert of the evening series at the Women's Centennial Music Hall at which, true to his reputation as a programmer of the best European music, Thomas surrounded the American pieces that had been commissioned for the Centennial with standard works that were sure to please the audience and assure that the evening would be appropriately dignified. The lengthy program was as follows:

Part I

Introduction—National Airs	
Overture, "Consecration of the House"	Beethoven
Invitation to the Dance	Weber
Aria from "The Magic Flute"	Mozart

Part II: Centennial Inaugural Programme

Grand Inaugural March	Wagner
Centennial Hymn	J. K. Paine
Cantata-Centennial Meditation of Columbia	Dudley Buck
Hallelujah Chorus	Handel

Part III

Waltz, "On the Beautiful Blue Danube"	Strauss
Serenade	Schubert
Overture, "Masaniello"	Auber[37]

In spite of Thomas's reputation and the quality of his orchestra, the concert series in the Women's Centennial Music Hall fared badly. The concert promoters assumed that, because the Exhibition closed at sundown and there were few cultural events planned for the evening hours, people would flock to hear Thomas and his orchestra, in spite of the out-of-the-way location of the Hall. But attendance proved to be sparse at best, as visitors to the Exhibition witnessed much less elevating spectacles, such as Simmons, Slocum, and Sweatman's Minstrels; The Mechanical Horse ($10 given to anyone staying on his back); James Bohee, the Great Banjoist; and John H. Clark's Sparring Academy.[38] For a brief period in June there was some healthy competition between Thomas's orchestra and that of the French composer and conductor Jacques Offenbach. Both groups performed concerts of light music, and attendance at the Music Hall improved somewhat as listeners compared the orchestras and their respective leaders.

Just as the high-wheeled bicycle (which would soon become a national craze), the refreshment bars, and the opportunity to consume ice cream and soda "pop" in a variety of flavors were highlights of the Exhibition during the day, the public gravitated at night toward amusements rather than the more educational and elevating fare that Thomas and his orchestra offered in the Women's Centennial Music Hall. The concert series was such a financial failure that the Women's Committees withdrew their backing, leaving Thomas responsible for its economic as well as its artistic health. He lost so much money on the venture that his entire music library, including scores, books, and arrangements, even his music stand and baton, were sold at a sheriff's auction. Ironically, one of the pieces sold at auction to make up for the debacle of the 1876 summer concert series was the original autograph copy of Wagner's *Grand Inaugural March*, which the Women's Centennial Committees had earlier presented to Thomas as a gift.[39] Although it seemed that Thomas's American musical career would have to begin again, there was some small help forthcoming. Dr. Franz Zinzer of New York purchased Thomas's entire collection at the auction for $1400. In 1878 he presented it to Mrs. Thomas for her husband's use on the condition that he treat the materials "carefully."[40] Thomas began almost immediately to reorganize his orchestra and to give concerts throughout the United States.

The American composers whose music appeared on the programs of Thomas's orchestra during the Centennial summer season expressed little interest in representing the special nature of their country in music. John Knowles Paine and other highly trained musical craftsmen of the period sought an audience in the middle- and upper-class patrons of the major symphony orchestras who were already accustomed to good music as defined by European standards. For the majority of Americans, music, if it impinged on their daily lives at all, took the form of community or ethnic celebrations and popular entertainment of the music-hall variety. It is not surprising that Thomas's concerts did not attract large audiences, as the general public was not accustomed to experiencing "culture" in the hushed atmosphere of the concert hall.

On April 25, 1890, President Benjamin Harrison signed a bill that would provide another major opportunity for the music of American composers to be heard by a wide audience, although American concert music was hardly the sole focus of the legislation. The law provided for the celebration of the four hundredth anniversary of Christopher Columbus's discovery of America with an international exposition of "the arts, industries, manufactures, and the products of the soil, mine, and sea in the City of Chicago in the State of Illinois."[41] Once again, the United States celebrated an event in its own history by sponsoring an international fair, and, once again, Theodore Thomas was the choice of the organizers to supervise the musical activities.

The World's Columbian Exposition, or the Chicago World's Fair, as it came to be called, represented what Henry Nash Smith designated a "Mark of punctuation in American cultural history."[42] The city of Chicago had competed successfully for the honor of sponsoring the event with the more prominent eastern cities of New York and Philadelphia. Civic leaders, many of whom had supported the idea of bringing the Exposition Fair to the midwestern metropolis as early as 1885, thought that it was appropriate that "the youngest, most enterprising and representative city in America . . . celebrate the landing of the great navigator of Genoa upon the new continent."[43] In answer to the concern that Chicago was not a fit cultural environment in which to celebrate such an important American anniversary, Henry Van Brunt, writing in the *Atlantic Monthly*, emphasized future promise for the nation as a whole and the West in particular:

> The Exposition will furnish to our people an object lesson of a magnitude, scope, and significance such as not been seen elsewhere. They will for the first time be made conscious of the duties, as yet unfulfilled, which they themselves owe to the civilization of the century. They will learn from the lessons of this wonderful pageant that they have not as yet taken their proper place in the world; that there is something far better worth doing than mere acquiring and spending of wealth. . . . They will be suddenly confronted by new ideals and inspired by higher ambitions; they will find in themselves qualities hitherto unsuspected, capacities for happiness and powers of production hitherto unknown.[44]

An optimistic tone was also reflected in the views of those who believed that the former village, now a burgeoning city, was "the heart of the nation already and would soon be the national centre of letters and art."[45] Indeed, the presence of the Exposition in an industrial city of "the West" was an indication of the forward visison of the Fair's planners, one which had prevailed in 1876 in Philadelphia with the Centennial's emphasis on industrial, technological, and commercial progress. According to Henry Nash Smith,

> the Garden of the World in the interior of the continent had become an industrialized region of the country capable of creating the enormous ugly mass of Chicago and a dozen other urban centers from Cleveland to Minneapolis and Kansas City. These cities belonged to the new age of steam and steel rather than to the frontier or the agrarian past.[46]

Prior to 1893 Chicago had experienced rapid, almost frenzied growth in commerce and industry, and it was not long before a wealthy and educated class of patrons for artistic activity of all types emerged. The city had seen its first concert series, featuring a piano imported from London, in 1834–35, and October 24, 1850, saw the inauguration of a Philharmonic Society that "formed the beginning of an organized musical culture which has affected and benefitted this city through its later life."[47] And, through the efforts of businessman Charles Norman Fay, fifty Chicago citizens pledged $1000 a year for three years in order to establish the Chicago Orchestra Association in December of 1890. The financial guarantee thus established, Theodore Thomas and the Chicago Symphony Orchestra began peforming on October 17, 1891.[48]

The Exposition provided an opportunity for the United States to demonstrate its continued remarkable industrial progress, but more important, it was also an occasion to show that Europe's stepchild in matters of art could boast cultural institutions, if not yet a culture, of her own. The planners of the musical events at the Chicago World's Fair held to the notion that culture could thrive in the commercial and material world. In 1893, with its own orchestra under the venerable Thomas, Chicago was prepared to present a series of musical events of which the nation could be justly proud. Consistent with Thomas's goal to educate as well as entertain his audience were the central ideas of the Exposition's Music Bureau, to "make a complete showing to the world of the musical progress in this country" and to "bring before the public of the United States a full illustration of music in its highest form, as exemplified by the most enlightened nations of the world."[49]

The Exposition was officially dedicated on October 12, 1892, although it did not open for visitors until the spring of 1893. Daniel H. Burnham, the chief architect for the Exposition, had conceived the notion of the "White City" as a structural theme for the project. He brought together the efforts of American architects to design buildings, sculptors to create statues, fountains, and decorative pillars, and painters to provide murals for walls and domes. In addition, Frederick Law Olmsted planned the lanscaping of the grounds. All of these efforts were intended to achieve a harmonious result, within the context of already familiar forms and styles.[50] The music of the concert programs also represented the finest examples of familiar forms and styles. Significantly, many of these compositions were created by Americans.

It was important to present the host country as an equal among nations, and the language of the speeches given at the Exposition's many ceremonies underlined the greatness of late nineteenth-century America, both in terms of the magnificence of the fair itself and with respect to the unique American environment that could produce such a marvel. Like the orations in Philadelphia in 1876, those in Chicago stressed progress. On opening day President Grover Cleveland lauded the

> splendid edifices, but we have also built the magnificent fabric of our popular government, whose grand proportions are seen throughout the world. We have made and here gathered together objects of use and beauty, the products of American skill and invention; but we have also made men who rule themselves.[51]

Among the "objects of use and beauty" to which President Cleveland referred were works of art and musical compositions, which the Exposition's audiences had ample opportunity to see and hear. Like the American painters who found at the Fair the chance "to show that their work could stand comparison with that of other nations,"[52] the American composers whose music was performed throughout the summer of 1893 found that their works shared programs arranged by Thomas with those of Europe's most important past and contemporary composers. Although there were occasional patriotic gestures during the summer in the form of "All American Programmes," music by American composers was generally integrated into concerts throughout the season.

The Exposition's Opening Ceremonies set the tone for the entire event, with its emphasis on grandeur and national pride. Before an invited audience of 100,000, with uncounted thousands more gathered outside the Manufactures Building, the "master artists" of the Fair, including Theodore Thomas and the composer George Whitefield Chadwick, received special medals in recognition of their contribution to the celebration, ministers asked God's blessings on the proceedings, and Thomas led an orchestra of 200 players in a performance of John Knowles Paine's *Columbus March and Hymn*, composed for the occasion. A chorus of 500 voices, led by William H. Tomlins, sang portions of Harriet Moore's massive 400-line *Columbia Ode,* which Chadwick had set to music. The program as a whole reflects the pride with which the World's Columbian Exposition's organizers presented their Fair to the public, and its extreme length attests to the patience of the massive audience.[53] Paine's *Columbus March* also welcomed visitors to the opening of the Fair's exhibits on May 1, 1893.

The Music Bureau of the Exposition engaged Theodore Thomas to plan and direct concerts throughout the summer. In contrast to the situation in 1876, wherein the concert series in the Women's Centennial Music Hall had been financed privately, mostly at risk to Thomas's personal finances, the Chicago concerts, of which there were fourteen types in all, were planned under the auspices of the Exposition and its Bureau of Music.[54] Almost all of the programs were held during the Fair's regular daytime hours or, thanks to electric lights, in the early evening hours in either Festival Hall or the Music Hall, and not in an out-of-the-way location like the former Edwin Forrest Mansion. These factors combined to assure a greater degree of artistic and financial success than could have been achieved seventeen years earlier in Philadelphia. In addition, Thomas's reputation as a conductor was now enhanced by the prestige that such composers as Paine, Chadwick, Foote, MacDowell, and Mrs. Beach brought to the event with their compositions. These were prominent American composers whose works could not be ignored in planning the Exposition's many concerts.

Thomas made an effort to seek out appropriate music by Americans for his concerts. Native composers of the "first rank" were asked to choose which of their works they wished to have played, while a large number of other American composers received the following notice:

> The Musical Director of the World's Columbian Exposition desires to include in the programmes of its concerts representative choral, orchestral, and chamber compositions by native Americans. All scores received before October 15, 1892, will be submitted to the following committee: Sir Alexander C. Mackenzie, London; Asgar Hammerich, Baltimore; B. J. Lang, Boston; William L. Tomlins and Theodore Thomas, Chicago. The favorable recommendation of this committee will be final and will insure performance.[55]

Thomas and the Exposition Festival Orchestra, which ranged in size from 100 to 150 players, presented three concert series during the six-month season of the Fair in 1893. The Festival Hall Series of twenty-seven concerts between May 22 and August 5 appealed to popular tastes. There were numerous choral concerts, including performances by a 1200-voice children's choir and programs by a variety of American

Table 2-1 American Composers and the Popular Orchestral Series

Composer	*Piece*	*Date(s) Performed*
Arthur Bird	Suite No. 3, Op. 32	June 12
Charles C. Converse	Overture, "Hail Columbia"	July 4
Arthur Foote	Serenade for String Orchestra	June 13 July 13
Frederick G. Gleason	Prelude, "Otho Visconti"	May 26
	two pieces, op 26	August 7
Margaret Ruthven Lang	Overture, "Witichis"	July 29
Edward MacDowell	"Indian" Suite	May 12
John Knowles Paine	Columbus March and Hymn	May 20 July 4 July 29
Henry Rowe Shelley	Suite, "The Ruined Castle"	July 19

choruses, including the Mannerchor of Minneapolis, the American Union of Swedish Singers, and the Choral Society of the Western States. On July 8, the last movement of Chadwick's *Columbian Ode*, composed for the opening day ceremonies, shared the program with music by Gluck, Beethoven, and Dvořák. Orchestral music by Richard Wagner occupied an important place on the programs in this series, as, by 1893, the American audience was beginning to develop a fondness for the music of the genius of Bayreuth, thanks in large part to the earlier efforts of Theodore Thomas. In general, American composers were only modestly represented on this series by the songs of Arthur Foote and Stephen Foster.

But there was considerably more music by American composers on the programs of the Popular Orchestral Series of fifty-three concerts between May 3 and August 11. (Table 2-1 provides a list of those Americans whose works were performed in this series.) Thomas's subordination of nationalistic inclinations to a high standard of artistic excellence can even be observed in the Fourth of July concert. Paine's *Columbus March and Hymn*, Charles Crozat Converse's *Hail Columbia* overture, *The Star Spangled Banner*, and *America* shared the program with music by Saint-Saëns, Schubert, Wagner, Strauss, and Moszkowski, whose suite *The Nations* provided musical portraits of Russia, Italy, Germany, Spain, Poland, and Hungary. This composition, selected for its international character, did not include any musical references to the United States.

The only series at the Exposition to offer programs of music exclusively by American composers was the one presented in the Music Hall between May 2 and August 4. Performances of Thomas's orchestra were supplemented by guest appearances by the Boston Symphony Orchestra, the New York Symphony Society, and the Cincinnati Festival Orchestra in this thirty-six concert series. An American Programme on May 23 featured music by Chadwick, Foote, and MacDowell. Chadwick was represented by his Second Symphony, and the Festival Orchestra played Foote's *Serenade for Strings in E.* The highlight of this concert was MacDowell's *Indian* Suite, which the composer conducted. Of the three works, this was the only one in which an American program figured. But this Suite places its Indian tribal melodies squarely in a Romantic symphonic context, and it is difficult to hear any "American" qualities in the music at all. July 6 saw the performance of a special concert of music by American composers in recognition of the work of the Music Teachers' National Association, a group that had encouraged the creative efforts of immigrant and native-born American composers since its founding in the 1870s. On August 4 Thomas and his orchestra presented three compositions that had been submitted to the examining committee chosen to review works in answer to the call for music that Thomas had issued in late 1892. Margaret Ruthven Lang's overture, *Witichis*, John A. Broeckhoven's *Suite Creole*, and a concert overture by Hermann Wetzler shared the program with the Mendelssohn Violin Concerto, played by the popular American soloist Maude Powell.[56] Another concert in this series featured the music of lesser-known American composers—A. M. Foerster, Henry Rowe Shelley, and Henry Schoenfeld—as well as Arthur Bird and Frederick Grant Gleason, whose reputations were somewhat better established.

But, in spite of Thomas's reputation, all was not well in Chicago, and the musical events, the Music Bureau that organized them, and the conductor who was the prime mover in the selection and performance of the music became the subject of considerable controversy. Not all visitors to the Exposition or writers on the event thought it was a good idea to present elevating musical entertainment that would educate, even as it provided pleasure for the crowds in the White City. The *Providence* [*R.I.*] *Journal*, setting its sights on the average visitor to the fair rather than the typical patron of concert music in this country, commented that

> the generality of people who attend a World's Fair do not care to spend time in sitting down for a couple of hours to listen to a severely classical concert without any particular feature of special attractiveness, more especially when they have to pay a large additional fee for so doing. . . . Who, for instance, visiting a World's Fair, after having come a long distance, will devote a couple of hours out of the afternoon to listen to a concert of chamber music, even of the best possible quality? There is a lack of proportion and of a sense of general fitness in the idea which is positively ludicrous. One might as well try to make a miniature do duty as a fresco in the dome of St. Peter.[57]

The writer from Providence leveled some valid criticism at the musical organization of the Exposition, as the one dollar charge for admission revealed "the intention of restricting the audiences for the higher concerts to the music lovers, who might profit by them, and the exclusion of mere loafers." Nevertheless, thousands of Americans attended Thomas's concerts, as well as those of the visiting bands, orchestras, and choral groups. During the month of June, many concerts were offered to the public for half the usual charge, and the Providence commentary neglects to mention that programs of popular music and all of the band concerts were free duing the Exposition.[58]

But the criticism of Thomas was more severe and the attacks on his artistic integrity were more personal. Throughout the spring and summer of 1893, even as he continued to conduct in Chicago, Thomas became embroiled in a controversy over commercialism rather than art that eventually led to his resignation as Director of Music for the Exposition. The trouble began when the piano manufacturing establishment of Steinway & Sons, along with several other eastern piano makers, elected not to exhibit their wares in Chicago, possibly, but by no means certainly, in protest of the Fair's location in Chicago rather than New York. In response, piano makers from the midwestern and western regions of the country demanded that instruments made by the absent manufacturers should not be used for performance, a demand to which Thomas obviously could not accede, given that many of the soloists he had engaged, some of whom had agreed to perform for no fee, had exclusive arrangements with particular instrument makers, agreements that could not be breached. Besides, as a matter of artistic integrity, Thomas believed that performers had a right to play on the instruments of their choice.

But the western piano makers, including the Sangamon County Piano and Jew's-harp Company, appealed to George R. Davis, the Director General of the Exposition, who ordered that only pianos made by exhibiting manufacturers could be used. Thomas went ahead with plans for a concert featuring pianist Ignace Paderewski (whose piano was a

Steinway), the concert was held, some of the Chicago newspapers (most notably the *Herald* and the *Post*) were up in arms, and Thomas continued with his artistic and administrative duties as usual. The controversy escalated with an accusation that Thomas had banned a harp made by the firm of Lyon & Healy, which also exhibited pianos at the Fair, and, eventually, charges that he had accepted payments from the absent eastern piano manufacturerers to use only their instruments, or, at the very least, that he had chosen certain performing musicians because they used "New York instruments." After testimony that suppported Thomas's contention that it was not he, but his chief harpist Edmund Schuecker who had banned the Lyon and Healy harp, the controversy should have subsided. But the official inquiry commission told the press after its meetings in early May of 1893 that Thomas "was partial to a New York concern and was using his position as Director of Music to bestow favors on his personal friends that could not be secured by exhibitors who were spending thousands of dollars in making displays at the Fair."[59] The commission called for Thomas's removal, and an official request for his resignation came from the office of George Davis on May 17.

In spite of the commission's opinion, Davis's formal request for his resignation, and vicious attacks in the press, Thomas continued to conduct, with the full support of the Board of Directors of the Exposition Company. A less strident Chicago newspaper, the *Tribune*, rallied to Thomas's defense, citing his prior reptuation for artistic and personal integrity, and the *New York Times* went so far as to call the actions of those newspapers supporting the Sangamon and other western piano companies "an exhibition of the Yahoo press." That assessment is borne out by the following commentary from the June 23 *Herald*:

> Theodore Thomas is unable to discern any melody in a piece of music unless it emanates from a German composer. Mr. Thomas's musical taste is decidedly foreign. All airs except those of the Fatherland are vicious in his ears. He loves the German musicians and he abhors all others. It seems never to have occurred to Mr. Thomas that it would be proper for him as musical director of the Exposition to consult the wishes of the people in the arrangement of his programs. The public really likes "Yankee Doodle" when played well rather than a Wagnerian symphony in E.[60]

Like the writer from Providence, this Chicago observer spoke with the voice of a public that had little knowledge of music and little interest in acquiring any more. This was precisely the musical situation that Thomas had worked to remedy throughout his long career. While he could never be called a champion of American music solely for the sake of patriotism, he did often support the efforts of American composers by performing their music if it conformed to his well-known high standards. These men and women were by no means absent from the programs of the World's Columbian Exposition.

Ultimately, the controversy over music merchandising versus high culture was resolved not by decisions based on artistic criteria but by the Panic of 1893. Attendance at the Exposition declined, and the Board of Directors was faced with the difficult task of cutting expenses. It began its work with the Bureau of Music, thus leaving Thomas with no funds with which to pay his musicians and guest artists. With this development, Thomas submitted his resignation on August 12. Even a declaration by the members of his former Exposition Orchestra that they would play without compensation could not induce Thomas to return to the event for which he had contributed his outstanding programming and conducting skills but which had become an emotional trial. He had presented a brilliant and controversial season for the World's Columbian Exposition that, while it diverged only a bit from the repertoire of standard European classics, still managed to contribute to an important American celebration a number of works by American composers that were likely to remain in the concert repertoire. In spite of the charges and attacks leveled against him, Theodore Thomas had succeeded in making the best European and American music for the concert hall available to a large public in Chicago.

The World's Columbian Exposition, which music historian Rupert Hughes called in 1900 the "artistic birthday of Chicago and possibly the most important artistic event in our national history,"[61] did not inspire the creation of American music that claimed a unique national character. In spite of the rhetoric of the Fair's orations, which emphasized American achievement and the promise of a future free of dependence on older European societies, only those American composers whose music sounded familiar, i.e., "European," found themselves able to obtain a hearing for their creative efforts.

The experiences of the Gilmore Peace Jubilees, the Philadelphia Centennial Exhibition of 1876, and the World's Columbia Exposition of 1893 illustrate a tension between the need or desire to provide cultural education and an equally compelling demand for popular celebration. Each of these events attempted to provide the best of high culture in America while also including "light" music, band concerts, and other varieties of popular music that were not associated with traditional symphony, opera, or chamber music performances.

Even in 1915, at the Panama Pacific Exposition in San Francisco, the dichotomy between popular entertainment and high culture in the European manner was apparent. For example, Exposition historian Frank

Morton Todd described Music Director George W. Stewart's views on what music was appropriate for the commemoration of the opening of the Panama Canal:

> . . . Instead of serious symphonic compositions to be rendered in a solemn temple, and of interest but to a limited cult, there should be great military bands playing in the open, and playing music that would appeal to all classes—not trash for that purpose, but good, popular compositions, and especially things that were new. Even the professional artist visiting an exposition would not be in a frame of mind to enjoy the more technical exemplifications of his art, and the general public could not be expected to. The public would not have any patience with efforts to educate it musically, and it would not derive any benefit from what it did not enjoy. The general music plan should have as its core a complete orchestra of about 80 players, around which could be built a scheme that would include something for everybody.[62]

But in spite of the popular focus of Stewart's views on the nature of music in relation to the public at the Exposition, there was no dearth of "classical" performances among the 2,206 concerts held during the nine and one-half months of the celebration. These included appearances by such artists as Fritz Kreisler, Ignace Paderewski, Camille Saint-Saëns, Victor Herbert, John Philip Sousa, and Karl Mück and the Boston Symphony Orchestra. The Exposition Chorus peformed such standard works as the Verdi *Requiem* and Mendelssohn's *Elijah*. And, as if to underscore the continued reliance on European music and artists (this, in spite of the absence of many European performing groups because of World War I), the highlight of the music at the Exposition was the appearance of Camille Saint-Saëns, who conducted many of his own pieces and also contributed the official Exposition Symphony, *Hail California!* to the event.[63] Once again, Americans celebated the glories of their past and the promise of their future with music contributed by Europeans.

The role of concert music at these patriotic events of such importance to the celebration of America in the nineteenth and the early twentieth century illustrates not only the tension between cultural education and elevation on one hand and popular celebration on the other, it also points to an ambivalence regarding the existence of a high culture in this country that could be called "American." As citizens of an emerging world power, Americans looked to the future with the perception that they needed few models with which to conquer a frontier, marshal an army, or Americanize new immigrants. But in the realm of culture, at least in music, Americans blazed few trails of their own prior to World

War I, accepting instead without question the models that they had inherited from Europe. After the turn of the century, when this country would become involved in a World War with Germany, that cultural dependence would be called into question, at least for a short time, in the name of patriotism.

3

World War I and the Challenge of 100% Americanism

In late October of 1917, orchestra and opera patrons in the United States learned that they would soon be paying for admission to their favorite cultural events. Program inserts and special announcements informed audiences that the new 10 percent tax on tickets for all entertainment and recreational activities had been mandated by Title VII, Section 700 of the federal "Act to provide revenue to defray war expenses and for other purposes."[1] Most concertgoers no doubt regarded this unusual surcharge as a necessary nuisance for the war effort and hoped that the call of patriotic sacrifice would not extend into the realm of the standard concert and operatic repertoire. But music lovers did eventually have to face the problem of reconciling their love for music by German, Austrian, and Hungarian composers with newly defined concepts of loyalty to the United States. In concert music, as in other areas of American life, the anti-German hysteria of the World War I years engendered a struggle against what many regarded as an enemy culture that had the potential to weaken the resolve of the nation. For a brief period, this struggle seemed to pit high culture against patriotism, although, in the long run, the special patriotic climate of the time had little impact on the music Americans paid to hear in the concert hall. The extent to which 100% Americanism was able to permeate the realm of concert music and opera and the responses of composers, performers, and orchestras to the special demands of the wartime emergency forms an important, if not a particularly happy, chapter in the history of American cultural identity.

To varying degrees German music and musicians were rejected by American musical institutions, and the war seemed to provide an opportunity for performing groups to express their patriotism by employing American artists and programming works by American composers. But this interest in American music was short-lived, and few of the compositions created for the war effort survived the enthusiasm of the moment. Henry F. Gilbert, an ardent musical nationalist in the years immediately preceeding the War, declared in 1920 that when music is inspired only "by a blind and perfervid sense of patriotism, the result is apt to be that of the traditional 'bull in the china shop.' "[2]

The war produced opportunities for music by American composers to be heard, but it did not contribute significantly to the development of American music. To the extent that the call for national musical expression was sounded, it went largely unanswered. Instead, in the name of patriotism, many individuals and organizations called into question the loyalty of those performers and conductors who maintained their artistic allegiance to what had become standard repertoire in this country.

The term "100% Americanism" denotes the patriotic mindset promoted by the Wilson administration in order to encourage and maintain support for the fighting in Europe and the necessary sacrifices on the home front. The tools for shaping a patriotic consensus in a diverse population of 100,000,000 were the slogans, parades, speeches, posters, and news articles generated under the auspices of George Creel's Committee on Public Information. While Creel did not use the term himself, the ideology of "100% Americanism" dominated his writings and speeches. He stressed the necessity of consensus and wartime loyalty, writing that what the national emergency required

> was no mere surface unity, but a passionate belief in the justice of America's cause that should weld the people into one white-hot mass instinct with fraternity, devotion, courage, and deathless determination. The *war-will*, the will-to-win, of a democracy depends upon the degree to which each one of all the people of that democracy can concentrate and consecrate body and soul and spirit in the supreme effort of service and sacrifice. What had to be driven home was that all business was the nation's business, and every task a common task for a single purpose.[3]

The goal of the Committee on Public Information was a unanimity of thought and action that would translate into victory on the battlefield and the realization of the ideal of the "melting pot" at home. The Wilson administration did not bring its patriotic crusade directly into the concert halls and opera houses of the middle- and upper-class music lovers, as their support for the war was generally assumed. But the ramifications of anti-German cultural propaganda that was intended to influence the immigrant and working-class groups whose loyalty was sometimes regarded as suspect were felt, however briefly, in the musical institutions that had relied so heavily on the performance of German music by German players, singers, and conductors.

George Creel considered the task of encouraging support for the war to be primarily an educational one. He wrote that this was a war that was not fought only on the battlefields of France. Indeed, it was the home front that occupied his attention:

> Back of the firing-line, back of armies and navies, back of the great supply depots, another struggle [was] waged with the same intensity and with almost equal significance attaching to its victories and defeats. It was the fight for the *minds* of men, for the "conquest of their convictions," and the battle-line ran through every home in the country.[4]

Despite President Wilson's frequent assertions that this was a war against the government of the Kaiser and not against the German people, issues of cultural values often formed the basis for judgments that Americans rendered regarding their German counterparts. Creel noted that other wars "went no deeper than the physical aspects, but German 'Kultur' raised issues that had to be fought out in the hearts and minds of the people as well as on the actual firing-line."[5]

In what Creel called "a vast enterprise in salesmanship, the world's greatest adventure in advertising," the Committee on Public Information, along with other government agencies, the National and State Councils for Defense, and a wide range of local patriotic groups, made World War I a crusade. Culture defined in various ways was at the center of that crusade, as speakers and writers with official government sanction contrasted American democracy with the authoritarianism of the Kaiser's rule. And although Creel disliked the word "propaganda," which, he felt, had come to be associated with deceit and corruption he labored to establish a pro-war, anti-German information apparatus to shore up the patriotic spirit at home.

The message of 100% Americanism filtered down to the average citizen through the activities of the Four Minute Men, 75,000 citizens who volunteered their voices for the war effort. At a variety of public gatherings, but especially in local movie houses, these speakers held forth on a variety of topics predetermined by the Committee. Matinee performances were even covered by a special Women's Division of the Four Minute Men. By September of 1918 the organization had discovered the power of music. Armed with slides containing the words to many popular and patriotic melodies, speakers urged their audiences to new heights of musical enthusiasm, if not to a high standard of performance, with such songs as *The Star Spangled Banner, Columbia, Gem of the Ocean*, and *Keep the Home Fires Burning*.[6] Following the example of the Army's Commission on Training Camp Activities and the United States Committee on Music for the Army and Navy, organizations that published song books and encouraged group singing at home as well as at the front, the Four Minute Men asserted the effectiveness of popular music in helping our fighting forces with the declaration that "The Singing Army, whether it be a fighting army or a working army, cannot be beaten."[7] Creel and his Committee recognized the value of popular music to their propagandizing efforts rather late in the game, but the Four Minute Men compensated for their lack of experience and expertise as leaders of group singing with an enthusiasm appropriate to the ideal of 100% Americanism.

But the music of the concert hall, unlike such popular songs as *Pack Up Your Troubles in Your Old Kit Bag*, was not so easily converted into a vehicle for selling the War. The Romantic symphonic tradition had long prevailed in the American concert hall, mainly in the form of works written by composers of German and Austro-Hungarian ancestry. From the perspective of orchestra managements, 100% Americanism, or even 100% anti-Germanism, was a virtual impossibility, as it was the familiar music of German, Austrian, and Hungarian composers that American audiences paid to hear. Given the prevailing ambivalence about the quality of American cultural production, it was unlikely that the symphonies of Mozart and Beethoven would be supplanted by music of unknown Americans, no matter how sharply the standard works may have been criticized by members of the Liberty Loan Committee as decadent products of German *Kultur*. Further, many of the conductors of this country's major symphony orchestras were either German by nationality or cultural identification or else German-trained. These men were unlikely to abandon a repertoire long considered standard. Their audiences generally concurred, but the American musical establishment would learn, as the country's involvement in the war became a certainty, that art could not be divorced from political reality. German music and musicians, like all aspects of German culture, came under attack for reasons that had little to do with artistic quality or popularity.

Antipathy to the German language during the war years contributed to the development of hostility to German music. Pro-war and anti-German sentiments were expressed in the excising of German names from buildings and street signs as well as the verbal replacement in the popular mind of the familiar frankfurter with sauerkraut by the hot dog with "liberty cabbage." Texts and titles of even the most familiar German songs were suspect because of the detrimental, even treasonous, effect that the hated tongue might have on Americans. Many educators and representatives of the various Councils of National Defense even advocated banning the teaching of German in the public schools. Teachers of the language were seen by the more rabid Germanophobes as having made more of an effort to "advance German Kulture [*sic*] than to teach literature. It has been propaganda to overthrow English, pure and simple. . . . Everything with the tag 'Made in Germany' must go. We resent any German influence."[8]

In California hostility to German culture even extended to songs that had been translated into English. State authorities ruled that young children would experience negative emotional responses to songs in their texts designated as "German folk songs" or "from the German." In order to prevent such damage to young minds, the State Council for National Defense decided to remove all such songs from California school music books. Of course, the result was warehouses full of mutilated books that contained many acceptable, but unusable, songs whose first or last pages had been excised because they happened to appear on the other side of the corrupt German melody.[9]

There was no question in the minds of officials who prohibited the teaching of the German language in the public schools and censored German songs of the close relationship between culture and the enemy German state. Indeed, the Kaiser's bureaucracy utilized the music of such standard German composers as Mozart and Beethoven to inculcate nationalist values as part of celebrations of German nationality and culture. Such an imposition of culture from the highest levels of government down to the people naturally went against the American political and cultural grain. But when the watchdogs of 100% Americanism imposed sanctions on activities that related to German language or culture, they failed to take into account that, for most Americans, German culture did not automatically connote the preeminence of the Kaiser. Without the added implications of the *Kaiserreich*, listeners in this country could regard a Beethoven symphony or even a Wagner opera merely as standard musical repertoire and not as a threat to their wartime loyalties.

As American involvement in the war increased, 100% Americanism found its way from the movie house and school house to the concert hall. There were no official policies regarding the performance of German music, but laws restricting the activities of enemy aliens did affect many orchestras whose conductors and players were German. These groups could not perform in Washington, D.C., for example, because of a ban on alien employment in the capital, and some orchestras hurriedly arranged for many of their players to apply for United States citizenship in order to assuage concern that enemy aliens were taking jobs away from Americans.

Anti-German feeling in the musical establishment varied in its intensity from mild to feverish, but in all cases it was short-lived. In general, German music, at least music by German composers who were long dead, was restored to its former prominence on the programs of America's major symphony orchestras by 1920. Table 3-1 illustrates the extent to which World War I influenced the programming of one such orchestra, the New York Philharmonic Society. In the second decade of the twentieth century, New York was a vital center of musical activity and opinion in the United States. If that city's musical institutions did not provide precise models for the rest of the country, and indeed, the very position of New York as a major cosmopolitan center rendered that city's musical activites different from those of the rest of the country, the city's orchestras and opera companies did set standards of activity and excellence that other municipalities could hope to emulate.

Founded in 1842 by some of the city's more prominent citizens, the orchestra in its early years was a plaything of wealthy subscribers who attended its four yearly concerts in the Apollo Rooms in order to be seen and admired by others of their class. Hardly known as inspiring musical events, the Philharmonic Society's concerts improved considerably in the late 1870s, when Theodore Thomas assumed the position of conductor. By 1900 the orchestra was entertaining a much larger and more diverse audience that paid from fifty cents to $2.50 for single concert tickets. The orchestra expanded its repertoire under the baton of Gustav Mahler during the 1909-10 season to include a Beethoven cycle, several tour concerts in Boston and Philadelphia, and a so-called Historical Cycle, in which music composed prior to 1830 dominated the programs. By 1917–18, the Philharmonic's Jubilee Year, its influence had spread throughout the eastern and midwestern portions of the country.[10] The Philharmonic Society's management was somewhat responsive to popular tastes, as the presence of numerous request programs during the first two decades of the twentieth century indicates. While this orchestra may not have been America's best in every respect, it did serve a large community, both within and outside of the country's most important city. Its responses to the patriotic impulses of the World War I period are important indicators of the impact of 100% Americanism on high culture.

In the years immediately preceding America's entry into the War, the New York Philharmonic Society played more music by French and Russian composers, even though familiar German music still dominated

Table 3-1 Nationalities of Composers Represented on New York Philharmonic Concerts, 1916–1922

Season	*Germany Austria-Hungary*	*Russia*	*Bohemia (Czechoslovakia)*	*Norway*	*Italy*	*France*	*U.S.A.*	*Britain*	*Other*
1916–17	60%	16%	3.2%	3.2%	0%	10.7%	3.2%	.6%	1.9%
1917–18	47%	10.8%	5.6%	1.5%	3%	15.5%	8.7%	3%	4%
1918–19	32%	24%	8.8%	1.7%	3%	12%	10.5%	2.9%	3.5%
1919–20	51%	22%	6%	2.3%	1.4%	10.3%	4.2%	.9%	1.8%
1920–21	67%	17%	4.4%	.5%	.5%	4.4%	4.4%	0%	1%
1921–22	65%	15%	1.5%	1%	1%	5%	5.5%	0%	4.5%

the programs. During the war, German music was never banned at Carnegie Hall, but the sharp decline in the number of pieces by German, Austrian, and Hungarian composers in 1917–18 and again in 1918–19 illustrates an uneasiness with art created by these artists and an unwillingness to argue that such art was not political but merely represented the standard musical repertoire.

The Philharmonic's management and conductors experienced some conflict between their confidence in what was "good" music and their feelings of American patriotism in a time of national emergency. At a concert on December 13, 1917, at which half of the program was devoted to the music of Richard Wagner, the management informed the audience that it might not be generally known that Wagner was

> as ardent a political revolutionist as he was a musical one. Whatever possibilities of a revolution may exist in Germany now, there was one in 1848–49. It was crushed, to be sure, by the Prussian "mailed first." Among the liberty lovers who fled from Prussian wrath were Carl Schurz and Richard Wagner. The former came to America and became one of our noblest and greatest citizens. Wagner seriously considered coming here too—doubtless he would have if musical conditions had been what they are now. . . . If Wagner had remained in Germany, he probably would have been put to death. It was twelve years before he was able to return to Germany. Wagner made speeches and wrote articles in favor of freedom.[11]

Philharmonic audiences retained a special fondness for Wagner's music, which appeared on three of the five request programs presented between 1918 and 1919. Anti-German political feeling dictated musical preferences only to a limited extent in New York. For example, the position of Philharmonic conductor Josef Stransky, who held the position between 1911 and 1921, was not threatened by the war with Germany. Although Stransky himself was Bohemian, he had conducted in Hamburg, Dresden, and Berlin before coming to New York. He took out preliminary United States citizenship papers in 1918. Until war was actually declared, Count Johann von Bernstorff, the German ambassador to the United States, continued to attend the concerts. Perhaps the most serious impediment to the success of the orchestra's playing was not politics at all, but the clicking of knitting needles throughout the audience, as patriotic ladies did their part for the Red Cross while partaking of the finest music New York had to offer.[12]

Sadly, the American entry into the conflict caused changes in the Philharmonic's board of directors. Oswald Garrison Villard, the chairman of that board and editor of the *New York Post* and *The Nation*, was asked to resign his Philharmonic post because of his opposition to the

United States entry into the conflict. Ironically, only a year before his resignation, during the Jubilee celebration of the Philharmonic Society, Villard had declared with some confidence that "art and our orchestra were unaffected by prejudice, even in the face of war."[13] By 1918, even though it was still possible to hear standard German Romantic music at Philharmonic concerts, tolerance for overt anti-war sentiments had all but disappeared.

While the New York Philharmonic Society did not ban German music from its concert programs, such music was conspicuously and understandably absent for those special programs played for soldiers at Camp Dix and Camp Upton as well as from a special benefit concert on October 17, 1917, the proceeds of which were donated to the Red Cross. Clearly, German music would have been inappropriate entertainment for soldiers about to cross the Atlantic to do battle with "the Hun," but it is less likely that the audience of soldiers, a group not selected for its interest in standard orchestral repertoire, would have missed Beethoven or Wagner as much as the orchestra's regular clientele would have.

An accommodation to the wartime situation included the playing of the *Star Spangled Banner* at Philharmonic concerts, beginning at least as early as October 1918, when it was formally listed on the program. In addition, some titles of German works were translated into English, and two noteworthy examples of this new practice applied to Wagner's music. The *Prelude and Liebestod* from the opera *Tristan und Isolde* was listed as *Prelude and Isolde's Love Death* for the first time during World War I, and the popular prelude from *Die Meistersinger* was translated as the prelude from *The Mastersingers*. There were also a few instances in which German songs or arias were sung in English, as at an all-Wagner program on January 27, 1918, that featured five of the composer's operatic excerpts, all sung in English.

Patriotism and enthusiasm for the war effort influenced the number and type of works by American composers performed by the Philharmonic. Some of those presented during the 1918–19 season were self-consciously "American" in theme. For example, Reginald Sweet's *Orchestral Sketches* were inspired, according to the composer, by the poetry of Walt Whitman. John Powell's *Rhapsodie Nègre* was based on Afro-American melodies and was consistent with the style of other nationalist composers for whom folk music was the key to creating an American idiom. Rubin Goldmark's *Requiem for Orchestra* bore the subtitle, *Gettysburg Address*. The latter two pieces were part of a program devoted entirely to the music of American composers on February 16, 1919. During the 1918–19 season, the Philharmonic Society played several special concerts for the Liberty Loan campaign. Such popular works as Dvořák's *New World* Symphony and Victor Herbert's *American Fantasy,* a collection of symphonically arranged patriotic melodies, were performed at these fund-raising programs. In addition, *Verdun,* a tone poem by the Irish composer Charles Villiers Stanford was played often immediately after the armistice. Although it was not by an American composer, this tone poem was composed for the annual Norfolk (Connecticut) Festival. Its inclusion on many programs and the prominent dedication, "to the brave people of France," that was printed every time the piece was performed, helped to foster a continuation of patriotic feelings on the part of the Philharmonic audience.

Not all musical organizations attempted to strike the balance achieved in New York between enthusiasm for the war and the maintenance of familiar programming that included German music. The experience of the Boston Symphony Orchestra and its famous conductor Dr. Karl Mück illustrates the extent to which patriotic feeling could and did obscure the artistic accomplishments of a man and a cultural institution. Mück had been brought to Boston in 1906 by the Orchestra's founder and patron, Major Henry Lee Higginson. As Mück was the principal conductor at the Royal Opera House in Berlin, it was necessary to secure approval for his Boston appointment from his employer, the Kaiser. After two seasons in this country, Mück was recalled to Berlin, but he was permitted to return to Boston in 1912. A strict disciplinarian who imposed his aesthetic standards on orchestra and audience alike, Mück was nonetheless popular in Boston because his direction had brought about a significant improvement in the orchestra's sound. At the end of the 1915–16 season, *Boston Herald* critic Philip Hale described the Boston Symphony as

> an instrument that, having been brought to a state of perfect mechanism by Dr. Muck, responds to his imagination and poetic wishes. . . . It is now hardly possible to think of this orchestra without the vision of Dr. Muck as the head interpreter of beauty and brilliance.[14]

But this artistic vision was soon clouded in a haze of hatred and anti-German hysteria.

Karl Mück's encounter with 100% Americanism began in Providence, Rhode Island, with an incident in which he was not even directly a participant. The Boston Symphony Orchestra was scheduled to perform in Providence on October 30, 1917. Prior to the concert, Orchestra Manager Charles A. Ellis received a telegram from members of the Chaminade Club, a local women's musical association, demanding that the concert begin with *The Star Spangled Banner* as a patriotic gesture.

This would have been an unusual practice, even in wartime, so it was not surprising that Ellis ignored the request from the patriotic ladies who were not even regular BSO subscribers. Major Higginson supported Ellis's action, and Mück was unaware of the controversy that was brewing. The BSO management halted ticket sales in order to allow entry to the performance only to those who had purchased them prior to the incident and the ensuing editorial in the *Providence Journal* that declared, "It is as good a time as any to put Professor Mück to the test. The Boston Symphony Orchestra should play 'The Star Spangled Banner' tonight in Providence."[15]

Ellis and Higginson tried to absorb the criticism that appeared almost immediately in newspapers from Boston to Baltimore, but it was Mück who was vulnerable. As the orchestra's conductor, he was visible, and his recent work as an employee of the Kaiser made him suspect as an enemy alien, despite his status as a naturalized Swiss citizen. In addition, those qualities that had made him so popular earlier in Boston, his strong sense of discipline and high musical standards, now were turned against him and labeled typical of the reviled German "character."

Major Higginson publicly defended his orchestra and its conductor, particularly in the wake of several anonymous accusations against them. He told the *Boston Globe*, "When Dr. Muck goes, the orchestra will go, and Symphony Hall, which costs me $13,000 to $18,000 to maintain, may be sold." Noting that it was not his practice to "meddle with the art side" of the Orchestra's management, Higginson nevertheless declared that the national anthem had "no place in an art concert. If it did, it would be played."[16] Mück also spoke publicly in defense of art. But if his reasoning was sound, his tone only aroused more suspicion of his political and cultural loyalties when he asked,

> Why will people be so silly? Art is a thing by itself and not related to a particular nation or group. It would be a gross mistake, in violation of artistic taste and principles, for an organization such as ours to play patriotic airs.[17]

Of course, for Mück's critics, *The Star Spangled Banner* was no ordinary air but a symbol of national unity in wartime. Even Mück's colleagues felt compelled to defend themselves in their comments on the situation in Boston. Walter Damrosch, the conductor of the New York Symphony Orchestra, whose interpretations of Wagner's music were well known and appreciated, did not defend the national anthem as art, although he did assert that it should be performed for its symbolic value. The *Boston Globe* quoted his assessment of that symbol's importance and his own suggestion to the Boston Symphony for preserving both art and national honor. Damrosch said that, while he did not believe in

> cheapening this symbol by producing it on every occasion, it is most fitting that a musical season this year should be introduced by a playing of the anthem. The issue in the case of the Boston orchestra could be met by having an assistant direct the anthem, for nothing would be gained by forcing Dr. Muck to do it.[18]

Damrosch spoke somewhat more forcefully to his New York audience, when he observed to the *New York Times* that

> Dr. Muck naturally does not care to conduct the national hymn at the present time, and I confess I should not enjoy hearing him do so. Considering his citizenship and his feelings toward our war, this would be an act of hypocrisy.[19]

The New York Symphony's conductor hoped to avoid criticism of the type to which Muck was being subjected. As the Providence incident began to receive national press coverage, Damrosch and Josef Stransky of the New York Philharmonic each opened his orchestra's season with the playing of *The Star Spangled Banner*, which, at the time, was not yet officially the nation's National Anthem. But official or not, *The Star Spangled Banner* and Karl Muck were in the midst of a growing controversy. Even Theodore Roosevelt got into the act, commenting in New York that he was

> shocked, simply shocked, to learn that anybody can apologize for Dr. Muck on the ground that the music is not artistic, but only patriotic. No man has any business to be engaged in anything that is not subordinate to patriotism. If the Boston Symphony Orchestra will not play "The Star Spangled Banner," it ought to be made to shut up. If Dr. Muck will not play it, he ought not to be at large in this country.[20]

Remarks like these emphasize the extent to which art and patriotism were brought together in a conflict that had less to do with the former than with a collective insecurity in wartime about the extent of the latter.

The opening of the 1917–18 concert season saw threats of violence in Baltimore if the Boston Symphony proceeded with plans to play in that city. Former Maryland Governor Edwin Warfield, who also happened to be a descendant of a Revolutionary War family, declared loudly that Mück "shall not lead an orchestra in Baltimore. I told the Police Bureau that this man would not be allowed to insult the people of the birthplace of 'The Star Spangled Banner.' "[21] Warfield did not confine his comments to the political dimensions of the situation. In the *Boston Globe* he ventured some judgments on the musical quality of *The Star Spangled Banner* and its merits relative to more standard symphonic music from Germany. He considered the anthem

> a symphony incomparable, at a time like this, greater than anything ever composed in Germany, more glorious and befitting the hearing of true Americans than the work of any composer, living or dead. We deny that our anthem jars with any harmony or symphony to which the American people should listen. "The Star Spangled Banner" will be sung when others are long since forgotten.[22]

It mattered little in the anti-German climate of the time that Warfield's aesthetic judgments were utter nonsense; it was his threat to lead a mob against Mück that eventually led to a ban on the BSO's performing in Baltimore. The city's police marshal heartily supported this action with his own assertion that Mück was "the Prussian who said, 'To hell with your flag and your national anthem.' We were after the man who said 'The Star Spangled Banner' was not fit to be included in an artistic program."[23]

The furor over Mück's national and cultural loyalties and the concern over his activities led to a federal government investigation in 1918 to determine if the conductor represented a danger to the United States in wartime. As this inquiry began, other German-Americans were asked to comment on the relationship of "The Star Spangled Banner" to art. Lieutenant William H. Santelmann, the German-born leader of the United States Marine Corps band, said that the former Anacreontic hymn was

> good enough for any musical program. [It] has a rightful place upon any program whatsoever, artistic symphonies not excepted. The National Anthem could in no sense detract from the beauty of any program of music, no matter how artistic it might be. In these times, it should be played and sung upon every public occasion, in school exercises, at church, and most decidedly at symphony concerts.[24]

Of course, there was no basis for rational argument between those who felt that art and anthems should be put to a common purpose in time of national need and those, like Mück and his supporters, who hoped to keep expressions of national consciousness or chauvinism out of the concert hall. Patriotism of a sort did triumph with the announcement on November 2 that the anthem would be a regular part of future Boston Symphony concerts. The *Boston Globe* noted that Mück conducted an arrangement of *The Star Spangled Banner* on November 2 that had been taken from Irish-American composer Victor Herbert's *American Fantasy*.[25] Perhaps Herbert's naturalized American citizenship prevented a furor over the presence of an Irishman's rendition of the American national anthem on the program. In any event, Mück continued to conduct this addition to his programs without incident, and public attacks on him and the BSO diminished in the press for a few months.

But the normal routine of Boston Symphony operations was disrupted again in March of 1918, when the orchestra was scheduled to perform a series of concerts at Carnegie Hall and in Brooklyn. Almost single-handedly, Mrs. William Jay, a director of the New York Philharmonic Society who had been instrumental in the banning of German works from the stage of the Metropolitan Opera, rekindled the antagonism against Mück. She asked why, "if Dr. Muck is a dangerous alien in Washington should he be considered a harmless alien in New York, the great American port and centre of all but Federal activities?"[26] Mrs. Jay even convinced the military commanders at Governors Island and the Brooklyn Navy Yard to prohibit their men from accepting free tickets to the BSO concerts, tickets that in previous years had been offered and routinely accepted. She contended that the practice subverted military loyalty, arguing that

> the abominable use that is being made of our soldiers and sailors to support an enemy alien in his arrogant conduct could only have sprung from the modern German brain. To use these fine men to support German propaganda through a love of music should be condemned by every loyal American and lover of fair play.[27]

The Carnegie Hall concert was played with a police guard and rave reviews for Mück's interpretation of Brahms's Third Symphony and Major Higginson's handling of the renewed crisis. He showed Mück's Swiss naturalization papers to the audience and reiterated his support for the conductor. The BSO was also warmly received in Brooklyn. For the 100% Americans, Mück was an enemy and his orchestra was suspect, but for the New York concert audience, these were consummate performers of the music they were accustomed to hearing, war or no war.

Outside the concert hall, the enemy-alien chasers won a victory of sorts with Mück's arrest without formal charges on March 25, 1918, his resignation from the Boston symphony on March 30, when there were still no charges against him, his imprisonment as an enemy alien by the federal government at Fort Oglethorpe, Georgia, and his deportation on August 21, 1919, nine months after the end of the "war to end all wars." Mück's deportation was based on a Justice Department investigation that discovered "alleged pro-German sympathies and utterances, and his close association with the State Leaders of Germany before the war." In spite of Mück's legitimate claim to Swiss citizenship (he had been naturalized in 1885) and his frequent assertions that politics and music in the concert hall should not impinge upon one another, Justice Department officials determined that "it would be dangerous for him to be permitted to remain at large."[28] At the time of Mück's deportation, the *Boston Post*, in an exercise in yellow journalism that bordered on the fantastic, printed a number of letters, purported to have been written by Mück himself, that proved not only the conductor's anti-Americanism but his positive guilt as a German spy. These were reprinted under headlines that screamed "Mück's Hate Is Fanatical," "How Mück Fooled His Friends," "Mück Active German Spy Many Years," "Mück's Wife Very Active German Spy," and "Loyalty Not in Makeup of Dr. Karl Mück."[29] With the war long over and Mück securely on his way back to Germany, The *Post* effectively stirred up the antagonisms of the war years to boost sales and fire one parting shot at the conductor who had once been so revered in Boston.

On April 28, 1918, Major Higginson severed his connection with the Boston Symphony in the wake of the furor over patriotism in Symphony Hall that had begun with the Providence incident more than a year and a half earlier. The *Sunday Herald* reported that the BSO's founder and patron had originally intended to allow the organization to fold but that friends had persuaded him to accept a compromise in which a board of trustees would take over the affairs of the Orchestra. Accordingly, the BSO filed for incorporation, according to M. A. DeWolfe Howe, who made the formal announcement of the new arrangements on Major Higginson's behalf. Howe commented that the new board members began their new responsibilities "with a full realization of the significance of the orchestra to the life of their city and country."[30]

Karl Mück, whose cultural identity *was* German despite the national designation on his passport, claimed a higher identification with his art. He understood many of the forces that were operating an American society that had a direct impact on the course of his conducting career. And as a musical interpreter who inspired both praise and criticism, he was inclined to see personal jealousies as a part of the "conspiracy" against him. He told the *Boston Globe* that he left the United States "with no regrets, as the country is being controlled by sentiments which closely border on mob rule." He cited the presence of "rivals" in the music world who had encouraged the public questioning of his fitness for the post he held in Boston.[31] While Mück left the United States with no immediate plans, he was welcomed in Europe and resumed a distinguished conducting career until his death in 1940. Taken as a whole, what Irving Lowens called "l'affaire Mück" proved to be an unhappy example of the ramifications of 100% Americanism in the realm of high culture. Ultimately, Mück's reputation resumed its prewar eminence, and the Boston Symphony lost one of its most prominent and important musical leaders.[32]

The search for Mück's replacement illustrates the extent of the BSO management's ambivalence regarding the advisability of appointing an American conductor. The orchestra had never had a non-German conductor, and even the patriotic attitudes of the time did not inspire serious consideration of an American for the position. *Musical America* reported that there were seven likely candidates: Ernest Bloch, Ossip Gabrilowitsch, Vincent D'Indy, Pierre Monteux, Serge Rachmaninoff, Leopold Stokowski, and Sir Henry Wood, all of whom were foreign nationals or foreign-born American residents.[33] The magazine responded to the absence of an American conductor on this semi-official list with the following comment, addressed at least in part to Major Higginson:

> It is passing strange that the names afloat on the currents of speculation should be made up wholly of foreign musicians. . . . Quite apart from chauvinistic or patriotic considerations, however, it would seem that the time is at hand when the leading spirit of the Boston Symphony Orchestra owes a word on this matter to American music-lovers, who have long devotedly supported his orchestra. . . . The Boston Symphony Orchestra long ago ceased to be merely a great civic institution. It is a great national institution, and as such, at a time when America's emancipation from European thraldom has become a happy reality, there are plenty of excellent reasons why the orchestra should be headed by an American conductor.[34]

Musical America added to the speculation by proposing its own list of "dark horse" candidates for the BSO post. These were Weston Gales, the organist and choral conductor who organized the Detroit Symphony in 1914 and conducted that ensemble until 1917; Henry Hadley, who had conducted both the Seattle and the San Francisco Orchestra; Alfred Hertz, who was best known for his opera performances and was, in 1918, the current conductor of the San Francisco Symphony; Walter Henry Rothwell, the conductor of the St. Paul Symphony from 1908 to 1914; Theodore Spiering, the violinist and conductor who had led the New York Philharmonic Orchestra during Gustav Mahler's illness in the spring of 1911; Arturo Toscanini, who had made a reputation as an outstanding operatic and symphonic conductor, but who was in Italy in 1918; and Arnold Volpe, the founder and conductor of the Young Men's Symphony Orchestra and the Volpe Symphony Orchestra.[35]

In November of 1918 the speculation ended with the appointment of the French composer and conductor Henri Rabaud. The new conductor's first statement to the press indicated that he had not yet made a decision regarding any future limitation of German music on the orchestra's concerts. He declared simply that he wanted to perform "only the most beautiful music."[36] For Rabaud and his successor, Pierre Monteux, who conducted in Boston from 1920 to 1924, the most beautiful music included a significant number of works by their countrymen, including Camille Saint-Saëns, Vincent D'Indy, and Jean-Jules-Aimable Roger-Ducasse. The French accent in BSO programming reached a peak in Rabaud's first season, when almost half of the works performed in Symphony Hall were by composers of that nationality.

Table 3–2 permits a comparison of Boston's wartime concert repertoire with that of the New York Philharmonic Society Orchestra conducted by Josef Stransky. While the number of works by German, Austrian, and Hungarian composers declined dramatically after the United States entered the War, German music recovered its former place in the repertoire more slowly in Boston than in New York. And while Boston audiences heard more French music during this period, concertgoers in New York listened to more pieces by Russian composers.[37] The New York and Boston Orchestras also approached the programming of pieces by American composers differently during the War years. The American presence on New York Philharmonic programs was most evident during the 1918–19 season, as audiences heard a variety of patriotic fantasias, works inspired by the Log Book of the *Mayflower* (Edgar Stillman Kelley's Symphony No. 2, *New England*), compositions based on Afro-American melodies, works inspired by historical personalities or documents (as Rubin Goldmark's *Gettysburg Address* Requiem), and concert pieces written specifically to pay homage to America's war dead. In contrast, the Boston programs included a few patriotic pieces, such as George Whitefield Chadwick's *Land of Our Hearts*, a hymn for chorus and orchestra, but the American music played in Boston displayed less of the emotion of the moment. Boston audiences continued to hear American composers who were already familiar, including Arthur Foote, Edward Ballantine, Frederick Shepherd Converse, Edward MacDowell, Henry Carey, Henry F. Gilbert, and George W. Chadwick during the war years. Representative pieces included Foote's *Four Character Pieces (Omar Khayyam)*; Chadwick's tone poem, *Angel of Death*; and the *Concertino for Piano and Orchestra* by John Alden Carpenter, another composer familiar to Symphony Hall audiences.[38] Boston differed from New York in the extent to which conductors in Symphony Hall sustained at least a minimal interest in non-nationalist American music after the War. The American composer never became a fixture on programs in

Table 3-2 Nationalities of Composers Represented on Boston Symphony Orchestra Concerts, 1916–1922

Season	*Germany Austria-Hungary*	*Russia*	*Bohemia (Czechoslovakia)*	*Norway*	*Italy*	*France*	*U.S.A.*	*Britain*	*Other*
1916–17	62%	6.1%	3.7%	0%	3.7%	12.3%	9.8%	0%	0%
1917–18	42.6%	8.5%	2.4%	2.4%	1.2%	26.8%	4.8%	0%	8.4%
1918–19	29.7%	8.9%	0%	1%	3%	46.5%	7.9%	2%	1%
1919–20	43.3%	9.6%	3.6%	2.4%	2.4%	26.5%	7.2%	1.2%	3.6%
1920–21	44%	7.6%	1%	0%	3.2%	17.2%	12%	5.4%	8.5%
1921–22	49.5%	12.6%	1%	0%	4.2%	18%	6.3%	0%	8.2%

either Boston or New York, but he faded back into almost total obscurity on Stransky's post-War concerts.

The war against Germany made it easier for the critical and educational elites in American music to adopt, at least for a time, a more favorable attitude toward pieces composed by their fellow citizens. *Musical America* reprinted a 1918 address by editor John C. Freund to the Musical Alliance in New York in which he remarked that "just as the time came when we declared first our political, later our commercial and industrial independence, so the time has come for us to declare our musical independence."[39] These sentiments were hardly new in 1918, and they were hardly surprising, given the climate of heightened patriotism and support for American culture. But such thoughts represent an interesting departure for *Musical America*, a journal that only a few years earlier had not looked kindly on attempts to declare America's cultural independence from its European models. A few months later, the same journal reprinted the comments of Frank Wright, the president of the New York Music Teachers' Association, who asserted that music composed here "must be made world known. Too much stress is laid on the German product. There is no reason why Americans should not take their place in music."[40]

A special issue of *Musical America* in the fall of 1918 was devoted exclusively to patriotic, anti-German articles, including statements by prominent American performers that the conflict would only strengthen this country musically because of the existence of considerable American talent and a growing receptivity to the homegrown musical product.[41]

The dismissal of many German orchestral players during the war imporved the position of American instrumentalists somewhat. For example, Frederic Fradken of the Boston Symphony advanced to the position of concertmaster of that orchestra in September of 1918. He was the first American-born violinist to achieve such a distinction with a major performing ensemble in this country. Although he described himself as "American from my head to my feet," Fradken, like most native-born performers and composers of his day, had studied in Europe.[42]

There were other ramifications of the overzealous expressions of 100% Americanism in the realm of concert music. The previously published plans for New York's Metropolitan Opera season had included only one work in German, Franz Liszt's *Saint Elizabeth*. But the company's management declared openly in November of 1917 that it was responding to public pressure of the type that had "demanded a change of attitude on the part of the Boston Symphony Orchestra" when it took formal action to ban productions of works in German for the duration of the War.[43] Much of this pressure emanated from the pen of Mrs. William Jay and her colleagues who held influential positions on the boards of directors of New York's major cultural institutions. In calling for a ban on German opera, Mrs. Jay made a spurious connection between the German language and the current wartime situation. She argued that "given in the German language and depicting scenes of violence, German opera cannot but draw our minds back to the spirit of greed and barbarism that has led to so much suffering."[44] Mrs. Jay won her case in the board room of the Metropolitan Opera Company. But not all of the Met's audience approved of such a fundamental change in the repertoire of the company. German opera was too popular and too important a part of the Met's artistic offering to be dismissed without protest, war or no war. The *New York Evening Post* commented in an editorial that

> for an excited public opinion to try to dictate what opera should be produced and what orchestral numbers played would be a grievous blow to musical art in America. It is stated that there will be no German operas at the Metropolitan this season. This we think regrettable, if only because it shows less breadth of tolerance than is to be found in London, where there they are giving German opera right along, or in Vienna, where Shakespeare's plays are frequently produced. These great works of art surely rise above international rivalries and warfare. Particularly is this true of Wagner's works. As we have already pointed out, Wagner was one of the most anti-Prussian Germans who ever lived. He hated Prussia and her officialdom, which he frequently denounced, and if he were living could surely be counted upon to be in opposition to-day.[45]

Two months after the announcement of the ban, *Musical America* ran a front-page story on the fact that French and English audiences were not being deprived of their familiar German Romantic music, in spite of the strong feelings aroused by the war. There the only concession in the concert hall to the climate of hostilities seemed to be the absence of music by the modern German composer Richard Strauss and the singing of Wagner arias in English in the opera houses of London.[46]

Throughout the country, musical organizations and individual artists responded to public pressure for gestures of American patriotism. The Metropolitan Opera opened its already modified 1917–18 season with the singing of *The Star Spangled Banner* by the entire company prior to the evening's performance of Verdi's *Aida*.[47] And Metropolitan Opera director Giulio Gatti-Casazza included two American works in that season's repertoire, Charles Wakefield Cadman's *Shanewis* (*The Robin Woman*) and the ballet pantomime, *Dance in the Place Congo*, by Henry F. Gilbert. Civic leaders in Pittsburgh forced the cancellation of a concert by the Cincinnati Symphony Orchestra because of the presence of the group's German-born conductor Dr. Ernest Kunwald.[48] There were even rumors that the Boston Symphony would have to disband because twenty-one of its one hundred one players were German-born. The Trading with the Enemy Act prohibited these citizens from doing business in the United States, and, presumably, this included playing in the orchestra for a salary. Several cities, including Washington, D.C., prohibited aliens from entering their borders, and police departments in many municipalities refused to grant the necessary permits for Boston Symphony tour concerts.[49] The orchestra did not disband as many feared, but the concern for its continued existence reflects the dilemma of American orchestras that wanted to maintain a patriotic posture along with their accustomed repertoire and personnel. The Philadelphia Orchestra averted a problem by dismissing eight German-born players who had not yet completed their applications for United States citizenship. More typical patriotic gestures in Philadelphia included the presentation of the American flag at concerts and the planting of trees in memory of fallen soldiers by members of the Orchestra's Women's Committees.[50]

In one of the more unfortunate incidents of the World War I period, the famous Austrian violinist Fritz Kreisler was forced to cancel all of his public appearances in the United States, with the exception of those at which he had agreed to perform for charitable organizations. Kreisler had been very popular with American audiences,[51] and *Musical America* estimated that the cancellation of fifty-five concerts that had long been booked would cost the violinist $85,000 in fees. Kreisler issued the following statement on the subject:

> Bitter attacks have been made upon me as an Austrian and because at the outbreak of the war I fought as an officer in the Austrian army at the Russian front. I have also been criticized for fulfilling engagements made long ago. I, therefore, am asking all concerned to release me from my obligations under existing contracts. My promise will be kept to play, without compensation, for those charities to which I have already pledged my support. I shall always remain deeply sensible of my debt of gratitude to this country for past kindnesses and appreciation of my art.[52]

100% Americanism in music was mixed with no small dose of ambivalence about this country's ability to do without its standard concert repertoire of German Classical and Romantic music. Indeed, when Olga Samaroff, the American-born pianist and wife of Leopold Stokowski, and Mrs. Ossip Gabrilowitsch (Mark Twain's daughter) journeyed to Washington to express their concern over the extreme actions of many local musical organizations in banning or restricting the performance of German works, they were assured by both President Wilson and Colonel House that, at the federal government level at least, it was not considered necessary to engage in wartime hostilities against long-deceased German composers.[53] Many cultural institutions agreed and limited or banned only music by living German composers. The advocates of 100% Americanism were hardly satisfied, as the publicly aroused antipathy to Karl Mück illustrates. But German music was not necessarily replaced with works by American composers, and the real measure of our cultural ambivalence was the speed with which German music reappeared once politics became less of an influence on programming with the cessation of hostilities.

For many formulators of musical opinion in this country, the immediate post-war period seemed to promise an awakening of creativity that would far surpass the patriotic efforts of the war years. Editors of music journals and critics who penned columns on the subject of the new American music held to the view that the familiar standards of beauty, inspiration, and quality, as defined by the Romantic aesthetic of the previous century, would continue to prevail in concert works composed here. Without specifying what the new music would sound like or what materials would be appropriate as its thematic or programmatic basis, some critics wrote in high-sounding phrases about what they saw as a new awareness of "good" music. For example, Robert W. Wilkes wrote in *Musical America* in 1919 that

> we seem to have emerged from the great war with a new national consciousness, more spiritual and somewhat purged of its former material character. American compositions of a serious order—not the light songs and ballads of previous years—are being exploited by concert artists and symphony orchestras. The great heart of the American people has throbbed to music during the last four years more completely than it has ever done before.[54]

But however great the popular interest in American music may have been during the war years, the country's major orchestras now looked to Europe, and especially to the music of German composers, for their repertoire.

In a few critical circles, commentary after World War I shifted from the issue of patriotism and American musical nationalism, however imprecisely defined, to what was perceived as a much larger issue, the challenge to the Romantic aesthetic and the emergence of modern music. The composer and conductor Alfredo Casella was quoted in *Musical America* as saying that "the war has conferred a greatly exaggerated importance on the problem of musical nationalism." Casella argued further that the music of the present should be *new* rather than national.[55] The defense of new currents in musical thinking sometimes even carried with it a defense of German music, so recently reviled but never completely eliminated from the American cultural scene. In her brief for modern music, Dorothy J. Teall castigated 100% Americans for continuing their crusade against German music and musicians. Even though many standard works had already found their way back on to American orchestral programs by 1919,

> the starless night of our de-Teutonized musical boredom is yet enlivened and enlightened from time to time by a pyrotechnical display of intolerance, when narrow-mindedness stalks abroad like the Queen of Hearts, crying "Off with his head!" as it points now at this gentle conductor and now at that mild-mannered virtuoso.[56]

In her defense of Mück, Kreisler, and other German musicians, Teall recommended that the American public and concert management establishment revive their former receptivity to German music and that they also look to that country for new musical ideas and techniques that foreshadowed the music of the future.

During World War I, it was easy, under pressure from patriots who knew nothing about art, to substitute standards of American patriotism for standard criteria of proven quality and popularity in the concert hall. This tendency was short-lived, but it was indicative of a narrow vision that did not recognize the interrelationship of American and various European cultures. The deportation of Dr. Karl Mück after the end of the war, for example, revealed that many Americans could not separate the perceived threat of an enemy alien from the contributions of foreign artists who had helped to forge American cultural patterns since the 1790s.

The World War I period was potentially a turning point for American composers and performers. The lacuna created by restrictions on German music on concert programs and in the opera house might have been filled with music by American composers. But conductors and orchestra managements were unaccustomed to programming American pieces in large numbers and were likely unconvinced that this country had a viable concert music repertoire of its own. In this respect there is an interesting comparison to be made with the musical situation in other countries whose armies fought against Germans on the battlefields but whose concert and opera audiences were accustomed to German music as an important component of their high culture. In London, for example, Hubert Foss and Noel Goodwin have pointed out that "German music was taboo for a short while only, but for long enough to show that the English public was not at that time ready to substitute and accept in its place the native product."[57] But German music did not regain its pre-war popularity in London to the extent that it did in New York. In the long run, music by British composers received first and second performances during the war and eventually achieved a more secure place on the programs of major symphony orchestras. Between 1918 and 1926, for example, the famous Proms Concerts in London saw the incorporation of works by Frank Bridge, Arnold Bax, York Bowen, John Ireland, Arthur Bliss, Gustave Holst, and many lesser-known British composers into the repertoire on a regular basis.[58] With less confidence than the British in their own cultural product, Americans could not reap a lasting benefit from the upheavals of the war years in terms of hearing more of their own music in the concert hall.

As we have seen, in the United States World War I did inspire some composers to write patriotic music, but most of these pieces simply used a historical text or a familiar tune in the context of what audiences knew to be the Romantic idiom to which they were accustomed. Like the nationalistic music of the pre-war years by Henry F. Gilbert and his contemporaries, these pieces could not be considered European because of their inspiration, popular materials, or simply the nationality and patriotic intentions of their composers, nor were they "American" in the sense their creators hoped they would be. They expressed the feelings of the moment, but they did not caputre an essential element of American cultural character and are seldom heard in the concert hall today. In short, the influence of German high culture in the United States could not be wiped away with the creation of government propaganda agencies, local attempts to excise manifestations of that culture from the everyday lives of Americans, or smear campaigns against individual artists who, German or not in their national identity, generally placed art before politics. During the war, the United States was not yet ready to blaze an independent path in the realm of high culture. Ultimately, given the rehabilitation of German music in most places after the war, 100% Americanism made very little difference.

4

Modernists in Search of an Audience

American composers whose careers were just beginning in the 1920s had a number of compositional possibilities open to them. Rapid developments in the realm of modern music rendered the period between the wars liberating for many composers caught up in the excitement of the modern movement, even as the period was one of dizzying confusion for many audiences and critics. In this country, the same composer could write dissonant avant-garde works in the mid-1920s, pieces that employed some of the techniques of jazz toward the end of that decade, songs whose texts contributed to the cause of the political Left in the early 1930s, and compositions with representative American titles and fragments of folk music or popular tunes in the decade after 1935. Needless to say, there were few such versatile American composers, but this description indeed serves as a sketch of Aaron Copland's carrer and illustrates the various possibilities available to the composer for whom the desire to be "American" coexisted with an equally stong need to compose in the modern idiom that he had so recently studied in Europe.

Ideas associated with the avant-garde transcended national identity. American composers could now be in the vanguard of change and innovation in Western music. They could escape the perception of the innate inferiority of American art that had haunted their forebears. In the 1920s, as in the decades since, one important and interesting way to contribute to the acceptance of American music, irrespective of its intended national inspiration or message, was to compose modern music.

By the early twentieth century, composers on both sides of the Atlantic were becoming dissatisfied with Romantic music, which they regarded as a limited vehicle with which to compose the music of the new century. Serialists claimed that the tonal system no longer had meaning and should be abandoned as an analytical framework within which to comprehend and create music; Dadaists asked performers to play "like a nightingale with a toothache" and argued in the name of musical satire that symphonies should take up only three minutes of an audience's time and operas even less; and Futurists intoned the irreconcilability of past and future traditions, opting instead for what they called "harmonic polyphony, a logical fusion of counterpoint and harmony."[1] The frenetic experimentation of the years after World War I eventually yielded to a more flexible approach to modern composition that could subsume the Romantic concept of melody or Classical symphonic form into a composer's individual style. But the innovators of this important musical period believed that their individual compositional ideologies could facilitate the creation of the music of the future from a tone row, the roar of an airplane propeller, or even American jazz.

The interest in jazz as a tool for modern composition on the part of Americans followed a similar strong but temporary passion for American popular music by European composers. During the early 1920s, when many young American composers couldn't sail for Paris quickly enough, composers in that city and other European capitals, fascinated by the versions of dance music, ragtime, and jazz that they heard, and intrigued by popular images of urban life in "Roaring Twenties" America, began to use elements of jazz in their own revolution against musical convention. Jazz was new, and its blue notes, quarter tones, muted trumpets, cymbals played with brushes, and glissandi were all grist for the modernist composer's creative mill. It also provided a technical legacy that American composers in the years after 1935 would exploit in works that developed other varieties of folk and popular music. This music, according to the intentions of its composers, could be both avowedly "American" and accessible to a broad audience and, in the context of the simplified and generally tonal idiom of the period, also modern.

Ragtime music and the cakewalk, which James Weldon Johnson had touted in 1912 was among those Afro-American cultural contributions "which demonstrate that they have originality and artistic conception, and, what is more, the power of creating that which can influence and appeal universally,"[2] attracted the attention of European composers early in the twentieth century. Claude Debussy used the rhythms of this music in the *Gollywog's Cakewalk* movement from his *Children's*

Corner Suite, composed in 1908. Although the composer was offering a whimsical device for holding the attention of young piano students rather than exalting an Afro-American dance form, Johnson's protagonist in his novel, *The Autobiography of an Ex-Colored Man*, took pride in the international appeal of the dance, arguing that in Europe

> the United States is popularly known better by rag-time than anything else it has produced in a generation. In Paris they call it American music. The newspapers have already told how the practice of intricate cake-walk steps has taken up the time of European royalty and nobility. These are lower forms of art, but they give evidence of a power that will someday be applied to the higher forms.[3]

For Debussy, Afro-American music was novel, but for the modernist composers of the 1920s, its application to the "higher forms" was a serious compositional effort. Even when the spirit of Dadaism pervaded a piece, as it often did in the works of Erik Satie and Darius Milhaud during this period, the use of ragtime and jazz was part of a larger attempt to create something new in the process of defying the conventions of the past.

American jazz, the music that Jean Cocteau called "une catastrophe apprivoisée," figured in the creation of such works as Milhaud's *Shimmy for Negro Dancer, Caramel Mou* (1912) and Georges Auric's fox trot, *Adieu, New York* (1921), both of which exploited American images and musical fragments drawn from jazz that were new and potentially shocking to audiences. Jazz mottos were intentionally used to evoke faraway Africa and to conjure up images of the Harlem nightclub where Milhaud heard the sonorities that would later appear in *La Creation du monde*.

The arrival of this new music in Paris from New York caused quite a stir. Milhaud described the enthusiasm for jazz, noting that

> a whole literature of syncopation grew up to convince a hesitant public. Stravinsky wrote his "Rag Time" for eleven instruments, his "Piano Rag Music," his "Mavra." [Jean] Weiner wrote his "Sonatine Syncopée," his "Blues," and almost caused a great public scandal by bringing a famous jazz band into the concert hall.[4]

In 1922 Milhaud came to New York, as he said, "looking for jazz." He looked, of course, to Harlem, which

> had not yet been discovered by the snobs and aesthetes: we were the only white folks there. The music I heard was absolutely different from anything I had ever heard before, and was a revelation to me. Against the beat of the drums the melodic line criss crossed in a breathless pattern of broken and twisted rhythms. A negress whose grating voice seemed to come from the depths of the centuries, sang in front of the various tables. . . . This authentic music had its roots in the darkest corners of the negro soul, the

John Sullivan Dwight, the Boston critic and arbiter of American musical propriety who described his own cultural tastes as "ultra-classical, pedantic, transcendental." (*New York Public Library*)

Criticized for his popular appeal based on "Bananiers and Bamboulas," Louis Moreau Gottschalk utilized the musical materials of the Americas in many of his compositions. (*New York Public Library*)

PHILHARMONIC SOCIETY.

FIRST CONCERT,—FIRST SEASON.

Apollo Rooms, 7th Dec. 1842.

TO COMMENCE AT 8 O'CLOCK PRECISELY.

PART I.

GRAND SYMPHONY IN C MINOR. - - - - BEETHOVEN.

SCENA, *from Oberon.* - - - - - - - - - WEBER.

MADAME OTTO.

QUINTETTE IN D MINOR. - - - - - - - HUMMEL.

PART II.

OVERTURE TO OBERON. - - - - - - - - WEBER.

DUETT—*from Armida.* - - - - - - - - ROSSINI.

MADAME OTTO AND MR. C. E. HORN.

SCENA, *from Fidelio.* - - - - - - - - - BEETHOVEN.

MR. C. E. HORN.

ARIA BRAVURA—*from Belmont and Constantia.* MOZART.

MADAME OTTO.

NEW OVERTURE IN D. - - - - - - - - KALLIWODA.

The Vocal Music will be directed by Mr. Timm.

Wm. C. Martin, Printer, 111 John st.

The New York Philharmonic Society offered its first concert on December 7, 1842, at the Apollo Rooms. (*Bettmann Archive*)

Theodore Thomas and his Orchestra at New York's Steinway Hall on April 17, 1890. (*Bettmann Archive*)

John Knowles Paine, best known as the standard-bearer of late nineteenth-century American concert music and as Harvard University's first Professor of Music. (*New York Public Library*)

Edward MacDowell, who composed in a variety of forms and who provided early musical leadership at Columbia University. (*New York Public Library*)

Karl Mück in 1915, between his two terms of service as conductor of the Boston Symphony Orchestra. Mück's second period in Boston was characterized by brilliant performances and bitter controversy over his German cultural identity. (*Bettmann Archive*)

As part of the World War I Liberty Loan campaign, Walter Damrosch conducted a military ensemble in front of New York's Liberty Altar. (*Bettmann Archive*)

Virgil Thomson, Walter Piston, Aaron Copland, and Herbert Elwell in 1926. All had been students of Nadia Boulanger. (*Bettmann Archive*)

Composer Marc Blitzstein, with Muriel Smith and Robert Chisholm, rehearsing for a 1947 revival of the controversial musical, *The Cradle Will Rock*. (*New York Public Library*)

Aaron Copland providing musical instruction at the Berkshire Music Festival at Tanglewood. (*Bettmann Archive*)

vestigial traces of Africa, no doubt. Its effect on me was so overwhelming that I could not tear myself away.[5]

The result was a ballet, *La Creation du monde*, based on a sketch by Blaise Cendrars drawn from African mythology. "At last in 'La Creation du Monde,' " Milhaud wrote, "I had the opportunity to use elements of jazz to which I had devoted so much study. I adopted the same orchestra used in Harlem, seventeen solo instruments, and I made wholesale use of jazz style to convey a purely classical feeling."[6] Actually, Milhaud enlarged the typical jazz orchestra to include solo strings, a bassoon, and an oboe, instruments not usually found in the Harlem bands of the 1920s. He used a few jazz mottos, or riffs, which by 1923 had become almost clichés, employing them as subjects in contrapuntal passages. The score also includes flutter-tonguing for the flute, blues passages for the oboe, saxophone, and muted brass instruments, and sections that sound improvisational, even though they are precisely notated. These sections in particular sound like the product of an avant-garde creative mind rather than the spontaneous entertainment produced at a Harlem night club. Indeed, music historian Joseph Machlis noted that *La Creation du monde* has "a sensibility that is wholly French."[7] To Machlis's assessment might be added the assertion that the sound of the piece is thoroughly modern for its time. It transcends the nationality of both its creator and of the jazz that inspired it.

If the Parisians were charmed by the exoticism of jazz, German and Austrian composers used it in a somewhat more ironic way. Jazz elements subsumed into a musical fabric of dissonant counterpoint or even serial technique have more in common with a George Grosz painting than with Pablo Picasso's lighthearted scene for Erik Satie's *Parade*, a piece that borrowed from the sounds of American popular music.

Ernst Křenek used jazz elements in his opera, *Jonny spielt auf*! in 1926. This stage piece has as its central character a black violinist and jazz-band leader. The work was immensely popular in Europe, but it failed in New York.[8] Audiences and critics looking for real jazz on the stage of the Metropolotian Opera House were disappointed that Křenek had not merely quoted American popular music but had developed it in his own style, which was often dissonant. Composer Vladimir Dukelsky, better known as Vernon Duke, commented on the distance between *Jonny* and other German works like it and the real product of urban America's clubs and speakeasies. He spoke derisively of two "crude exercises in Americanomania" in Germany in 1928:

One was "Jonny Spielt Auf," Krenek's tuneless and jazzless jazz opera; the other was "Evelyne," an elephantine operetta by Bruno Von Gran-

> ichstadten, fully as unpalatable and Teutonic as the composer's name. The badly lipsticked and atrociously garbed chorus girls kicked sausagelike legs and shrilled "Yes," "Okay," and "Get hot," at the top of their beer-greased lungs, to the accompaniment of three trombones, a tuba and the inevitable celeste and xylophone, all played in unison, which, to anyone familiar with German musical comedy, is an orchestrator's "must."[9]

Berthold Brecht and Kurt Weill's *Das kleine Mahagonny* (1927), later expanded into *Aufsteid und Fall der Stadt Mahagonny* (1929), used images of the American Wild West, gangster films, and Florida hurricanes, as well as American place names, such as Pensacola, Memphis, and, of course, Alabama. Their opera, *Der Dreigroschenoper*, owes more to American popular music in the form of ballads, blues pieces, torch songs, and fox trots. Such music was appropriate to Brecht's declamatory style and sharp social commentary.

By the end of the 1920s, European interest in jazz and American popular music had diminished considerably, but, for a brief period, the path of serious cultural transmission was reversed, as French and German composers of modern music for the concert hall looked to the United States for fresh musical and programmatic material. The varieties of song, ragtime, and jazz that appeared in modern European concert and stage pieces revealed a fascination with stereotypic American images and, more important, a creative interest in the technical possibilities inherent in jazz. Not all Americans thought of their era as a "Jazz Age" or a roaring decade, but the images that took hold in these European works were those of decadence and a Harlem subculture that brought vestinges of Africa to life after dark. Even though "Europa Jazz" seldom sounded like the popular music of the real Chicago, Kansas City, or New York clubs, it was important that composers were using their creative sense to see jazz as a tool for composing modern music rather than as a finished musical product. The goal was not to rewrite jazz, an impossible task, but to create something modern. European composers "discovered" the New World in the early 1920s, and their American counterparts were to follow soon.

American modernist composers in the 1920s also experimented with jazz and other varieties of American urban music for a variety of reasons. For some, it was sufficient to quote jazz riffs simply because these short melodic patterns were recognizably jazzy and "American." For others, jazz evoked the fast pace of modern America, as in Adolph Weiss's *American Life*, subtitled *Scherzoso Jazzoso*. And for still others, most notably Aaron Copland, rhythm was the essence of jazz, and the jazz approach to rhythmic organization provided another modern compositional technique.

In addition, the music of the speakeasy and the dance hall was popular in the 1920s. Composers who returned to the United States from study in Europe well schooled in the craft of writing original music that stretched the tolerance of audiences beyond their capacity to comprehend or enjoy were often hard-pressed to find receptive listeners for their new pieces. Jazz sometimes helped the modern American composer to reach the contemporary audience.

As early as 1915, Henry F. Gilbert had composed *Dances in Ragtime Rhythm* in response to the popularity of piano ragtime music, and John Alden Carpenter incorporated a few blue notes, some ragtime rhythms, and a fox trot into his ballet, *Krazy Kat, A Jazz Pantomime*, composed in 1922 and based on George Herriman's popular cartoon character. Carpenter did contribute a major jazz work to the repertoire in his *Skyscrapers, a Ballet of Modern Life*, commissioned for performance at the Metropolitan Opera House in 1926. This work is more modern than its predecessor, with the inclusion of syncopation and polyrhythms in addition to blues harmonies. Carpenter intended to use jazz as he understood it to portray modern America. In the preface to the musical score, he described *Skyscrapers* as a work that reflected

> some of the many rhythmic movements and sounds of modern American life. It has no story, in the usually accepted sense, but proceeds on the simple fact that American life reduces itself essentially to violent alternations of WORK and PLAY, each with its own rhythmic character.[10]

Whether or not Carpenter provided an accurate analysis of the rhythms of America, he chose to express the moods he described with sounds that came from jazz and popular music.

An important event that helped to encourage interest in American popular music among composers and performers in the realm of concert music was Eva Gauthier's "Recital of Ancient and Modern Music for Voice" in New York's Aeolian Hall on November 1, 1923. In addition to songs by Byrd, Purcell, Bliss, Bartók, Schoenberg, Milhaud, and Hindemith, Miss Gauthier, a noted performer of modern music, programmed a group of seven American popular songs, including pieces by Irving Berlin, Jerome Kern, and George Gershwin, her accompanist for this portion of the concert. The performance of a group of tunes from Tin Pan Alley with accompaniments rooted in the harmonies and rhythms of jazz was more than a novelty: it placed these pieces in the context of the formal recital, where audiences were unaccustomed to hearing jazz or popular music. This program also produced favorable notices for the young pianist and composer who would soon make his own contribution to the synthesis of jazz and popular music.[11]

George Gershwin began his career as a pianist and song plugger for the firm of Jerome H. Remick in New York. His interests ranged from Jewish music to the blues. His formal piano study was limited, but he pursued lessons in counterpoint and orchestration briefly with Rubin Goldmark. In 1927, when he met Nadia Boulanger in Paris, she refused to accept him as a student, saying, "I can teach you nothing." It is likely that the teacher who helped to shape the individual personalities of so many original American modernist composers meant that Gershwin's style was already so well developed that she could no longer have an impact on the development of this already successful and popular composer.

Gershwin's melodic gift was particularly apparent in smaller pieces, such as the popular songs in AABA form. His Piano Preludes, published in 1926 but composed earlier, illustrate both his talent for melodic invention and the influence of jazz and popular music. His flair for developing the short motive as well as longer, more lyrical passages is amply illustrated in the *Rhapsody in Blue* first performed by the Paul Whiteman Orchestra in 1924. Whether we consider the glissandi, blue tonalities, and the use of a "wha wha" mute for the trumpet to be simply jazz devices tacked on to a Lisztian piano concert or the product or a genuine synthesis of Romantic music and Tin Pan Alley, the *Rhapsody* is clearly an important contribution to American concert music.

The first theme of the *Rhapsody* in Blue is a bombastic display by the full orchestra that is leavened by a teasing three-note chromatic figure that gives the ensemble the feel of a jazz band. The second theme, which is played mainly on the piano, is lighter and more playful in character. Gershwin demonstrated his ability to fuse concert music and jazz in other large works, most notably the *Concerto in F* commissioned by Walter Damrosch (1925), *An American in Paris* (1928), the *Cuban Overture* (1932), the *I Got Rhythm Variations* (1934), and the opera *Porgy and Bess* (1934–35). The composer's modern harmonic sense, along with his use of jazz mottos and his manipulation of the symphonic forces in the *Rhapsody*, prompted pianist and critic Samuel Chotzinoff to assert in 1924 that Gershwin was "thoroughly conversant with the harmonic secrets of Stravinsky and the latest French 'Six,' even though he acquired his knowledge through trial and error as a song writer rather than as a student of Nadia Boulanger."[12] Of course, in 1924 Gershwin, who along with Darius Milhaud was bringing American popular music into the concert hall with some success, had not yet encountered Mlle. Boulanger.

Many of the American composers who looked to American jazz in the late 1920s with technical interest, if not the intention of creating a unique American musical style, had studied abroad earlier in that decade, and one of the most prominent influences on these American modernists was the teaching of Nadia Boulanger. June 26, 1921, saw the opening of the Conservatoire Américaine at Fontainebleau under the auspices of the École des Hautes Études Musicales de France, with Mlle. Boulanger among the instructors of harmony. At the opening ceremonies, conductor Walter Damrosch, who had been active in securing funding and other crucial support for the school, told its students: "Learn French and the French people, they have the civilization of the ages. . . . Their civilization must be kept for the benefit of the world and it is a supreme privilege for you to share in its rewards."[13] Damrosch had organized and contributed his talents and cultural contacts to the American Friends of Musicians in France, a group that raised money for humanitarian purposes and eventually developed the idea of a music school for Americans in post-World War I France. Even before the opening of the Conservatoire, he and General Pershing had convinced the French high command of the utility of opening a school for American bandmasters, and that facility was in operation at Chaumont under the direction of Francis Casadesus by 1919. The school for bandmasters and the Conservatoire were seen as examples of Franco-American cooperation in which Americans would contribute financial resources and the French would provide the benefits of their musical culture.

It was not the French culture and civilization of the past but the excitement of Paris in the 1920s and the quality of instruction and encouragement for talented composers at Fontainebleau that attracted such young composers as Marion Bauer, Melville Smith, Douglas Moore, Elliott Carter, Virgil Thomson, Herbert Elwell, Roger Sessions, and Aaron Copland to the Boulanger studio. The proximity to Paris, the center of modern musical life, was also critical in the decision of many composers to come to Fontainebleau. Virgil Thomson has described the importance of that city to the vitality of new music and the extent to which, for him at least, the long-standing dominance of German music had ceased to be important:

> Paris can admire you and let you alone. New York withholds its admiration till assured that you are modeling yourself on central Europe. This is still true; a French musical influence is by definition heretical and only that made in Germany (or to its east) esteemed worthy. As H. L. Mencken put it, "There are two kinds of music, German music and bad music." Right there was my reason for living in France. I believed then, and still do, that German music, after being blessed above all others and having led the world for two hundred years, had failed to keep contact with our

century, that it had long since become self-centered, self-regarding, and self-indulgent.[14]

Thomson also criticized the American musical establishment for its continued adherence to German cultural patterns. "As an American," he wrote, "I had to keep contact with Europe." For Thomson, Paris was the only place in which he could remain free of the Germanic influence in modern music (including serialism, which he found to be "a combination of the progressive and the retrogressive in a most uncomfortable proportion"). And Paris, he believed, was the best place from which to "remind my country that it was not obliged to serve another country's power set-up."[15]

There were more personal reasons for studying in Paris in the 1920s. For example, Aaron Copland described his visits to the Left Bank cafés and such influential bookstores as Shakespeare and Company, where he could encounter the literary elite of modern Paris. And he expressed satisfaction with his composition study with Boulanger, not only because she knew "every musician of any importance in France," but also because she knew "everything there was to know about music; she knew the oldest and the latest music, pre-Bach and post-Stravinsky, and knew it cold."[16] And Virgil Thomson, a composer who established his own contacts with Gertrude Stein and other members of the Parisian avant-garde and who depended less on Mlle. Boulanger's influence to gain a hearing for his music, nevertheless described her commitment to the young American composers who came to study with her in glowing terms:

> A certain maternal warmth was part of her charm for all young men; but what endeared her most to Americans was her conviction that American music was about to "take off," just as Russian music had done eighty years before. Here she differed with other French musicians, who, though friendly enough toward Americans (we were popular then), lacked faith in us as artists.[17]

Study with Mlle. Boulanger for the American composer in the 1920s could be a liberating experience in which the development of a personal style took precedence over imitation of established models, even as this demanding pedagogue insisted that her students know thoroughly the music of the past as they were creating the art of the future. For some of the American modernists of Fontainbleau, a return to the United States meant a search for new musical materials. That search led to dance music, jazz, and other varieties of American popular music.

In the early 1920s, Copland had shown little interest in either American musical expression or the adulation of the average concert audience. Mlle. Boulanger introduced him to Walter Damrosch in Paris in May of 1922, and the conductor promised to perform a piece by the young American with his New York Symphony. The premiere of the *Symphony of Organ and Orchestra* took place on January 11, 1925, as part of Mlle. Boulanger's American tour as an organ soloist. The work is characterized by its irregular rhythms and uneven patterns of accents, and Copland noted that the Scherzo movement was his "idea of what could be done to adapt the raw material of jazz."[18] In this work, as in later pieces in which the composer abstracted minute elements of jazz rhythms or tonality, Copland was less interested in jazz as an expression of American or Afro-American identity than in its potential as a rich source of ideas for development in modern music.

The premiere of the *Symphony for Organ and Orchestra* was followed by Damrosch's famous remark to the audience that "if a gifted young man can write a symphony like that at twenty-three, within five years he will be ready to commit murder." Copland understood the remark to be a joke intended to "smooth the ruffled feathers of his conservative Sunday afternoon ladies faced with modern music." But he also notes than many critics were unreceptive to his work, both because it was jazzy and because it was modern.[19] Copland continued to attract the attention of conductors and audiences who expressed a willingness to hear his modern ventures into the realm of jazz. A performance of *Music for the Theatre* by Serge Koussevitsky and the Boston Symphony Orchestra on November 11, 1925, provided not only a reading of this five-movement chamber suite that is characterized by its asymmetrical rhythms reminiscent of jazz and moments of modern bitonality, it also brought remuneration, something on which the American concert music composer could rarely rely in the 1920s.[20]

Copland felt that American composers could find more of lasting value in the jazz idiom than had their European modernist counterparts who had considered popular music in this country to be a useful, but clearly temporary, novelty. He wrote, "Jazz offered American composers a native product from which to explore rhythm; for whatever the definition of jazz, it must be agreed that it is essentially rhythmic in character." Earlier, Copland had told critic Oscar Thompson that the two American elements in jazz were its rhythm, notably its syncopation, and something that he called the "jazz spirit." These two qualities, the first clearly definable and the second ineffable, were the tools with which this young composer in the 1920s hoped to capture the attention of the American concert audience.[21] Copland continued his exploration of the technical and expressive possibilities of jazz elements in the *Concerto for Piano and Orchestra*, composed in 1926 and first performed with the Boston Symphony with Copland as the soloist. The work is scored for orchestra, including alto and soprano saxophones and a variety of additional percussion instruments that could be called exotic, if not jazzy—a tam-tam, Chinese woodblock, and xylophone. According to the composer the piece illustrates two of the basic moods of jazz, the slow blues and the "snappy number." It lacks the steady beat of most popular music, however, incorporating numerous rapid changes in time signature and unusual rhythmic patterns.

Copland's *Concerto* was met with a variety of negative critical reactions ranging from assertion that it was "a harrowing horror from beginning to end" and descriptions of the piece as a portrayal of "a jazz dance hall next door to a poultry yard" to characterizations of Copland as "the ogre with that terrible concerto." After a New York peformance, Samuel Chotzinoff called the work's jazzlike theme in the second section

> a pretty poor pick, as these things go. But Mr. Copland surrounded it with all the machinery of sound and fury, and the most modernistic fury at that. The composer-pianist smote his instrument at random; the orchestra, under the impassioned baton of Mr. Koussevitzky, heaved and shrieked and fumed and made anything but sweeet moans until both pianist and conductor attained such a climax of absurdity that many in the audience giggled with delight. Mr. Copland was evidently seriously engaged in saying something of vital importance to himself, and played away, frantically aided and abetted by the orchestra, which made barnyard and stable noises in the intervals of proclaiming imposing Scriabinish fanfare.[22]

These remarks on Copland's last serious jazz composition reveal more hostility to the modern qualities of the music than to the attempt to incorporate elements of American popular music into a concert piece.

Even when composers exploited jazz for its pure sound possibilities and created symphonic works that clearly quoted from popular music, critics were often brutal in their censure. The following remarks sound as if they might have been directed at a bizarre Futurist tribute to the anarchy of random notes: "The honks have it. Four automobile horns, vociferously assisted by three saxophones, two tom-toms, rattle xylophone, wire brush, wood blocks, and an ensemble not otherwise innocent of brass and percussion blew or thumped the lid off Carnegie Hall." But these comments were written about George Gershwin's *An American in Paris*, a work that is melodic and evocative of a modern, bustling, urban panorama. The piece never loses its attachment to the easy, jazzlike style of Tin Pan Alley, and, for this reason, Oscar Thompson wrote that it was a display of "buffoonery" and "blatant banality." As for its lasting value to American culture, Thompson wrote that "to conceive of a symphonic audience listening to it with any degree of pleasure or patience twenty years from now, when whoopee is no longer even a word, is another matter. Then . . . there will still be Franck with his outmoded spirituality."[23] Critics like Thompson found fault with Copland's less accessible modern music that used jazz rhythms and melodies as well as the symphonic jazz of Gershwin on two grounds—it was modern and difficult, and it brought a popular music genre that many considered "low class" into the concert hall.

Other American concert music composers devoted some attention to jazz in their music during the 1920s. But like their European counterparts, this interest did not dominate their artistic output beyond that decade, as sounds and techniques derived from jazz and popular music became part of their compositional repertoire. Louis Gruenberg's first two violin sonatas (1918 and 1924) included syncopations and blues harmonies, and the composer's interest in dance music is reflected in the titles of the movements ("Fox Trot," "Blues," "Waltz," and "Syncopep") of *Jazzberries*, a piano piece composed in 1925. There is also jazz inspiration in *The Daniel Jazz* (1925), a cantata for tenor and chamber based on a poem by Vachel Lindsay. *Jazzettes* (1926), for violin and piano, and the orchestral *Jazz Suite* (1929) also reveal Gruenberg's interest in jazz in this decade. He also utilized some of the sounds of jazz in the score to the opera *The Emperor Jones*, based on a play by Eugene O'Neill, which was performed at the Metropolitan Opera House in 1933. But in later stage and film scores and the violin and piano sonatas of the 1940s, the jazz element is absent, having served its purpose for Gruenberg during one productive decade of his career.

This was also the case with the music of George Antheil and Henry Cowell. Antheil's *Jazz Symphony* (1925) represented a temporary flirtation with the jazz idiom and was neither as controverseial as the *Airplane Sonata* and *Ballet Mécanique* nor as lyrical as later film scores, operas, and symphonic works. Hints of jazz influence can also be heard in two operas, *Transatlantic* (1930) and *Helen Retires* (1934). Ever the experimenter, Cowell played with jazz in his *Suite for Clarinet and Piano*, but the influence of popular music on his creative mindset was minimal. He had much more success with exotic instruments such as the Japanese koto and with such new musical devices as his famous tone clusters.

Wallingford Riegger's *Triple Jazz* (1918), a piece in which he attempted to evoke the feeling of jazz in triple meter, was unusual, as very few examples of jazz or popular music used three beats to the measure. It was a good example of Riegger's interest in reconciling disparate rhythmic elements and is unique in the composer's oeuvre as a piece that includes elements of jazz. Finally, one of America's first nontonal composers and Arnold Schoenberg's first student from this country, Adolph Weiss, composed *American Life, Scherzoso Jazzoso* in 1929. The piece was published in 1932 under the auspices of Henry Cowell's *New Music* magazine and called for soprano, alto, and tenor saxophones, a suspended cymbal, and a snare drum played with brushes. There is a "Fox Trot" section, and another part of the piece is marked "Blues tempo, slow, rubato." One solo in the "Blues" section begins with an English horn, then the melody is picked up by a saxophone, an interesting juxtaposition of sounds common to the traditional orchestra and the dance band. Weiss did not continue to experiment with jazz sounds and effects after the 1920s.

As early as 1924, composer Virgil Thomson had warned that jazz might not be the salvation for American concert music. Chiding those who saw this country's musical future only in terms of the blues, the fox trot, or the fast, syncopated dance number, he argued that the worship of jazz was "just another form of highbrowism, like the worship of discord or the worship of Brahms." He cautioned American composers against abandoning the lessons they had learned in Europe, saying that "to be an American, one need not be ignorant" of developments in the larger musical world. He also remarked that he liked jazz, not because it was American, but because it was good music that more and more American composers were becoming adept at using as a compositional tool.[24]

Aaron Copland saw his interest in jazz as a product of his commitment to the new music. By the late 1920s, Copland had begun to compose more abstract pieces, such as the *Dance Symphony* (1929, adapted from an earlier ballet, *Grohg*), the *Piano Variations* (1930), and the *Symphonic Ode*, which was first performed in celebration of the fiftieth anniversary of the Boston Symphony Orchestra in 1931. Of the *Symphonic Ode*, Copland wrote that it

> resembles me at the time, full of ideas and ideals, introspective and serious, but still showing touches of youthful jazz days, reflections of a Jewish heritage, remnants of Paris (Boulanger's *la grande ligne*), influences of Mahler (the orchestration) and Stravinsky (motor rhythms). Looking ahead, one can hear in the *Ode* the beginnings of a purer, non-programmatic style, an attempt toward an economy of material and transparency of texture that would be taken much further in the *Piano Variations*, the *Short Symphony*, and *Statements for Orchestra*.[25]

Copland the modernist found in his deepening interest in form and musical structure an abstract perspective that allowed for the use of a broad range of musical materials, whether they were derived from jazz or were the product of the composer's creative imagination. He wrote in 1941 that modern music was "the expression in terms of an enriched musical language of a new spirit of objectivity, attuned to our own times. It is the music of the composer of today—in other words—*our* music."[26]

Roy Harris, who had studied with Nadia Boulanger and who would later make his reputation as a distinctly "American" composer, commented in 1930 on the variety of influences on his craft and the impossibility that any single style could represent the whole of American cultural character. With regard to attempts to compose American music by quoting jazz, he wrote that "music does not lend itself to the portrayal of literal ideas and concrete facts." He described the essence of music as abstract, "springing naturally from abstract impulses and formulating itself into abstract autogenic forms. The abstract nature of music can awaken as many associations as there are auditors: in this fact lies its unique social significance."[27] Copland and Harris both saw the art of composition as having its basis in such nonprogrammatic aspects of art as formal structure and melodic invention. By the end of the 1920s, both composers favored a more abstract idiom than Copland had utilized in his "jazz period." Harris composed the *Concerto for Piano, String Quartet, and Clarinet* (1927), a Piano Sonata (1928), and a String Quartet (1930) during this period.

Looking back on the mid-1920s from a lectern at Harvard University in 1952, Copland described his compositions of this period as "American" in character. "Gradually," he said,

> the idea that my personal expression in music ought somehow to be related to my own back-home environment took hold of me. The conviction grew inside of me that two things that seemed always to have been so separate in America—music and the life about me—must be made to touch.

Despite the assertion, "The desire to make the music I wanted to write come out of the life I lived in America became a preoccupation of mine in the twenties,"[28] it is not clear from Copland's music that he had a strong inclination toward national expression or that his music was a reflection of American life. After all, his interest in jazz was born of a modernist, experimental temperament, and his more difficult and cerebral works of the late 1920s revealed even more clearly a variety of international influences. It was the modernist composers of the 1920s, including Copland, who, through their experiments with jazz and modern music, set the stage for the creation of music that would "sound" American. Copland did not assume the role of "nationalist" in music until the following decade.

As modernist composers in the 1920s looked for a receptive audience for their new music, they generally found few interested ears, in spite of the efforts of Damrosch and Koussevitzky to educate the cosmopolitan concert audience to an appreciation of experimentation. Critical commentary often did little to encourage audiences to approach modern music with open minds. Richard Aldrich, music critic for the *New York Times* from 1902 to 1923, witnessed the invasion of modern music into the concert hall in the 1920s. While most of his writing on music was relatively mild-mannered, Aldrich was openly hostile to the new. In a 1923 column, "Some Judgments on New Music," he was sarcastic about the tendencies of many modern composers:

> It is nothing less than a crime for a composer to write in any of the idioms that have been handed down, or to hold any of the older ideas of beauty, however touched both may be with a new spirit and extended in adaptability to new and independent thought. Any who do not throw overboard all the baggage inherited from the past, all transmitted ideas of melody and harmony, are reactionaries, pulling back and hindering the onward march of music.

Aldrich's hostility to the proponents of the modernist ideal was as pronounced as was his disapproval of the new music itself. He considered himself to be among the reactionaries who were reluctant to jump on the bandwagon of modern music, describing the admirers of the avant-garde as "strangely uncritical personalities." "Whatever is presented to them as acrid ugliness or rambling incoherence," he wrote, "is eagerly accepted as emanations of greatness and originality. It never occurs to them that it may be really simple, commonplace ugliness." While he left the final verdict on modern music to future generations of critics and audiences, he thought that it would be useful in his own time "to have some means of judging whether possibly there may be some geese in the proud flotilla of swans that sail under the banner of new music."[29]

Arthur Farwell, a prominent Romantic nationalist composer and proponent of the cause of an American concert music based on folk sources, also attacked the modern movement. He feared overspecialization and reliance on technical criteria for judging music and the very real possibility that modern composers would never reach a broad audience. He wrote in 1927 that the music of what he called "our secular epoch" was

> assuming a character so technically over-refined and strained as to remove it beyond recall from the possibility of reaching the sympathies and satisfying the needs of more than a microscopic proportion of the people. This follows naturally the technical and materialistic bias of the time.[30]

Farwell still looked to national or regional musical expression based on folk music for the creation of something uniquely "American." He hoped that composers would cooperate with local performing groups to create as "people's music." His reliance on the small community as the locus of musical activity, in contrast to the international focus of many modernist composers in the late 1920s, is reminiscent of the Wilsonian strand of Progressive thinking that promised the improvement of society through a return to the values of the small town of the nineteenth century. But by the time Farwell was writing, both the small-town ideals and the concept of a national music based simply on the quotation of popular and folk music were part of America's history. Farwell's criticism was in tune with much contemporary critical opinion that saw little value in what appeared to be a complete rejection of the past.

What many critics failed to hear in the new music was a reliance on past traditions that lay beneath the surface of total rejection of traditional tonality and rhythm. As Aaron Copland's comments on his *Symphonic Ode* indicate, by the latter part of the 1920s, many composers did recognize a debt to earlier sources. And an interest in older forms on the part of Igor Stravinsky and other composers during what has been called a "Neoclassical" period in modern music demonstrated that the new music could allow composers to reject the portions of past traditions that no longer served the needs of their individual styles while using what remained interesting of older music from the Middle Ages to the nineteenth century.

If modern composers did not always feel that their music was understood by the critics who brought it to the attention to the public, they did have a journal of their own that championed the cause of new and experimental music. *Modern Music* spoke to a small audience, but its writers were among the more important composers and critics who were receptive to new creative currents. Begun in February of 1924 as the *League of Composers Journal, Modern Music* (which assumed its new title in November of 1925) consistently supported the efforts of contemporary European and American composers.

Internationalist in outlook, this journal offers the modern reader insights into the opinions of new music specialists on the important issues of national music and modern music. For all the assertions by Henry F. Gilbert and others that the only great art is *national* art, many writers for *Modern Music* took an opposing position. Louis Gruenberg spoke for universality through internationalism in art, Frank Patterson called national characteristics "as accidental in music as in life," and A. Walter Kramer wrote that "no composer of parts can hope to be considered a significant figure until he has achieved international acceptance. The American composer must battle for that goal, if he would be ranked with the composers of the world."[31] By the end of the 1920s, many modern composers recognized that they could achieve artistic, if not popular, acceptance in their own country not by removing themselves from developments in Europe but by continuing to participate in the search for an individual modern style.

Throughout the 1930s, contributors to *Modern Music* aired their views about the latest compositional techniques and the uses to which these devices could be put in the creation of expressive American music. The journal never abandoned its commitment to innovation, even after many composers had come to feel that it was time to slow the rapid pace at which new musical innovations created a sensation.

The international language of musical modernism provided some American composers with the tools they needed to create useful and accessible American music in the 1930s. In general, they surpassed in originality the hybrid symphonic works of the Romantic nationalist group of composers who were most active prior to World War I. Henry F. Gilbert saw the potential for the new music to contribute to a synthesis of modern and characteristically American elements when he wrote in 1930 that Aaron Copland

> is a young man. He and I belong to different generations. We are poles apart as regards style of musical expression. Yet the principle which actuates us both is about the same. He also desires to write some music which, in its content, shall reflect and express American character rather than European. But America, to him, is New York. He is a great believer in Jazz, and its possibilities regarding symphonic development. And his technique is in the up-to-the-minute style of modernity.[32]

But the modernists' approach to composition could do little to bring audiences into the concert hall. In general, few composers wanted or could afford to create music that no one understood or would pay to hear, and the challenge of the committed modernist as the decade of the 1920s came to a close was how to hone the qualities of his individual style and still reach an audience in his own country. The answer no longer lay in an attempt to transplant jazz into the concert hall. Having exhausted most of the possibilities of the so-called "jazz spirit," many composers now turned to a more cerebral and, for most audiences, a less attractive exploitation of the more technical elements of jazz. To the average ear, these works were indistinguishable from the most modern, nontonal, and difficult pieces of avant-garde composers who expressed no interest in using popular music for any purpose.

The stock market crash and the ensuing Depression placed many composers in dire economic straits, just as it affected other Americans. The desire to be heard and to create useful music, along with the dramatic shift in economic and social realities, contributed to a change in creative direction on the part of many composers. If few Americans could support modern music, then perhaps the composer could find a medium in which his creative imagination could reach a larger audience. Moreover, the impact of the Depression encouraged a new perspective on the role of the American composer in his society.

For many artists a heightened interest in the nation's social and economic conditions during the early Depression years brought forth an awareness of future political possibilities as defined by the American Left, while for others a similar involvement led to a greater recognition of the potential of American historical narrative and contemporary problems as subject for art outside of a particular political context. Commenting on the latter phenomenon, cultural commentator Maxwell Geismar wrote in 1941 that "the depression brought our artists back from the shadows of apathy or hostility to a more fruitful share in our common heritage."[33]

The American composer who had utilized some aspect of jazz in his music was often distanced from a large audience by the very modern artistic point of view that had helped to awaken him to the possibilities inherent in jazz in the first place. But in the 1930s, more American composers sought to reach the audience on its own terms. They simplified, but they did not abandon completely, their modern styles and techniques. Their claim to audience attention was based not on assertions that they had invented a new American music, but rather that they had used the new music in one form or another to compose program music on subjects in which the intended audience was interested.

A small but significant number of American modernist composers in the early 1930s felt that one way to reach a mass audiecne was to contribute to the work of the political Left. They wrote articles for *New Masses*, composed songs for political rallies, and participated in cultural events sponsored by the Communist Party and its various affiliated organizations, even as they often continued outside of a political context to compose modern music as they had learned to do in Europe. It is important to remember that political attitudes and activities do not always inspire what might be called "political music." Notes on the printed page achieve political content only when their creator attributes such an interpretation to them. Thus, it was possible in the 1930s for the most committed political activists to compose songs for workers while they also created the most difficult and abstract music that claimed no nonmusical content or inspiration at all.[34]

American left-wing political music had generally been derived from the musical traditions of various immigrant groups. This was particularly so before and during the Third Period of 1928–35, in which Nicolai Bukharin articulated the notion of continued class struggle in all areas of life, including culture. In keeping with the philosophy of the Third Period, which advocated international class struggle over national political development, including cultural expression, Mike Gold lamented in 1931 that, while the Freiheit Gesang Farein, with its three hundred members, was a highly accomplished vocal group, its emphasis on German culture did not advance the larger cause of worldwide revolution. He complained that "there are no new workers' songs and music being written in this country."[35] Two years later, he asked, "Why don't American workers sing? The Wobblies knew how, but we still have to develop a Communist Joe Hill."[36] The answer, of course, was that no one was composing new music to further the class struggle that workers could sing and understand.

In 1931 New York's John Reed Club set out to remedy the lack of workers' songs by forming a Music Committee whose goal was the "creation of songs expressing and projecting the class struggle."[37] In June of the same year, the Workers' Music League, the music section of the Workers' Cultural Federation, which described itself as "the central organization of all musical forces connected with the American revolutionary working class movement," was founded for the purpose of providing "ideological and musical guidance" to those American groups and organizations involved in the class struggle.[38] The League's leadership in its composition, publishing, and performance divisions came from the Pierre Degeyter Club (the musical counterpart of New York's literary John Reed Club) and adopted as its slogan, "Music for the Masses." The League's *Red Song Book,* published in 1932, contains music that workers would be likely to know, such as Degeyter's *The Internationale, Red Marching Song,* with its tune derived from the last movement of Beethoven's Ninth Symphony, and the traditional *Hold the Fort* and *The Preacher and the Slave,* both of which had appeared in the *Red Song Books* of the Industrial Workers of the World early in the twentieth century. Lan Adomian, Hanns Eisler, and several anonymous composers also contributed pieces to this small volume. Most of the music is quite easy to sing, and there is little modernist influence in these works that derive from the German marching-song tradition.

The Composers' Collective emerged out of the Workers' Music League in February of 1932 as a workshop for the creation and performance of revolutionary music and as a forum for discussing how modern music could be used to further the workers' cause. The Collective described itself as a group in which "conservative and radical musical thought and taste meet in free and vigorous clash upon the question of the definition of a musical style 'national in style, proletarian in content.' "[39] The diversity of compositional points of view is amply illustrated in the membership of the Composers' Collective, which included Henry Cowell, George Antheil, Lan Adomian, Charles Seeger, Jacob Schaefer, Wallingford Riegger, Elie Siegmeister, Marc Blitzstein, Max Margulis, Herbert Haufrecht, Henry Leland Clarke, Janet Barnes (Jeannette Barnett), and (from time to time) Aaron Copland. While most of the composers who attended the weekly reading and discussion sessions of the Collective were not members of the Communist Party, the Party did provide loft space and a forum for some of the work the Collective members produced. There was no remuneration for Collective activities, and members survived the worst years of the Depression by conducting, playing the piano, and teaching, just as composers with no interest in politics did. The modernist aesthetic is evident in the early music of the Collective, and some pieces demonstrate a remarkable synthesis of political inspiration of text and avant-garde musical style. An example of this synthesis appears in Elie Siegmeister's *Strange Funeral in Braddock,* after a poem by Mike Gold for baritone and piano. This song is dissonant and quite difficult to sing. It represents a genre of political music that was intended to be heard by workers but not performed by them. The text expressed outrage at the death of Jan Clepek, a Bohemian steel worker, in the Pennyslvania mills.

The modern composers in the Collective in its early years often used advanced techniques such as changing meters and angular melodies in their songs, but they also sought in their political music to learn from the working class about its cultural and political needs. Aaron Copland, whose *Into the Streets, May First!* won the 1934 *New Masses* song competition, wrote that "composers will want to raise the musical level of the masses, but they must also be ready to learn from them what species of song is most apposite to the revolutionary task."[40] Copland asserted that the mass song was the most appropriate vehicle for communicating the political message of the "day to day struggle of the proletariat." He was convinced that "as more and more composers identify themselves with the workers' cause, the challenge of the mass song will more surely be met." He reminded *New Masses* readers that those composers who had turned their creative talents to the writing of workers' songs were owed a debt of thanks "by those of us who wish to see music play its part in the workers' struggle for a new world order."[41]

Copland's remarks appeared in a review of the first *Workers Song Book,* a publication of the Workers' Music League that contained music by Collective members and others. While the songs in this volume were intended to inspire revolutionary fervor in a musically untrained working class, they are by no means simplistic in musical terms. The compositions of L. E. Swift (Elie Siegmeister), Carl Sands (Charles Seeger), and Jacob Schaefer were often characterized by changing time signatures and some interesting melodic twists. Many have texts that reflect the political situation of the early 1930s, such as Swift's readily singable round, *Poor Mister Morgan,* whose text is satirical:

> Poor Mister Morgan cannot pay his income tax,
> Pity poor Morgan, he cannot pay.
> He's dead broke, he hasn't got a cent!

Other pieces in this collection express a generalized revolutionary spirit, such as Sands's *Mount the Barricades.* And compositions such as Janet Barnes's *God to the Hungry Child,* with a text by Langston Hughes, are mildly dissonant and thematically timeless:

> Hungry child,
> I did not make this world for you.
> You didn't buy any stock in my railroad,
> You did not invest in my corporation.
> Where are your shares in Standard Oil?
> I made the world for the rich.
> And they will be rich, and they have always been rich.
> Not for you,
> Hungry child.

1931 had seen the indictment and conviction of nine young black men in Birmingham, Alabama, on charges of raping two white women. The flimsy evidence and blatant racism of the case brought notoriety to the Scottsboro Boys at a time when the Communist Party and its affiliated organizations were making a concerted effort to overturn the verdicts. Elie Siegmeister, while not a member of the Party, contributed *The Scottsboro Boys Shall Not Die* to the first *Workers Song Book.* Writing both text and music under his *nom de musique,* L. E. Swift, Siegmeister captured the spirit of the labor movement in general and the Industrial Labor Defense organization that played a particularly active role in rousing public indignation at the plight of the Scottsboro Boys:

> Workers, farmers, Negro and white,
> The lynching bosses we must fight.
> Close your fists and raise them high,
> Labor defense is our battle cry.

Chorus: The Scottsboro boys shall not die,
The Scottsboro boys shall not die.
Workers led by I. L. D. will set them free.
Set them free!

By mass action we will defend,
Our own class brothers to the end.
Death to lynchers we declare,
Frame-ups and lies to bits we'll tear.

Chorus:

The first *Workers Song Book* contains pieces with revolutionary texts and some examples of relatively sophisticated music, considering the purpose for which the music was composed. Folk melodies, most of which are easy to learn and sing, played practically no role in the Workers' Music League's 1934 vision of the class struggle. Collective members like Charles Seeger, who would later embrace folk music with considerable enthusiasm as authentic American cultural expression, even considered folk tunes to be detrimental to the cause of creating political music for struggling workers. Writing as Carl Sands in *The Daily Worker*, he noted that most folk songs were "complacent, melancholy, defeatist—originally intended to make slaves endure their lot—pretty but not the stuff for a militant proletariat to feed upon."[42] Sands was interested only in those traditional songs that expressed what he called the "spirit of resentment toward oppression" or "vigorous resistance." And Henry Cowell contended that modern music that was "revolutionary" in the sense that it broke with traditional patterns was still the best vehicle for expressing the spirit of class struggle in cultural terms. Cowell was unwilling to give in to easy solutions to the problem of an absence of popular acceptance of modern music, although he did concede that "technical innovations must be steadily and slowly introduced into workers' music" so that those who were intended to benefit from its revolutionary content could come to appreciate its musically revolutionary sound."[43]

But even as Sands and Cowell attacked folk music as bland and nonrevolutionary and as they defended political music of a complex and often difficult nature, a theory of "socialist realism" was taking hold. This doctrine was first articulated by Maxim Gorky and Andrei Zhdanov at the first All-Union Congress of Soviet Writers in the summer of 1934. The artistic expression of socialist realism was intended to emerge from the daily lives and experiences of the people. Works of art created within this political framework were to inspire their audiences by presenting familiar and easily understandable forms and style as media for revolutionary content. In the United States, the shift toward socialist realism in art was encouraged in 1934 by the Communist Party's attempt to broaden its appeal with less emphasis on international class struggle and a clearer focus on Earl Browder's slogan, "Communism Is Twentieth Century Americanism." On the relationship of musical form to political meaning and the newly perceived need to derive both form and content from the experience of American workers, Mike Gold wrote in *The Daily Worker* that "a new content often demands a new form, but when the new form gets so far ahead of all of us that we can't understand its content, it is time to write letters to the press."[44] Such notions implied a rejection of the difficult music to which Elie Siegmeister had set Gold's own poem, "Strange Funeral in Braddock." This approach also encouraged composers and critics to accept American folk tunes, or melodies that sounded like folk tunes, in music that claimed a political purpose. Of course, folk music had long served as a means of popular expression outside of a specifically political context, and, as Gold had earlier pointed out, the American working class had a long history of music associated with its struggle for recognition.

Although not all of the Composers' Collective members were quick to modify their styles to include the folk idiom, Lan Adomian defended cowboy songs, spirituals, and other varieties of folk music as

> a colorful addition to our repertoire. Such an approach [composing with folk music or in a folk style] would carry us a long way toward rooting our work in the tradition of American music. It would give the lie to those who would insist that our music is nothing but an importation from the outside.[45]

The change in the political line prompted a change in musical thought for left-wing political composers. With less embarrassment than in the past, they looked to the music of their own country.

The second *Workers Song Book* (1935) contains pieces by twelve composers, and six of the eight Americans represented were Collective members. The influence of the new socialist realism is evident in this collection. In contrast to the songs in the first volume, these pieces are virtually devoid of rhythmic or melodic complexity. Copland's *Into the Streets, May First!* (a piece that wanders through several keys before ending where it began, in C major, but which is easily learned with the help of a strong piano accompaniment that doubles the vocal line) appears here, as do songs by Earl Robinson, the composer of *Ballad for Americans*, Swift, Sands, and the German refugee composer, Hanns Eisler. It also includes two Afro-American protest songs, *I Went to 'Tlanta*, and *Sistren and Brethren*, both contributed by Lawrence Gellert.

With the publication of *Workers Song Book 2,* there also seems to have been a realization on the part of many composers that their earlier confidence in the ability of untrained workers' choruses to sing difficult and complex music may have been somewhat premature. Commenting on Elie Siegmeister's *Park Bench* (with words by Langston Hughes), one of his *Three Workers' Rounds* in the first volume, Charles Seeger had noted that there was, in a fast tempo, "alternation of four-four and five-eight meter that would cause difficulty for most bourgeois choruses. But workers' choruses that have tried it do not have any trouble."[46] But despite Seeger's claims for the proficiency of workers' choruses, it appears that by 1935, simpler, less challenging compositions were required for the continuation of the class struggle. *Workers Song Book 2* contains none of the musical barriers to easy performance of the first volume.

By 1935 the impact of socialist realism was apparent in both the music and the writings of several modernist composers. Henry Cowell, the musical experimenter and advocate of the more dissonant and less accessible works of Charles Ives, also supported the cause of left-wing political music in the 1930s. He wrote for *New Masses* and published numerous original manuscripts by Soviet composers in his own journal, *New Music.*[47] Cowell, who was not known for composing singable melodies or simple rhythmic patterns, nevertheless responded to the call for political music that workers could understand and create for themselves. His *New Masses* article, "Useful Music," described the evolution of an original protest song from a familiar melody as workers marched on a picket line. Cowell wrote that it was the creation of the new song and the act of singing together that created unity among the marchers.[48] Where the social function and ideological content of music had earlier been of little importance to Cowell and other modernist American composers, thse two facets of the larger creative process of composition assumed new meaning to many who now identified with the Left and whose work was affected by the political concept of socialist realism.

The notion that music should have a social or political purpose and not merely exist for its own sake was also articulated in the pages of *New Masses* by Marc Blitzstein. Describing a Town Hall symposium in which he had participated with Aaron Copland, Henry Cowell, and Hanns Eisler, Blitzstein approvingly quoted Eisler's comments: "To the criteria of 'Invention,' 'Technical Skill,' 'Emotion,' the decisive criterion of the 'Social Function' [of music] must be added." Blitzstein called this credo the "manifesto for the revolutionary music of our time."[49]

Eisler had a long history of revolutionary ideas about musical composition, although he had not always subscribed to the ideas of the political Left. He had studied composition with Arnold Schoenberg and Anton Webern between 1919 and 1923, and his technique in the 1920s combined serialism, an interest in American jazz, and a commitment to experimentation. By 1926 Eisler's political convictions had prompted him to join the German Communist Party and to re-examine his views on the nature and future direction of music. He wrote for the Party's journal, *Rote Fahne,* and he attempted to turn his creative energies in the direction of his political beliefs. This change in perspective, away from the purely abstract aesthetic and closer to what he would later call the doctrine of "art for society's sake," led to a break with Schoenberg. Once the Nazis came to power, Eisler's music was banned in Germany, but he continued to compose, especially stage pieces and film scores, and to lecture throughout parts of Europe and the United States. His lecture series on "The Crisis in Music" at the New School for Social Research in 1935 presented the idea that music had a relationship to its environment and could be an instrument for social change. Eisler's hope for a synthesis of modern musical style and revolutionary social and political content was also articulated in the pages of *Modern Music,* where he argued that the creative output of his colleagues could serve both composers and audiences "only when there is a new, modern style, pertaining to all, and useful to society."[50]

For the Left, Eisler's ideas had direct implications for the revolutionary potential of music. A year before the Town Hall Symposium, Eisler had analyzed what he perceived to be a crisis in modern music and asserted that the only important music was that which came out of the life of the American people. According to Eisler, the crisis in modern music

> has been caused by the general crisis in society. In music it appears concretely in the technique of composing. This, in turn, has contributed to the complete isolation of the modern composer from social life. The modern composer meanwhile has become a parasite, supported by wealthy patrons out of personal interests, and no longer carries out any rational work in society.

Experimentation in modern music, no matter how interesting it may be to the composer, does not appeal to the public nor does it serve to resolve broader social issues of the day. For Eisler, it was irrelevant:

> At a time when modern music no longer has a public but is only promoted privately a composer can do as he pleases. He can compose like Czerny and with a few false basses write a "Book of Exercises for *non*-Dexterity." He can copy Brahms with the twelve tone technique or sit on top of the piano declaring he is expressing his innermost soul. Since these methods are as useless as they are unsalable the difference is minute.

As composers debate the fine points of how to create an avant-garde musical aesthetic, "another type of man with a rough voice and hard hands would appear, bang on the table and demand, 'For whose benefit?' " Eisler asserted that "the modern composer will have to leave his airtight room and find his place in society"[51] and that this was the only way to stem what he saw as the tide of decay in new music and find a new style that will also attract new listeners.

By 1935, when the Communist Party itself was taking a broader view of culture and politics with the Popular Front, a number of American composers defined the social function and political ideology of their music in most flexible terms. Works for performance by amateur groups, pieces that presented the melodies and scenarios of everyday American life in the theater or concert hall, and music composed with the idea of representing some aspect of American history or society (even if it did not quote specific popular melodies) all served a valuable social, if not revolutionary, function.

The music of Marc Blitzstein reflected the idea that art can serve a political, if not a specifically partisan, ideology. After a period of study with Nadia Boulanger in France and Schoenberg in Berlin between 1926 and 1928, Blitzstein brought his modern musical training to the task of composing music for the theater. He explored the possibilities of theater music for expressing social commentary, even as he continued to compose abstract works, including the *Sarabande for Orchestra* (1926), the Piano Sonata (1927), a Piano Concerto (1931) and *Variations* (1943). *The Condemned,* a work inspired by the trial and execution of Sacco and Vanzetti and composed in 1932, was a synthesis of Blitzstein's modern style and his emerging social consciousness.

The idea of creating "useful music" influenced Blitzstein's theater music. His works from the mid-1930s until his entry into the Army Air Force in August of 1942 reflected Eisler's position that it was not enough for an artist to exist in his society and create only within the boundaries of his own aesthetic—he must use his talent to struggle for the improvement of that society.[52] Perhaps the most representative example of Blitzstein's social commentary was his play, *The Cradle Will Rock,* performed outside the auspices of the Federal Theatre Project because of fears that its prolabor message was too radical. Other works that confirmed his reputation as an activist composer were the opera *No For an Answer* (1940) and the film score for *Native Land.* Of Blitzstein's "political" music of the late 1930s, Aaron Copland wrote:

> Marc Blitzstein's life exemplifies a truism that bears restatement today: Every artist has the right to make his art out of an emotion that really moves him. Those of our composers who are moved by the immense terrain of new techniques now seemingly in their grasp would do well to

remember that humanity's struggle for a fuller life may be equally valid as a moving force in the history of music.[53]

Blitzstein was no stranger to modern compositional techniques, and he utilized a broad range of strategies for conveying the poignancy of American life, from the twelve-bar blues to the twelve-tone row. His was modern theatrical music that addressed the concerns of the American people in a time of economic dislocation and potential political turmoil. He spoke to an audience that recognized the message of his art as the message of the daily headlines.

The turn toward the Popular Front made it possible for composers who had previously seen their commitment to the Left and to social change only in terms of the victory of an international proletariat now to identify with struggles against fascism and for democracy within their own countries. For Blitzstein and many other American composers who had begun to write music about their own country and its problems in the mid-1930s, there was little need to look for class struggle in an international context. The struggles of American workers and farmers provided ample inspiration for music that reflected the contemporary reality of the Depression. The Soviet regime abandoned its antagonism to the Western capitalist countries in favor of a policy of cooperation, as Stalin feared that his country would be isolated in a war with Nazi Germany. In the United States, Communist Party leaders such as Mike Gold proclaimed that

> the chief battleground in the defense of culture against fascist barbarism is this question of national tradition. . . . In our pamphleteering, we should learn to use naturally and easily, examples and metaphors out of the American past.[54]

Popular Front ideology helped to unite composers who had previously been active on the Left and those who had not in the pursuit of a national rather than a specifically political message in their music.

Of course, without programmatic titles, folk or other familiar melodies, or an American subject or source of inspiration, it was as difficult to recognize uniquely "American" concert music as it was to detect the "proletarian" quality of notes and rests without a text on a printed page. But for about a decade after 1935, many American composers did create works about their own history or present reality, they developed folk tunes in a modern musical context, and they wrote operas and overtures for high school students or scores for Living Newspaper productions. On February 10, 1936, the Workers' Music League, the parent body of the Composers' Collective, dissolved itself in favor of the formation of a more broadly based organization, the American

Music League, whose purposes were to promote the Popular Front in American music and to encourage the study and collection of native folk music. Without its Party affiliation, the Composers' Collective continued to function under the auspices of the new American Music League, but by 1936, only Siegmeister, Blitzstein, and Robinson remained of the original membership. Party identification and the furtherance of the international class struggle had been supplanted by a less clearly defined but ultimately more fertile vision of America. The cowboy, pioneer, railroad man, and balladeer once again found their way into the concert hall through the folk music that depicted them. The difference was that the folk characters, as well as the composers who brought them to life, wore distinctly modern dress that could consist of quartal harmony, occasional dissonance, syncopated rhythms and other references to jazz, and even serial technique.

Virgil Thomson possessed a modernist's musical perspective, and he looked at his homeland with a vision that was both European and American. Thomson himself has observed that his musc attempted to bring Paris to the banks of the Missouri River, and a touch of Kansas City, his home town, to the banks of the Seine. As a Boulanger student in the early 1920s, he wrote with a flair for dissonant counterpoint in works such as the *Sonata da Chiesa* for E-flat clarinet, trumpet, horn, and trombone, and he also experimented with some of the Dadaist techniques with which Erik Satie had earlier caused such a stir in Parisian musical circles.

Thomson's employment of simple melodic patterns, a disjointed relationship between music and text, and passages that parody more "serious" compositional styles coincided with his collaboration in Paris with Gertrude Stein, one of the twentieth century's most famous manipulators of the English language. The opera, *Four Saints in Three Acts* (1927), was one result of this collaborative effort. It is a work that conveys "American" images in its dance tunes and Stephen Foster-like ballads but also contains Sapnish-sounding passages, numbers written in the style of an Elizabethan madrigal, and deliberate discontinuities between music and text.[55] Thomson also worked with Gertrude Stein on *The Mother of Us All* (1947), an opera based on the life and influence of Susan B. Anthony.

As a participant in the Federal Theatre Project, Thomson contributed a score for the fanciful stage production of the nineteenth-century farce *Un Chapeau di paille d'Italie,* originally written by Eugene Labiche and translated for the Project by Edwin Denby and Orson Welles. The American title was *Horse Eats Hat*. He also wrote the music for the more topical Living Newspaper production of *Injunction Granted*. Thomson used an orchestra of sixteen percussion players who performed on "sixteen bass drums, snare drums, cymbals, sixteen of everything, including bronx cheers" to accompany this collection of scenes from the history of the labor movement in the United States.[56] He is also remembered for his "American" film scores of the late 1930s that were written on specifically American subjects in collaboration with director Pare Lorentz and subsidized by the Resettlement Administration. *The Plow that Broke the Plains* (1936) deals with conditions in the dust-bowl region and the problem of soil erosion, and *The River* also portrays life under adverse natural conditions in America's heartland. Thomson wrote that his own background helped to inspire these scores. The music of *The Plow that Broke the Plains*

> had poured forth easily. I knew the Great Plains landscape in Kansas, Oklahoma, New Mexico, Texas; and during the World War I had lived in a tent with ten-below-zero dust storms. I had come to the theme nostalgic and ready to work; and the film itself, when I first encountered it, was ready to be worked on. The subject, moreover, was highly photogenic—broad grasslands and cattle, mass harvesting, erosion by wind, deserted farms.[57]

Thomson arranged these film scores in concert suites, as he did with the score to the Robert Flaherty film, *Louisiana Story*, composed in 1948.

Thomson's music was particularly well suited to film and stage works, as his contributions to the Federal Theatre Project amply show. His description of the music and scenario for the ballet, *Filling Station*, shows his intention to portray popular America:

> For "Filling Station" [Lew] Christenson and I worked out a suite of "numbers" and "recitatives" to tell the story in appropriate timings. And I wrote a score made up of waltzes, tangoes, a fugue, a Big Apple, a holdup, a chase, and a funeral, all aimed to evoke roadside America as pop art. The painter Paul Cadmus designed clothes and a setting for it inspired by comic strips. Christenson, as a filling-station attendant in white translucent coverall, filled the stage with his in-the-air cartwheels and held us breathless with his twelve-turn pirouettes.[58]

Filling Station premiered in Hartford in January of 1938 and, in the spring of the same year, was performed in New York under WPA auspices.

Thomson has been called a Neoclassicist in the French mode because of his early training, a Neoromantic because of his melodic gift, and an American nationalist composer because of the inspiration for his film scores and many stage pieces. A variety of musical materials, from Baptist hymns to Gregorian chant, served his artistic purposes, and he developed an individual, modern style with the techniques acquired from his study and work in Paris in the 1920s.

Many composers joined in the quest for a modern music that would reflect the American experience and appeal to American audiences. Some of these men and women composed major works that remain in the concert repertoire today, while many others contributed to the programs of their local bands, orchestras, and choruses. Aaron Copland pointed out that the "great young American composer"

> will not appear suddenly out of the West with an immortal masterpiece under his arm. He will come out of a long line of lesser men—half geniuses perhaps, each one of whom in his own way and with his own qualities, will prepare the way for our mature music.[59]

But in the minds of many writers on music in the 1930s, such a great young composer would emerge out of the American West, and emerge he did in the person of Roy Harris. Born on Lincoln's birthday in Lincoln City, Oklahoma, in 1898, Harris made his mark as a composer of music that reflected the American scene. Like many of his colleagues, he had received his training modern composition in the studio of Nadia Boulanger between 1926 and 1929. Some writers praised Harris as much for his background as for his musical training. "Leaving his original West," wrote Arthur Farwell of Harris in 1932, the young American composer went to Europe

> to steep himself in technical resources. Now he feels the urge to go back and identify himself again with the Western earth-rhythm, the Western social consciousness, to refresh and reinforce his original vision and integrate it with his newly-gained technical resources.[60]

The idea that Europe might be the source of technical instruction in composition but that it was America that would provide inspiration for her composers was consistent with Farwell's musical philosophy.

Whatever the extent of Harris's training in the music of the avant-garde, his compositions of the 1930s inspired critics to focus on his "Americanism." Aaron Copland described his colleague as having a strong musical personality, one which was often equated with the "woolly West." He wrote that Harris's music was "American in rhythm, especially in the fast parts," and that it was characterized by "a jerky, nervous quality that is particularly our own."[61] To a greater extent than Copland, Thomson, or Siegmeister, Harris simplified his style in his "American" compositions, mainly by using folk materials as he found them and not subjecting them to much melodic or rhythmic transformation. This is particularly true in the *Folk Song Symphony* (1940), in which the chorus sings several familiar American folk songs in unison.

Even after World War II, when American composers as a group expressed less interest in the problem of national identify in their music than they had during the Depression, Harris continued to write such "American" pieces as *Kentucky Spring* for orchestra (1949), and the Eighth Symphony (*San Francisco,* 1962) and Tenth (*Abraham Lincoln,* 1965) Symphony. Harris's music had become anomalous at a time when most concert music composers had abandoned any interest they may once have had in portraying their nation or its people. Commenting on the lack of interest in the national theme in American concert music, Aaron Copland noted in 1967 that "today's gods live elsewhere."[62] Copland understood this dynamic in American music well, as he had made the transition from popular "American" works such as *Billy the Kid, Rodeo,* the *Outdoor Overture, Lincoln Portrait,* and the Third Symphony with its *Fanfare for the Common Man* in the decade after 1935 to a more cerebral, sometimes even serial, style after World War II.

American composers who consciously neglected national identification in their music in favor of a continuing search for new means of expression or the re-definition of concepts of classicism or romanticism in modern terms often had to forego audience recognition and acclaim. But they contributed to the development of modern music in original ways and demonstrated through their innovation that the excitement and experimentation of the 1920s had not given way completely to a consolidation of previous technical advances.

It is perhaps most useful to see the work of Roger Sessions as representative of an international modern music, one that speaks a highly technical language and claims no national identification. His style is original, taking from its predecessors those techniques that best suit his creative objectives. During the early part of the 1920s, when both he and Aaron Copland were studying and composing in Europe, their approaches to composition were compatible, and they collaborated on a series of concerts of modern music in New York between 1928 and 1931. But they soon took different creative directions, with Sessions remaining committed to a process of musical creation that took little or no account of national identity. Of Copland's attempts to bring American national consciousness into his music, Sessions remarked,

> I don't believe in that and don't believe it can be done like that—you create music and if it's genuine and spontaneous music written by an American, why then it's American music. These things have to grow naturally. For me, nationalism is the wrong approach.[63]

Most of Sessions's writings on music were confined to sophisticated analyses of the creative process and to issues raised by the difficulty of modern music,[64] but he did occasionally offer advice to his colleagues on the subject of national identity in art. In a letter to *Modern Music* in 1940, he described the demand for a national art as defensive and indicative of unwarranted feelings of inferiority. He said that the composer who is afraid to be influenced by international cultural currents, such as serialism or the various models provided in the music of Igor Stravinsky, or who is too insistent on the purity of the "American" content in his music tends to wither

> from lack of nourishment. A consciously "national" style, in any field, inevitably becomes a picturesque mannerism, a kind of trademark, devoid of significant human content, irremediably outmoded the moment the novelty has worn off.[65]

Sessions succeeded in avoiding the national trap, as he built upon the work of Schoenberg, Bartók, and Stravinsky, composers whom he considered to have "left music decisively changed from what it was before them."[66]

Walter Piston also approached his art from a distinctly international perspective. Aaron Copland, noting Piston's use of traditional musical forms, wrote that "there is nothing especially 'American' about his work. It falls naturally into a category of modern music that has been well represented both here and abroad since the introduction of the Neoclassical ideal."[67] This "Neoclassical ideal," which found expression in works such as Prokofiev's *Classical Symphony* (1918) and Stravinsky's *Pulcinella* (1919–20), implied a rejection of the large orchestration of late Romantic music as well as a return to the forms and procedures of eighteenth-century composition. Piston was adept at casting the organizational structures of the absolute music of the past, such as sonata form, in a modern musical language. At a time when some of his contemporaries eschewed the sonata, symphony, and string quartet, Piston infused these forms with modern musical content. He can also be considered a classicist in his belief that music needs no nonmusical associations to enhance its expressive quality or give it meaning. He stressed the need for the composer to find his own style through the development of melody and formal architecture. Piston was hardly involved in the search for an American music through historical scene-painting, the use of popular melodies with familiar nonmusical associations, or the use of jazz. But his music was played, especially in Boston, where he had a long-standing association with Harvard University and the Boston Symphony Orchestra, and his neoclassical approach was an important facet of twentieth-century American concert music.

While Piston sought to bring the styles of the eighteenth century into his modern compositions, Howard Hanson achieved the reinvigoration of a music that composers of his generation had generally rejected. His musical voice was romantic, and he believed that a new romanticism would emerge that would diverge from its nineteenth-century predecessor in sound but not in its essential spirit. Hanson was the first American composer to win a Prix de Rome, and he resided in that city between 1922 and 1924 as a student of Ottorino Respighi. Hanson's music was also influenced by the symphonists Sibelius and Grieg, and his works appealed to music lovers who were not quite ready to abandon the familiar music of the nineteenth century and not at all certain that the new modernist aesthetic was anything more than a passing fancy.

Hanson worked hard throughout his life to promote the music of other American composers. He was the director of the Eastman School of Music from his return to this country to 1964. In 1925 he founded the American Composers' Orchestra Concerts, and throughout his career he gave numerous first performances of music by his colleagues as the conductor of the Eastman-Rochester Symphony Orchestra. Hanson conducted Copland's *Cortège macabre* at the first of the American Composers' Concerts on May 2, 1925. Copland later withdrew the piece from circulation, but he allowed Hanson to play it again in 1971 at the last Festival of American Music. Copland did not explain why the piece was withdrawn, but in a revealing remark on Hanson's judgment, he wrote that "if Hanson liked it, there must have been something good about it!"[68]

Hanson's works are not particularly "American" in content or inspiration—two of his six symphonies are subtitled *Nordic* (1922) and *Romantic* (1930), and his two best tone poems are *Lux Aeterna* (1923) and *Pan and the Priest* (1926). He also composed chamber works and songs. His opera, *Merry Mount* (1934), was based on the antics of Thomas Morton and his followers at Plymouth in the 1630s. It is one of the few compositions in which Hanson made any reference to American history, although the titles of his other pieces indicate that he had no aversion to program music. *Merry Mount* was first performed by the Metropolitan Opera Company.

The music of Sessions, Piston, and Hanson represented three divergent approaches to musical modernism that did not rely on nationalism. The career of Otto Luening exemplifies the eclecticism of the nonnationalist American composer. In addition, Leuning's work helps to illustrate the connections between the varied styles of composers in the 1920s and 1930s and the explosion in musical creativity that followed

World War II. In the 1950s and 1960s, the composers in the international musical community who looked to *musique concrète* or to synthesized sound for new tools with which to experiment did not include the national theme in their musical aesthetic. Organized sound once again became truly international for such composers, and the pace of creative and technological innovation rivaled that of the avant-garde years around World War I. The roots of Luening's style of the 1950s and 1960s, like those of other modernists, can be found in his work in the 1920s and 1930s.

Luening received his early musical training in Munich and Zurich, and he also studied composition with Ferruccio Busoni and Philipp Jarnach. Some of his early works, such as the *Sextet* (1918) and the *First Quartet* (1919), exhibit polytonality and nontonal writing. He progressed from these "objective chamber works" of the years immediately after World War I to writing vocal and instrumental pieces composed in a modern idiom but based on Romantic texts during the period from about 1925 to 1952. And in the 1950s and early 1960s, he was an innovator in electronic music.[69] Luening was among the first composers to produce a work calling for tape and recorded sounds in combination with live performers, the *Rhapsodic Variations,* of 1954. In the 1970s, he again turned his attention to chamber music for traditional instruments.

Luening's career represents the transition from one modernist mode in the 1920s and early 1930s to another in the 1950s and 1960s. Like Sessions, Piston, and Hanson, he emphasized individual creative development and the discovery of new sounds and techniques. If the siren, buzzer, and airplane propeller were the media with which to do this in the 1920s, the synthesizer became a major producer of "organized sound" after World War II. The articulation of a specifically national idea in music was not important to the modernist experimenter, as it was not to the modern Classicist or Neoromantic, in the context of an international modern musical language.

The search for a national music and the quest for a modern musical language that would reflect the spirit of its time and also allow for expanded creativity and innovation were separate developments in twentieth-century American music. Prior to World War I, the concerns of nationalists and modernists did not seem to intersect at all. But the generation of young modernists who studied abroad immediately after the War, specifically Copland, Thomson, and Harris, did begin to make some connections between their modern aesthetic and the national theme in American music. This process came to a full flowering after 1935, after a period of experimentation with cerebral and symphonic jazz and the most advanced avant-garde techniques in the 1920s and a foray on the part of some into left-wing politics in the early 1930s.

These composers and many others appealed to large audiences with works that were intended to inspire renewed faith in this country's past and her expectations for better times ahead. But their music did not merely quote folk tunes. They subjected familiar music to the same process of development that they used for any original theme. After World War II, the national theme receded somewhat in importance, as many of the composers who had been modernists in the 1920s and proponents of a broadly defined Americanism in the late 1930s turned again to experimentation in a modern idiom.[70]

The composers who never abandoned their focus on experimentation and a definition of music as "organized sound" did not contribute to the search for a national music, but they were important to American concert music because of their continued exploration of the possibilities of form and sound. They did not seek a wide audience, but a wider realm for their creativity, and they provided important links between the avant-garde period around World War I and that of the 1960s. They cared little for the expression of national identity in their works.

The composer Elliott Carter called the tendency to reduce musical development to a few national traits

> a game that quickly wears thin in the artistic world, as in life itself. In earlier years when American music was just beginning to take shape, such an attempt may have been useful; but now that a substantial number of works has accumulated, neither critics nor composers feel it any longer necessary to emphasize national characteristics. On the contrary, instead of insisting that American music stands apart from that of Europe, it becomes interesting to consider the many foreign influences by which it has been influenced.[71]

By the time Carter made these remarks in 1955, American concert music had clearly "arrived" through the success of this country's composers in the larger international artistic community. The American composer had gained this recognition by writing *modern* music in a variety of ways.

5

The National Government and National Music

The presence or absence of art that is intended to reflect "national character" or some aspect of the national experience raises the question of the extent to which that art is supported, not only by individual creative personalities and patrons, but also by the national government itself. Government support of music in the United States prior to the twentieth century was sporadic and limited. But from the turn of the century to the dismantling of the Federal Music Project in 1943, the national government began to take a more active role in support of the arts, although not without considerable debate over the legitimacy of spending tax dollars for culture.

The generous and far-reaching involvement of the federal government in a variety of musical activities under the auspices of Federal One represented a significant effort to bring American music to an American audience and to provide work relief for people involved in music, from composers to performers, copyists, and collectors of folk music. This chapter explores various ways in which music became a concern of government, culminating in the efforts of the WPA during the Depression. An important concern here is the extent to which government involvement in music encouraged creativity and how much of that effort was directed to the creation of music that was intentionally "American" in character.

National government support for music in the United States was often influenced by a concern that such aid produce a tangible return on the investment of public money. It is not surprising, then, that the first example of federal government support for music was the formation of the Marine Corps Band, whose function was to perform at state occasions and recruiting activities. When the Continental Congress authorized the creation of the United States Marine Corps on November 10, 1775, it also permitted the organization of a group of fifers and drummers to accompany the new fighting unit. Interestingly, the English military bands on which the American group was modeled were not officially sanctioned by Parliament but were informally organized and paid for by regimental officers. The new United States supported military music during the Revolution by providing uniforms and salaries for soldiers who performed musical duties.

The original Marine Corps did not survive the Revolution, but on July 11, 1798, President John Adams signed a bill that brought a new Marine Corps into being. This legislation allocated funds for a drum major, a fife major, and thirty-two players who performed on naval warships during the troubles with France between 1798 and 1801; offered public concerts in Philadelphia, which was then the capital; and participated in recruiting drives.[1] During the presidency of Thomas Jefferson, the band became more diversified, consisting of a drum and pairs of clarinets, bassoons, oboes, and French horns.[2] This group played at Jefferson's second inauguration and at a number of other special appearances by the president.

The Marine Corps Band was appreciated for its decorative, ceremonial, and recruiting value and not for the quality or national character of its musical performances. The original group of fifers and drummers imitated the English military tradition of accompanying the flag on parade and into battle. The second Marine Band performed duties that were less strictly military in nature, as its new function was to serve the president. The marches, arrangements of concert pieces, and dances that the band performed were very likely English in origin. The *History of the Marine Band* mentions no music in the group's early repertoire by American composers.

The nineteenth century saw little government involvement in music, as private development in the areas of publishing, instrument manufacture and music merchandising, and the organization and support of performing groups, especially symphony orchestras, mirrored economic development in all areas of American life. These economic advances occurred in the context of the belief that it was not the proper role of government to become involved in aspects of life that the private sector could develop for itself at a profit, either in monetary or cultural terms. If the residents of a city desired a symphony orchestra, they raised the capital and found players and a concert hall on their own, to the greater glory of the municipality and generally with little government involvement beyond local support.

Congress approved the establishment of the Library of Congress in 1800, although it was 1897 before the Music Division was organized. Three important municipal or private collections preceded the Music Division and contributed to musical scholarship in this country. These were located at the Boston Public Library (1859), the Lenox Foundation (1870), which became the basis for the New York Public Library's Music Division, and the Newberry Library in Chicago (1887). It was not until the period from 1902 to 1917, under the leadership of Oscar Sonneck, that the Music Division expanded its Music, Music Literature, and Teaching collections. But private donations continued to be important. In 1925 Mrs. Elizabeth Sprague Coolidge provided the endowment for a chamber music foundation which has commissioned new works and built a concert hall for their performance. In 1936 Gertrude Clarke Whitall gave the Library five Stradivari violins, five Tourte bows, and an endowment sufficient to care for them and to present concerts featuring these rare instruments. And in 1949 Serge Koussevitzky established a foundation under the auspices of the Library of Congress to commission modern works. Such donations supplement the Library's collections, as does the deposit of all copyrighted music and works about music.[3]

In the nineteenth century, there were two attempts to establish a "national" music conservatory, both of which were private efforts and only one of which received any attention from the national government. There is a brief record of a National Conservatory of Music at the Cooper Institude in New York as early as 1863. This institution was located on Madison Avenue by 1868, the year in which it presented its first concert season. The first concert program noted proudly that the school "affords its pupils facilities for acquiring a thorough classical education, so that they may aspire to the highest degree of excellence as musicians, while the price of tuition is so low as to be within the means of all."[4] From the few concert programs available, it is clear that the "classical education" mentioned in the first program was one in which music by American composers received little, if any, attention.

By September 21, 1885, the first National Conservatory had been superceded by another school of the same name, this one founded by Jeannette Myers Thurber. Mrs. Thurber's Conservatory operated in New York with a state Certificate of Incorporation, and its trustees included Andrew Carnegie, August Belmont, and Francis B. Thurber. Tuition in the early years of the school was free, although graduates who earned an income from music were required to contribute to the school for a period of five years, an arrangement that was formalized in 1899, when the state of New York permitted the Conservatory to enter into contracts for future contributions with students who were still minors. An 1892 brochure indicates that tuition charges were in effect by that time. Nevertheless, it was Mrs. Thurber's generosity that kept the Conservatory in operation. She contributed $100,000 in the first year alone and made total donations of $1 million.[5]

The National Conservatory was imbued with its founder's spirit of American cultural nationalism, as a statement in the school's first concert program makes clear: "It is believed that the National Conservatory addresses itself to all patriotic and music loving Americans as a National Enterprise of the utmost importance to the artistic future of the land."[6] The Conservatory was also committed to musical excellence, and its teachers included the Irish immigrant composer, Victor Herbert, and New York newspaper critics Henry T. Finck and James Gibbons Huneker. Finck commented that "no American conservatory ever had one half as many famous musicians on its staff as Mrs. Thurber's had."[7] The school's reputation was also enhanced by the hiring of Antonín Dvořák as director from 1891 to 1894. Mrs. Thurber personally paid the composer's $15,000 annual salary. His teaching duties were limited to small classes of advanced composition students. Dvořák lent prestige to the school because of his personal reputation and his earlier use of Indian and Afro-American melodies in concert pieces, but he did not encourage the performance of American music during his tenure at the National Conservatory.

Although the Conservatory bore the name "National," it had no government affiliation or subsidy. In 1888 Mrs. Thurber requested $200,000 in government aid from Congress. Part of her plan to make the school truly national in scope was a provision that "each Senator and Member of the House shall have the privilege of nominating one pupil who, upon passing the requisite examination as to talent, shall be taught free of charge."[8] Failing to get any financial assistance from Congress, Mrs. Thurber launched a short-lived scheme in 1890 to garner support from the thirty-three states whose residents attended the Conservatory, but this plan attracted no favorable attention at all. On March 3, 1891, Congress passed Public Law No. 159, a federal charter for the school that included the statement that "said corporation shall have the power to grant the degree of doctor of music," making the National Conservatory the first American school to have such authority. The Charter also included a provision that the Conservatory move to Washington, but this move never took place.[9]

The National Conservatory continued to function in New York until some time in the 1920s. The precise date of its closing is not clear from available sources,[10] but there is evidence that Mrs. Thurber attempted to revive her school with government assistance in the 1930s. In 1937 Congressman James W. Wadsworth from New York's thirty-ninth district introduced a bill that authorized the Director of Public Buildings and Public Parks of the National Capital to

> set apart an appropriate and suitable site in the public grounds in the District of Columbia for a building to be used for the corporate purpose of the National Conservatory of Music of America, founded in 1885 by Mrs. Jeannette Thurber, a corporation under the laws of the United States.[11]

The bill made it clear that Congress was not authorizing the construction of such a building but was only providing a site, should the now-defunct Conservatory be able to secure the funds for such an undertaking. Wadsworth's bill was referred to the Committee on Public Buildings, where it was shelved.

The economic conditions of the Depression and Congress's preoccupation with more pressing issues of national recovery help to explain why assistance to the National Conservatory was not a high priority in 1937. Two years later, in response to a request from Mrs. Thurber that he try to revive the issue of direct government aid to the school, Wadsworth wrote that

> the Congress is overwhelmed these days with problems of national and international importance and this situation bids fair to continue for a long time to come. Frankly, I think it would be wiser that I should not attempt to push through legislation for the establishment of the Conservatory. Such an attempt, I am sure, would fail, and through such failure the prospect of success some time in the future would be diminished.[12]

Mrs. Thurber died in 1946 without having realized her dream of a national conservatory that would operate with government assistance to facilitate its efforts on behalf of American music and musicians.

Even while Mrs. Thurber's Conservatory was active, the idea that American music students should be trained at home in a school supported by their government appeared in the musical press. Many writers expressed concern that private music schools had to depend exclusively on the sponsorship of wealthy and generous patrons or pay their way as strictly commercial enterprises. Frank Damrosch, a noted music educator in the early decades of the twentieth century, decried the commercialism of the private music conservatory. He noted that such a school generally was organized by an entrepreneur "whose commercial instincts are stronger than his musical conscience and who, banking on the ignorance of the average citizen in matters of art, offers what seems to be a great bargain in the acquisition of musical ability in one form or another."[13] Damrosch told his colleagues in the Music

Teachers' National Association that American music students deserved a better education than such entrepreneurs could provide. Two years later Frederick W. Root raised the issue of direct government involvement in the training of musicians before the same audience. Root compared American musical education unfavorably with that provided by government-supported conservatories in Europe. He argued that the United States government *should* become involved in the training of musicians. Inspired by the idea that, as a great nation, the United States deserved great music created and performed by artists trained at home, many writers filled the pages of *Musical America* with proposals for tangible government support for music.[14]

Oscar Sonneck, the head of the Library of Congress's Music Division, also expressed support for a government-sponsored music conservatory in the pages of *Musical America*. He wrote that competition from such a national school would only enhance the efforts of the private music schools and that such a conservatory would help to provide the country with the trained musicians it needed. His argument included an answer to critics of the plan who maintained that the venture was not specifically permitted by the Constitution. While conceding that "our Constitution has not provided for such an institution," he noted that "once Congress in its wisdom looks upon the idea of a National Conservatory with favor, there may be found in our Constitution, so others believe, a paragraph elastic enough for the purpose."[15]

The opportunity to see if the idea of a national conservatory would meet with Congressional favor came in 1917. Responding a few years earlier to what he saw as a "protest of some papers why our music students were flocking to European countries to study," a young civil engineer and amateur musician, Jacob Hayman, concluded from his own investigation in the form of letters of inquiry to American consulates in various European countries on the state of musical education that some form of national government support for the training of musicians was in order. He submitted a set of recommendations to President Wilson in 1914 for the founding of a national music conservatory. Wilson referred the report to the Department of the Interior, which, in turn, suggested that Hayman find a Congressional sponsor for his idea. In October of 1917, Representative Henry Bruckner from Hayman's New York City district introduced H.R. 6445 "to establish a national conservatory of music and art for the education of advanced pupils in all its branches, vocal and instrumental, as well as painting, drawing, and etching." The Bruckner bill was accompanied by similar legislation in the Senate introduced by Senator Duncan U. Fletcher of Florida.

The Bruckner Bill, which was subsequently modified and reintroduced by Bruckner's successor, Jerome F. Donovan, was the subject of hearings held by the Committee on Education on June 17, 1918. Interestingly, proponents of the bill were not necessarily devotees of American music. Representative Donovan, for example, anticipated that American students would have difficulty studying abroad immediately after the War. He felt that the time was ripe for the United States to step into the vacuum created by wartime destruction in order to educate our musical artists at home. He told the Committee that "we are more or less embarrassed to think that America can not provide as great artists as Europe. Personally, I believe we can and I believe the time is opportune to create this national conservatory."[16] In his testimony, Hayman defended the proposal on the grounds that a national conservatory would produce good music that would be an Americanizing influence on new immigrants. He did not specify, however, that it was *American* music that would serve this salutary function. Hayman argued that a nation like the United States,

> constantly receiving new blood from different nationalities, needs good cementing material to make one strong unified nation in peace time as well as in war time, and music as well as science and literature, cannot be destroyed by an enemy. Greece survived because of her art, while Rome, being only military and commercial, fell to pieces and [was] buried forever. Music should be part of education required by any individual.[17]

Later in his testimony, Hayman returned to the specific issue of the need for a national conservatory, calling for such an institution "to make America a singing America and the United States a center for music and art in this hemisphere."[18]

The most concrete proposals presented to the Committee in the 1918 hearings on a national conservatory and government support for music came from the National Federation of Music Clubs, represented by Mrs. David Allen Campbell. The Federation, originally organized to promote musical activity in local communities, came to support not only music in America but also American music. It sponsored competitions for music by American composers, presented concerts at which American music was performed, and included in its publications articles that promoted American musical creativity. The Federation supported the idea of a national conservatory and also called for the appointment

> of a minister of fine arts at Washington, thus placing ourselves for the first time on a governmental level with our great sister republic—France. The new minister must have a seat in the Cabinet, and the one taking first departmental rank under him must be the secretary of music.[19]

The Federation also voiced its support for the organization of community bands, the appropriation of state funds for orchestras to provide free symphony concerts, and more government support for music at all levels. Mrs. Campbell's testimony on behalf of the national conservatory idea was echoed by representatives from the American Federation of Labor and the American Federation of Musicians. But in spite of this support and the absence of any negative testimony in the Committee hearings, H.R. 6445 did not progress beyond its initial hearing in 1918.

In May of 1919, Senator Fletcher introduced a new bill that would have authorized the founding of a national conservatory and the establishment of a cabinet-level arts ministry. Despite the Senator's good intentions, his bill came under fire in the musical community because it gave considerable power to the new conservatory's director-general, who would most likely be a political appointee, and because his legislation provided government subsidy for the conservatory for only ten years.[20] In response Representative Donovan introduced legislation similar to the Fletcher bill that ensured that the conservatory's regional directors and director-general would be appointed on a nonpartisan basis and allowed for government support for the school after its first ten years of operation.[21] Neither bill received serious legislative consideration.

In 1924 the issue of a national music conservatory emerged again in the House of Representatives. H.R. 7011 was designed to create a commission to study the feasibility of establishing such a school. The debate focused less on the abstract capacity of good music to elevate American popular tastes or Americanize new immigrants and more on the proper role of government in providing musical or any other resources for its citizens. For example, Representative E. Hart Fenn, when asked if his opposition to the bill rested on the assumption that the federal government lacked the constitutional authority to establish a national conservatory, replied that his concern focused on "whether we are to adopt that principle of the National Government engaging in matters which I think are peculiarly the province of the State. . . . the problem with me is whether this is properly a national function."[22] One need only read the tenth amendment to the Constitution to see that Fenn had a valid point, from a strict constructionist perspective. Fenn went on to argue that, even though he supported music, to begin to involve the federal government in the cultural life of the nation would have ramifications for other areas of American life that had not previously been the province of Congress. He described himself as

> strenuous in regard to national agencies. If we are going to begin with music, the next thing we will have colleges and high schools under the National Government, we will have schools and mines and all these things that are desirable, but the question is whether thay are properly functions of the Federal Government.[23]

Fenn distinguished between what he considered to be legitimate federal responsibilities and "what the people ought to do for themselves, and not be running to Washington and asking every 15 minutes because something is a good thing to put our hands into the public treasury to help."[24] H.R. 7011 died in the House Committee on Education.

When the issue of federal government support for music arose again, it was under very different economic circumstances. The Depression created the need for the various relief projects that were instituted by the Works Progress Administration and its predecessors. In the debates of the 1930s, assistance to the unemployed, not art per se, was at issue. But art did emerge from these federal government projects, whose primary goal was to get trained artists off the relief rolls. The unanticipated benefit of such economic aid was that many creative artists, including modern composers, produced works that were intentionally "about" America. Historian Warren Susman commented that American artists whose work in the late 1930s expressed an "American" point of view were committed to the search for a common, yet pluralistic, national culture. Such culture would have "an increased emphasis on strengthening basic cultural institutions seriously threatened by newer cultural forms (especially associated with the machine age), and the profound experiences of depression and war."[25] The economic circumstances in which American composers found themselves encouraged in many a commitment to creating music that could be heard and could serve a larger cultural purpose in American society.

For musicians, economic troubles had begun even before the stock-market crash of 1929. With the increasing popularity of sound films after their introduction in 1927, theater managements found that the orchestras, organists, and pianists who accompanied the action on the screen were no longer a necessity. Further, mechanical or "canned" music on phonograph records was regarded by many as the enemy of the performing musician. The onset of the Depression only worsened the plight of the pit or radio orchestra player who now practiced an obsolete craft. According to the American Federation of Musicians, by 1929 five thousand performing musicians had lost their jobs to the "talkies" alone. In 1933 twelve thousand of the fifteen thousand union members in the New York City area were out of work because of the combined effects of technological change and economic distress.

Even the early private relief efforts of such groups as the Musicians Symphony Orchestra in New York City and the American Federation of Musicians throughout the country were inadequate to alleviate the plight of performers and conductors. The Musicians Symphony Orchestra employed players from New York City's relief rolls and volunteer soloists and conductors. According to *The New York Times* of May 16, 1932, the group had raised $325,000 to aid 1,227 musicians since its founding under the auspices of Walter Damrosch's Musicians Emergency Aid Organization in December of 1931. The American Federation of Musicians distributed $150,000 in direct relief funds to members between 1931 and 1933. The union also attempted to impose a system of taxes on its working members to aid those out of work, but this was soon abandoned in favor of staggered work schedules in which employed members gave up one work day of every seven to an unemployed colleague. The union also gave concerts to collect funds for its relief efforts.[26] Extensive as these efforts were, they were of only minimal assistance to the thousands of performers who were out of work. And composers who were not also performers or conductors did not benefit from these activities at all.

The federal government was not quick to respond to the specific relief and employment needs of artists because of the enormity of the problem in the population as a whole. But there was one rare instance of the use of Reconstruction Finance Corporation funds, which generally went to finance assistance to large industries, for a successful arts project. The Musicians Project 8047 in Los Angeles began in October of 1933 with RFC funds under the auspices of the County Department of Recreation, Camps, and Playgrounds. Nine hundred musicians shared three hundred jobs performing on a rotating basis in the county's various recreational facilities. By November of 1933, the Project was operating under the control of the Civil Works Administration.

In contrast to the situation at the federal level, the New York state legislature, at the request of Governor Franklin Roosevelt, set up the Temporary Emergency Relief Administration with the passage of the Wicks Act in 1931. Under the direction of Harry Hopkins, who would later supervise President Roosevelt's federal relief operations, the TERA gradually moved from an emphasis on manual labor to the creation of jobs for professionals. Hopkins established the following guidelines for a music program within the TERA:

1. The character of the plan must be a definite program of "educational, cultural, recreational, and remoralization value" for the public;
2. The program must be non-competitive;

3. The scope of the program must include a broad range of activities to include all types of musicians.

These guidelines were later incorporated into the philosophy of the Federal Music Project.[27]

The Roosevelt administration's serious efforts at alleviating some of the distress of the Depression for artists began with the formation of the Federal Emergency Relief Administration on May 13, 1933. Like the RFC, the FERA accepted only limited federal responsibility and control of the relief, leaving the administrative organization for specific programs to state and local officials. The FERA under Harry Hopkins sought to substitute work relief for the more demeaning direct form of assistance. Hopkins felt that it was important to diversify work relief programs to overcome the stigma of the "make work" label on government programs and to put the skills of unemployed people to productive use. He articulated these goals in a radio broadcast in October of 1933, arguing that "there would be no sense in giving an unemployed needy teacher a brush hook and telling him or her to go out and cut weeds along a road, when there are thousands of unemployed people who need some more schooling."[28]

The life span of the FERA was from June 1933 to August 1935. For a brief period, from December 1933 to March 1934, FERA funds were used for projects under the Civil Works Administration, which was a centralized federal project whose workers came from the relief rolls as well as the segment of the unemployed population that had not yet exhausted all of its resources. Workers were paid prevailing wages to build roads, schools, and recreational facilities, to teach school, and to participate in community cultural projects. These white-collar employment opportunities were provided by the Civil Works Service, a branch of the CWA. Despite criticism, the CWA sent opera singers to tour the Ozarks, sponsored free band, orchestra, and chamber music concerts, presented a variety of performances in hospitals, schools, libraries, and on the radio, and encouraged group singing by establishing community choruses. In some areas of the country that lacked a pre-existing musical infrastructure of performing groups and interested citizens, it is likely that government funds were not put to the most productive use because many local projects were poorly conceived and administered by inexperienced people. George Foster, who directed the WPA Music Program in its last years from 1940 to 1943, wrote that early attempts at work relief in the arts, of which the CWS projects in most of the country were typical, were characterized by

> shoddy performances by shoddy musicians who operated without careful planning. "Made work" was the rule rather than the exception and ragged groups of musical "reliefers" gave concerts in municipal lodging houses, rescue missions, county poor farms, and orphan asylums. In some states the reputation of ERA music impeded the WPA efforts to improve conditions.[29]

In contrast, CWA activities in New York had a large pool of unemployed musicians on which to draw, musical organizations already in place, and a precedent for using public or privately raised funds to aid unemployed musicians. Such projects were often a continuation of New York State's TERA or the City's Emergency Relief Board efforts. The Civil Works Administration and its projects for unemployed artists helped the country to survive the winter of 1933–34, as musicians worked in their communities in the occupations in which they were trained.

With the appropriation of $4.8 billion on May 6, 1935, and the signing of Executive Order 7034, President Roosevelt created the Works Progress Administration to "recommend and carry on small useful projects to insure maximum employment in all localities." As an operating agency within the federal government, the WPA was not permitted to compete with private industry, nor could it pay the prevailing minimum wage in its state and local projects, a demand made by American Federation of Labor. Nevertheless, it was the WPA that provided more than relief to millions of workers—it offered the dignity of a job. Federal Project no. 1 was the Arts Project, which was divided into four smaller projects in Art, Music, Writers, and Drama (later referred to as the Federal Theatre Project), each with its own director. The goal of the WPA as a whole was clearly articulated by its director. Harry Hopkins advised his staff never to forget that the objective of the program was

> taking 3,500,000 people off relief and putting them to work, and the secondary objective is to put them to work on the best possible projects we can, but don't ever forget that first objective, and don't let me hear any of you apologizing for it because it's nothing to be ashamed of.[30]

The emphasis on work relief over specific project content was reiterated in the original document that authorized the formation of Federal One, the umbrella organization of the four arts projects. The purposes of Federal One were

> (1) To provide proper employment for unemployed eligible artists, musicians, theater workers, and writers.
> (2) To provide valuable services to the community.[31]

At no point in these early statements of purpose was the type or level of sophistication of the art involved specified because the purpose of

Federal One was to provide relief and not to dictate in matters of artistic taste. Occasionally individual Music Project directors closed a local project if they felt that the level of performance was less than acceptable, but the Project did not tell composers what to write or performers what to sing or play. Occasionally, however, the bureaucratic demands of accountability in a relief organization could lead to some strange questions about the operation of a music project. Arthur Cohn, a composer and director of the music-copying project at Philadelphia's Fleischer Collection, employed as many as one hundred music copyists under the Federal Music Project. These federal workers provided scores for performing units and prepared manuscripts for permanent storage. He described a visit to the Project by a WPA administrator whose main concern was how many notes each copyist could put on paper per hour![32] In spite of the different needs of art and relief administrators, the Federal Music Project supported activities as varied as modern composition, community concerts, and the collection and preservation of traditional folk music.

While other projects in Federal One encountered their share of administrative interference or censorship, the Music project was relatively free of such encumbrances. The Project's first director, Dr. Nicolai Sokoloff, no doubt assuaged the fears of potential critics who saw him as a man of traditional musical tastes and impeccably high standards of performance. To those, especially in Congress, who might have been frightened by the political bent of some of the activities of the Writers' or Theatre Projects, the work of the Federal Music Project seemed reassuringly neutral.[33]

Sokoloff was not a proponent of the national cause in American music, and there was little evidence in his early career that he considered American music to be particularly important. He came to his administrative post from a distinguished conducting career. A native of Russia and a member of a musical family, Sokoloff came to the United States at the age of thirteen. His violin playing so impressed Horatio Parker that the young musician received a scholarship for study at the Yale University School of Music. By the age of eighteen, he was a member of the Boston Symphony Orchestra. Sokoloff studied conducting in Europe and was appointed to lead the Cleveland Orchestra in 1920, the year of that Organization's founding. He left that post ten years later to come to New York and found his own orchestra. At a time when concert music had recently undergone major upheavals with the emergence of a myriad of "modern" compositional styles, Sokoloff as a conductor remained staunchly Romantic in his musical preferences. A composition student of Charles Martin Loeffler, Sokoloff, like his teacher, had little interest in musical innovation of the type that had caused such a stir in Europe and some cities in the United States in the 1920s. He expressed little interest in specifically American music, although he was not unwilling to program pieces by American composers that conformed to his Classical/Romantic ideal. The Federal Music Project was supervised in its early years by a man whose musical preferences were rooted in the nineteenth century and reflected neither the most current trends in modern music nor an interest in compositional Americanism.

As an administrator, Sokoloff was convinced that an educated public would create a demand for "good" music by native-born and immigrant American composers. He hoped that through its performances, educational activities, music therapy research, the Index of American Composers, and collections of American folk music, the Federal Music Project would contribute to a greater appreciation of American music. By the beginning of 1936, he could point to evidence of a good start toward this goal. Ten regional directors of the Federal Music Project were at work (the system of regional directors would later be replaced by organization of the Project along state lines), there were 270 different local projects in which about thirteen thousand musicans were at work in some capacity, generally as performers. Relief workers were performing symphonic, chamber, choral, and band music, and the Project also employed copyists, tuners and repair specialists, and librarians.

In general, the Federal Music Project's early activity in the realm of folk music was limited, particularly in comparison to the Federal Art Project's Index of American Design and the state guides, ethnic studies, and collections of slave narratives of the Federal Writers' Project. One reason for this was the absence of existing groups dedicated to the collection and preservation of folk music. In addition, Dr. Sokoloff's own interests were primarily in the area of concert music. There was some Depression Era collection of folk music with federal government support, however, such as the project that composer Charles Seeger supervised for the Special Skills Division of the Resettlement Administration.

In the debate over providing relief for as many musicians as possible versus presenting professional-quality performances, Sokoloff placed himself among those who valued the high standards of musicians defined as "professionals." This philosophy caused some difficulty in the Project's relationship with local musicians unions that sought to employ as many of their members as possible, even if some of them did not meet Sokoloff's criteria for "professional" status. For example, a competent jazz musician who could not pass a sight-reading test but who performed without written music might not be considered a professional. This attitude was idealistic in terms of making the federal Music Project a showcase for national talent, but it was inconsistent with the WPA's emphasis on providing work relief for as large a portion of the unemployed population as possible.

As the director of the Federal Music Project, Sokoloff exerted considerable control over the work of state and local projects. He often intervened when he felt that a particular activity was either inappropriate or lacking in artistic merit. In January of 1936, he criticized the content of some of the Denver Music Project's programs, declaring in no uncertain terms that "such novelties as Mr. Krevas and his musical bottles, Miss Matlick in a Whistling Novelty, and skits of the John Reed Club" had no place on a federally sponsored concert.[34] Later that year, the director closed the Detroit Music Settlement Project because of the poor quality of its performances.

Even as Sokoloff was embroiled in the debate over quality control within the Federal Music Project, Congress continued to debate each year whether the projects in Federal One were performing a worthwhile function and whether it was proper for government to support the arts under the guise of work relief at all. The impermanent nature of the federal sponsorship of the Federal One projects was compounded by the fact that, even though Congress allocated WPA funds on a year-by-year basis, money for the arts projects was released only by presidential letter. These authorizations could run for the entire year of the WPA budget, but, more frequently, they lasted for periods as short as six, three, or one month. When all WPA projects were cut by 25 percent in July of 1937, Federal Music Project employment in forty-two states and the District of Columbia was reduced to about ten thousand workers from its peak of 15,842 employees in May of 1936. In addition, Congressional concern that relief projects should not become permanent fixtures in American society inspired a new clause in WPA funding legislation that required that employees who had been on the government payroll for eighteen months or longer were to be dropped from all WPA projects. The provision brought Federal Music Project employment down to 5,449 workers in September of 1939.[35] But in spite of the cuts in government support, the Federal Music Project provided work for many musicians where none had previously existed, and it offered entertainment and education for millions of Americans who could now enjoy the benefits of free or very inexpensive performances of live music as well as instruction in music.

The Federal Music Project, in spite of its name, sponsored few national musical events and left few national accomplishments. The Project was most successful at the regional, state, and local levels. In 1936 state projects superceded the earlier regional organizational pattern, each under a state director. Several urban projects, such as those in New York, Chicago, San Francisco, and Los Angeles, were large enough in terms of the scope of their activities and the number of musicians that they employed to have virtual autonomy.

Although the performance of compositions by Americans and the creation of recognizably American music were not among the Project's stated goals, the Administrative, Concert, and Educational branches of the Project's central organization did employ composers in a variety of capacities (although seldom *qua* composers) and authorized the creation of performing units that presented American music to American audiences. The Administrative branch operated from Washington and dealt with such matters as budgets, state employment quotas, technical standards for employment, job descriptions for specific positions within each local project, and general financial, procedural, and policy matters. The Washington administrators also set guidelines for projects' relationships with the American Federation of Musicians.

The Concert branch of the Project concerned itself with performances and sponsored, according to figures compiled by William F. McDonald:

28	symphony orchestras employing	1,907	musicians
90	small orchestras,	2,075	
68	bands,	2,114	
33	opera and choral units,	1,100	
55	dance bands and orchestras,	663	
15	chamber ensembles,	114	
1	soloists' unit,	10	

These figures account for 7,983 Music Project workers and are a good picture of employment for performers in the Project's Concert Division after the 1937 reduction. John Tasker Howard cited distribution figures for 15,382 musicians employed by the Project as a whole in 1936; 2,428 in teaching, copying, arranging, and administrative work; and

168	symphony orchestras employing	6,059	musicians
85	bands,	2,684	
	dance and theater orchestras,	2,085	
35	choral groups,	1,204	
	opera projects,	440	
30	chamber ensembles,	265	
	soloists giving recitals,	217[36]	

Both portraits reveal the Project's emphasis on concert music. McDonald's figures reveal that only 8.3 percent of the Concert Division's employees performed jazz or popular music, and Howard's statistical picture of the entire Project at its peak of employment shows that only 13.5 percent of the Project workers were hired to perform popular music.

The Education branch of the Project was formed in response to the particularly high level of unemployment among music teachers. For private pupils, music lessons soon became a luxury during the Depression, and school districts throughout the country found themselves unable to continue music instruction. The relief goal of the Federal Music Project was the "rehabilitation" of music teachers who were now unemployed by getting them off the relief rolls and into various projects where their skills could be utilized. The Education branch set up research and music therapy projects, programs in which instrument or voice lessons were provided by teachers on the government payroll, and community activities that encouraged participation in bands or choral groups for recreation rather than performance. Participation in these recreational classes and ensembles was widespread, with a June 1939 survey of the Project's education effort claiming that a total of 13,849,919 students had attended 1,197,936 classes in twenty-two states and the District of Columbia.

Federal Music Project teachers also worked with other educators to devise techniques and materials for integrating music into school curricula in social studies, language, and literature classes. The Project attempted to prevent music from disappearing from the lives of American school children during difficult economic times. The Education branch was most active during the tenure of Earl Vincent Moore as director of the Federal Music Project between 1939 and 1940. This was understandable, as Moore's background was in education rather than conducting or performance.

Several problems emerged in the consideration of the American composer as a potential employee of the Federal Music Project. At first the Project's administrators did not envision providing employment for composers functioning as composers at all. The Federal Theatre Project did pay composers to write musical scores. In addition to Marc Blitzstein's works, Virgil Thomson wrote music for a production of *Macbeth*, collaborated with Paul Bowles on the 1936 adaptation of *Horse Eats Hat*, and composed music for the Living Newspaper's *Injunction Granted*. Thomson's score for *Androcles and the Lion* was a Federal Theatre commission, as were stage compositions by Herbert Haufrecht, Frederick Jacobi, and Earl Robinson. Robinson contributed the *Ballad of Uncle Sam* (later revised and retitled *The Ballad for Americans*) for the revue, *Sing for Your Supper*, produced by the New York Theatre Project and also wrote for the satirical revue, *Pink Slips on Parade,* that was produced as a benefit by Project workers to protest the 1937 WPA cuts.[37] And Thomson also wrote film scores for the Resettlement Administration, another New Deal Agency. Even when Federal Music Project administrators recognized that the best way to encourage American composers was to pay them to write music, the problem of compensation was not easily solved. Was the composer to be paid by the hour, by the piece, or according to some measure of the public's response to his work? Using limited funds provided by the American Council on Education, Sokoloff attempted to commission three new works for the Project in 1935. George Antheil refused the invitation to compose a choral work, Ernst Bacon wrote *Country Roads Unpaved* for orchestra, and Hilton Rufty composed a piano trio, later expanded into the orchestral *Suite in A.* But commission funds were not often available to the Project, and the decisions as to who would be asked to contribute new works naturally were potentially vulnerable to criticism.

One proposal for compensating composers through the Federal Music Project was to offer a ten-dollar honorarium for each work accepted for performance. But no such compensation was ever actually paid. Instead the Project developed a philosophy of encouraging composers to create new works by offering both a performance and commentary from an interested audience that was certain to attend a free or very inexpensive concert of new American music. Most American composers were grateful to get a hearing for their new works, something that was often unavailable in the current economic climate. What this willingness to accept a performance as compensation also points to is the conclusion that many American composers were making a living by using their other skills as teachers, performers, or conductors. A few examples underscore this point: Ernst Bacon ran the San Francisco Music Project, Charles Seeger worked for the Resettlement Administration collecting and recording folk music, Ashley Pettis was active in the Education branch of the New York Project, and Arthur Cohn supervised music copying at the Fleischer Collection in Philadelphia. The economic conditions of the period made it more difficult than usual for an American composer to earn a living solely through his craft.

Free concerts with an enthusiastic audience eager to comment on new works were provided through the Music Project's Composers' Forum-Laboratories that were instituted in a number of cities under the direction of Ashley Pettis. Composer participants in the Forum-Laboratories sometimes presented an entire concert of their own music, and sometimes they shared a program with one or more colleagues. Performers were paid by the Project, and rehearsal time was often virtually unlimited. This made it possible to introduce new and unusual music to audiences that, in many cases, commented on the music after it was performed.

Different cities used different formats for their Forum-Laboratory performances. In Portland, Oregon, and Dallas, for example, composers submitted their manuscripts to advisory boards that provided substantive suggestions in addition to their final judgments on the merits of a particular work. If the board accepted a piece, it was then recommended to appropriate performing units within the city's Music Project. The composer benefited from a performance and from suggestions from fellow musicians. In these cities, audiences do not appear to have been involved in the critical process. In Detroit, Cincinnati, Milwaukee, and San Diego, Composers' Forum-Laboratory concerts were held only occasionally and featured the music of local composers. They offered an opportunity for audience participation in post-performance question-and-answer sessions.

Audience participation was an important feature of the best organized Forum-Laboratory in New York. The format of these concerts was generally a presentation of the works of one composer followed by questions and comments from the audience. Sometimes audience members submitted their questions on slips of paper inserted into the concert programs. This device allowed the concert moderator a measure of discretion in choosing only those questions that he felt would maintain a high level of discussion. Occasionally, however, questions of all types were fielded directly by the composers. The first New York Composers' Forum-Laboratory concert took place in October of 1935 and consisted of recorded performances of the music of Roy Harris. Soon ensembles were formed to provide live performances. The composer whose works were to be presented at a Forum concert was invited to attend rehearsals, and he could conduct the ensemble if he chose to do so. A major goal was to provide professional performances of new music as well as employment for the singers and players involved, and rehearsal schedules and unusual ensembles were provided to meet the demands of the music.

Transcripts of some of the Composers' Forum-Laboratory concerts in New York and Boston have been preserved, and the questions and answers reveal that a variety of issues, from the structure and sound of modern music to the importance or lack thereof of creating a national music, were discussed. Ashley Pettis described the questions over the life of the series in New York as progressing from "more impertinent than pertinent" to "increasingly intelligent," an indication that the audience was growing in its sophistication, if not its appreciation, with respect to new music.[38] Modern, abstract music often met with audience confusion and hostility. One listener to the music of Ruth Crawford Seeger wrote, "Please inform one bewildered auditor of the intent and purpose of your writing. Why is it so difficult to grasp?" and another inquired, "Do you really believe that your music is the future of America? If so, then I pray for deliverance."[39] The composer agreed at this concert that her compositions were difficult, and while she recognized the importance of writing music that could be easily comprehended by an audience, she also defended her own inclination to compose for those who already understood and appreciated modern music.

Sometimes composers took the criticisms of their audiences to heart. To the remark that "Your string quartet is too modern, too dissonant. I do not like it," one composer replied simply that he would try to write better music.[40] But to criticism at a concert a year later that, "Your composition for violin and piano could make out very well without the piano and might do as well without the violin," there was no possible response. But "a lady modernist" did have a good answer to the audience member who asked her, "Would you sing your baby to sleep with your 'berceuse' for piano?" She replied, "A modern baby? Yes! Why not?"[41]

Occasionally a composer at the Forum-Laboratory concerts was castigated for not being modern enough, although it was also common for such traditional American composers as Daniel Gregory Mason and Arthur Foote to receive a warm response from Forum audiences. At the end of a particularly difficult question-and-answer session, at which most of the comments implied criticism of the tonal character of his music, one composer reached the limit of his endurance: "I would like to have you people know that I believe in God. I believe in the sanctity of the home. I believe in the Constitution of the United States, and, by thunder, I believe in the C Major triad."[42]

The debate over musical modernism was not the only issue that was raised at the Composers' Forum-Laboratory concerts. Given the inclination of many modern American composers to look to their own history or contemporary circumstances for subjects and inspiration for concert music as well as a renewed interest in varieties of American folk music, it was not surprising that composers and audiences were also interested in the problem of Americanism in music. In other creative efforts of New Deal agencies and Projects, specifically in the musical productions of the Theatre Project and the film scores of the Resettlement Administration, it was easy to identify "American" music because it was part of a larger work with a regional or national theme. But to what extent could, or should, something as difficult to define as "national character" define the content of music composed for the concert hall, where there was likely to be no evocative title or non-musical program to guide the audience?

It was not unusual for American composers to discuss the issue of cultural identity in the press, and the debate over Americanism at the Forum-Laboratory concerts was an extension of the discussion that composers had been having among themselves for years.[43] When asked about her feelings on American music and whether or not she approved of nationalistic expression in contemporary compositions, Marion Bauer commented on the fact that music need not quote folk tunes to express something "American." She did not feel that music had to reflect

> the Negro, Indian, Cowboy, or our Plains . . . I do feel that music in order to be sincere must reflect an inner national something which comes from the life of the people. It must be something so inbred in us, so much a part of our unconscious thought that if it comes out of a national idiom, so much the better, but to speak of nationalism is, perhaps, not as artistic as some people believe.[44]

Bauer's own music was not rooted in indigenous folk traditions and made no references to popular music. In her compositions, as in her theoretical writings, she was committed to individualism and an exploration of the possibilities of the modern idiom.

Aaron Copland, who was beginning in the mid-1930s to use the techniques he had sharpened as a student of Nadia Boulanger to compose works that had historic, regional, or patriotic inspiration and that sometimes included American folk tunes, was less than precise in his own definition of American music. When he was asked at a Forum concert to delineate the recognizable characteristics of American music, he replied that the specific national qualities in our music "are now in the making. Therefore, it is difficult to say with any certainty exactly what they are, but one can already see a certain vigor and a certain rhythmic impulse which are recognizably American." Interestingly, at the same concert, when he was asked to describe his own musical style, he made no reference to any particularly American qualities in his music. He stressed

> a certain massive sense and a certain attempt at quite a large and grandiose effect. Not so much "effect" but a large and grandiose feeling in the music. And the third characteristic, I should say, is an attempt to write music which is logically construed.[45]

Later, specifically in *Our New Music* (1941) and *Music and Imagination* (1952), Copland would claim a greater degree of national and regional inspiration in his music of his period.

Rhythmic vitality was the characteristic to which composer William Schuman pointed as uniquely "American." He also noted that the music of this country's composers was "terse, sinewy, direct, sentimental." Schuman maintained that "American composers feel rhythm, while to modern Europeans it is more of an intellectual process." In a comment that was reflective of American political thinking about culture in 1938, Schuman commented that "creative art functions best in a society where freedom of thought is every man's right. I believe that America is the white hope of the new music."[46] And Roy Harris, a composer whose reputation as a representative American composer was being established in the late 1930s, stressed rhythmic intensity and universality of experience as the aspects of life in this country to which he responded in his music. He noted, "in the final showdown the creative artist puts into his art the time spirit in which he lives, as he reacts to it, and if my reaction is found to be broadly enough experienced by the American people, it is American music."[47]

The Composers' Forum-Laboratory concerts provided opportunities for new American music to be heard and for composers to express their views on a broad range of topics, including the nature and difficulty of modern music and the particular characteristics of American music. The comments cited here reveal the difficulty that the participants had in defining what was specifically "American" about their creative output. That they, in many cases, were trying to create a musical category, even one that proved to be so elusive in its definition, underscores the importance of cultural Americanism to their thinking.

The various units of the Federal Music Project, of which the Composers' Forum-Laboratory was an important but relatively small part, performed many types of American music; modern, traditional, symphonic, popular, and participatory (there were many sing-along concerts planned and performed by local Music Projects). If the Project did not set out to encourage the creation of new American music, a goal that *was* achieved through the Forum concerts, it did present a significant amount of American music to American audiences. In March of 1936, for example, 220 American composers were represented on Project Performances nationwide with a total of more than five hundred compositions of all types. The Project claimed an aggregate audience for these concerts of 2,300,000. The presentation of so much music to so many people represents an important accomplishment by the national government in the realm of popular and high culture as well as relief during the depths of the Depression.

A governmental penchant for the compiling of statistics is revealed in the figures above as well as in those cited earlier on the accomplishments of the Education branch of the Project. Another example of the importance of numbers to WPA administrators was the Index of American Composers, a statistical effort that did not describe the work of the Federal Music Project, it *was* the work of the Project. The Index listed music performed by all WPA units on file cards that also contained important information about American composers and particular pieces. According to its compilers, Mrs. Margaret Kerr and Mrs. Harry Hewes, the Index, when published, was to contain

1. An alphabetical list of composers with biographical information, giving date and place of birth, current place of residence . . . notes and dates of performances, performing units, conductors and soloists.
2. An alphabetical list of compositions by form giving date of composition, performance time, and previous performances (where, when, and by whom performed, not necessarily under WPA auspices); data as to whether compositions had been published or were still in manuscript form.
3. Program notes, excerpts from reviews by reputable critics.
4. Notes showing derivations of folk tunes, legends, settings, etc.[48]

Unfortunately, the Index was never published, and the process of gathering information for it ended with the withdrawal of government funding in 1940. At that time the Index consisted of more than 20,000 index cards with entries on approximately 7,300 pieces by 2,258 American composers, of whom 1,297, or 55 percent, were still active. More than a research effort, the Index reflected the music that had actually been used by various WPA units from the inception of Federal One in 1935 to 1940. Although it did not incorporate popular music or jazz into its file, the Index did include folk music, teaching pieces, and special music written for WPA occasions, including several "Roosevelt Marches," ceremonial music, and arrangements of patriotic tunes. Margaret Kerr, one of the Index's compilers and the assistant commissioner of Work Projects, saw a connection between the size of the Index and the progress of American music. "A new, organic and idiomatic music, reflecting the spirit and cadence of America," she noted, "is in the making. Musically we are coming into our own. We have found much music that is vivid, vital and refreshing."[49]

The content of the Index reveals the breadth of music performed by units of the Federal Music Project by 1940 within the confines of traditional categories of concert music and opera. And some of the titles of works that received WPA first performances indicate a programmatic interest in America. Operatic works that referred to the national experience included Morris Hutchin Ruger's *Gettysburg*, for example, along with more typical productions such as *Gay Grenadiers* by Vern Elliott, and Clarence S. Metcalf's *The Town Musicians of Bremen*. Choral works composed by Americans on regional or national themes and performed by WPA Music Project performing units included Seth Bingham's *Wilderness Stone*, a cantata based on Stephen Vincent Benét's epic, *John Brown's Body, The Bridge Builders*, a rhapsody-cantata based on an American scene, and *An Abraham Lincoln Song*, a choral work by Walter Damrosch.[50] Composers whose symphonic works appear in the Index included the well-known Frederick Shepherd Converse, Felix Borowsky, William Schuman, and Wheeler Beckett, and the less famous composers Robert S. Whitney of Louisville, Theodore Bayne of Grand Rapids, Howard C. Christian of Fort Worth, Nicholas Gualillo of Syracuse, and Willy Stahl of Los Angeles.[51] The Index reflects the extent of local support for home-town composers.

But the broad scope of the Index probably brought about its demise. Federal Music Project administrators and the staff at the Library of Congress's Music Division, where the file cards were ultimately deposited, were reluctant to support the continuation of the Index under Library sponsorship because of its all-inclusive nature, an indication to some administrators that it was a less than serious research undertaking. George Foster, the director of the Project from 1940 to 1943, commented to his predecessor, Earl Vincent Moore, that there was no limitation "on the type of compositions included, and I fear that along with symphonic poems there are five finger exercises written by our teachers for their pupils." Foster feared that the completion and publication of the Index would make the leaders of the Federal Music Project "the laughing stock of the musical profession."[52] Whether or not that is a correct assessment of how the Index would have been received, it reveals the emphasis on "professionalism" among Project administrators.

The employment of composers as creators of new musical works was not part of the Project's original plan, and the creation of such new music for the Composers' Forum-Laboratory concerts was an ancillary benefit of federal involvement in the cultural life of the nation. Indeed, if government employment implies monetary compensation, the Federal Music Project accomplished little for American composers. Fortunately, many composers were simply glad to have their works performed.

Even though the Federal Music Project did not put composers to work as composers, a strong case can be made that the Project did help the American composer in its attempts to widen the audience for concert music in this country. In several communities the Federal Music Project took over the operation of existing orchestras and improved these performing groups to the point that they continued to receive community support even after government assistance ended in 1943. Some of these orchestras were in Providence, Rhode Island; Buffalo, New York; Worcester, Massachusetts; Akron, Ohio; and Richmond, Virginia. Orchestras in Bridgeport, Connecticut; Lynn, Massachusetts; Manchester, New Hampshire; Jackson, Mississippi; Patterson, New Jersey; Toledo, Ohio; and St. Petersburg, Florida; were established after World War II in large part because of the presence of a Music Project unit in the city that inspired community interest in establishing such a performing group. In addition, orchestras in Oklahoma City and Salt Lake City had their origins in the Federal Music Project. The government presence in the area of high culture was sometimes a catalyst to further development of community musical resources.

The argument that the work of the Federal Music Project encouraged more performances of works by American composers is not as strong but is certainly worthy of consideration. Cornelius B. Canon cited figures compiled by the American Composers' Alliance to demonstrate that performances of music by native-born and immigrant American composers increased between the end of World War I and the middle of World War II. In a survey of thirteen major symphony orchestras between 1919 and 1925, only 5.3 percent of the compositions performed were written by Americans. The following figures show a marked increase:

Season	*Percent of Works by Americans*
1939–40	9.7
1940–41	15.5
1941-42	17.1
1942–43	20.8[53]

The increase is significant, but it would be difficult to attribute it to the impact of the Federal Music Project alone. First, the survey does not specify what types of pieces were included, so it is possible that a medley of patriotic tunes arranged for a popular concert on a national holiday would receive as much weight as a modern piece by Roger Sessions. Second, the importance of wartime patriotism, difficult as its impact in the concert hall is to measure, cannot be discounted, as the experience during World War I indicates. No doubt, American orchestras performed more American music (and, it is likely, less German music) between the survey years of 1939 and 1943.

Federal government support for music during the Depression had an important impact on the shape of concert music in America, if not American music. Through its concerts, educational activities, research projects, and other efforts such as radio broadcasts, the Federal Music Project brought music to Americans. Specifically, the Concert branch helped to enlarge the audience for concert music, and the creation of paying jobs for performing musicians on relief was important to the post-World War II increase in the number of American players in this country's formerly European-dominated major symphony orchestras.[54] If the Project did less for composers directly, it helped them indirectly in its efforts to make concert music an important part of American cultural life.

At the height of the Project's success, there was support for a larger role for the federal government in support of the arts, even as the WPA as a whole and Federal One in particular were subject to deep personnel cuts. As the pink slips went out to government arts workers, The *New Republic* asked:

> Why should we enjoy such a necessary luxury [as Federal One] only when we are poor, and then dismantle it at the moment when we are beginning to be able to pay for it? Why should we encourage potential creators to think that at last the nation has recognized their value and that of their work, and then suddenly cut off their hope of creation, expecting them at best to find occupation as dishwashers or machine-tenders?

The editors saw the solution to the problem of unemployed creative Americans in the separation of the issues of relief and art, supporting the idea that the federal government

> ought to make permanent the art and theatre projects which it has developed under the WPA. At the same time, it ought to abandon the idea that they are for purposes of unemployment relief. They ought to be operated to produce works of esthetic and social significance, and to sustain and encourage talent.[55]

It was also possible to see the problem of unemployed musicians as essentially a product of competition with European artists who had long dominated the realm of performance, just as European composers had provided most of the material for symphonic and operatic events in this country for generations. Citing his concern to protect the "earning opportunities" in the United States for American performers and conductors, Representative Samuel Dickstein of New York introduced a bill in January of 1937 that would have prevented foreign musicians, actors, and dancers from entering the country without prior permission from the Secretary of Labor to accept professional employment here. Under the proposal, the Secretary of Labor would have to find, in an investigation held prior to the departure of the "alien artist" from his or her home country, that the permanent admission

> of such an alien artist would not immediately displace, or prevent employment of, a citizen or lawful permanent resident alien having similar professional qualifications to those possessed by the alien seeking admission.[56]

According to Representative Dickstein, the measure also provided that "the number of those admissible aliens admitted during any calendar year shall be limited to the number of Americans with similar qualifications which the government of such foreign country has granted permission to enter such foreign country for professional engagements during the same calendar year."[57] Clearly protectionist in nature, this piece of legislation took into account not only the domination of performance in America by European artists but also the unemployment problem for American musicians.

The Committee on Immigration and Naturalization, of which Dickstein was chairman, held hearings on the bill that sparked lively commentary on both sides of the issue. Lawrence Tibbett, the famous baritone and president of the American Guild of Musical Artists, supported the bill, arguing that immigration restriction "has long been in practice against Americans in Europe." He also noted that this longstanding practice had met in the past with numerous legitimate complaints on the part of the artists involved as well as considerable emotional opposition from the American artistic community as a whole, and that the advantage of the Dickstein bill was that it would improve the employment situation for American musicians in their own country. And Tibbett claimed further that the passage of immigration restrictions on the part of the United States government against alien artists "would go a long way toward breaking down the restrictions that are in practice in Europe, and toward bringing about the condition of free international exchange that is necessary for the good health of musical art from all points of view—aesthetic, economic, and social."[58] Tibbett did not explain to the Committee how the imposition of American restrictions in response to similar European quotas would inspire a climate of free international artistic exchange.

The opposition to the Dickstein measure came from a number of artistic quarters. Testifying on behalf of the major concert management organizations in the United States, F. C. Schang, the secretary of the Concerts Association of America asserted that

> a) The competition of foreign artists with Americans in the United States is negligible; and
> b) It is not true that Americans cannot appear with profit in Europe.

To support his first contention, Schang noted that it is the public, not concert managements or governments, that determines which artists are "drawing cards" in this country and which are not. He noted that the American public seemed to prefer sporting events to recitals by famous soloists or operatic performances by European stars. Therefore, given what he regarded as the small proportion of the American entertainment budget that was spent in the realm of high culture, it was not necessary for the government to restrict the access of European artists to the small American market. The second portion of his testimony focused on the large number of American artists, including Rose Bampton, Harold Bauer, Paul Robeson, Mischa Elman, Beveridge Webster, Jascha Heifetz, and Marian Anderson, who had recently completed successful European tours. He implied not only that these artists were justly popular in Europe but that, in many cases, their talents had not been appreciated in their own country. He concluded:

> What decides whether an American artist is going to get engagements in Europe is exactly what decides whether a European artist is going to get engagements in America, i.e., Are they any good? The growth of musical appreciation in this country has been extraordinary, but it is still in its infancy. . . . The country at present is in no condition whatsoever to place any limitations on its normal growth. The shutting off of the market or the restriction on it can have only one effect: that of arresting its progress.[59]

Walter Damrosch also spoke against the bill on the grounds that foreign artists were crucial to continued American musical development, and Alfred R. Allen, manager of the Philadelphia Orchestra, also noted that American audiences needed these performers.[60] A final series of hearings on February 25 and March 3 was the scene of more conflicting testimony from the musical community, with Mrs. August Belmont, president of the Metropolitan Opera Guild, opposing the measure and asserting that foreign artists were not taking away jobs from American musicians and Dr. Nicolai Sokoloff, the director of the Federal Music Project, supporting the bill on the grounds that, of the 13,000 unemployed American musicians, many could be put to work if there were no foreign competition.[61] In the end, in spite of a number of modifications to the bill that would have made it easier for world-famous artists to perform in this country without prior Department of Labor approval, the Dickstein measure did not succeed and the previous cultural "free market" conditions in the United States prevailed. The Congress was not swayed by arguments that unemployed musicians and other artists needed and deserved government support in the form of protectionism.

But the cause of American musical art, if not that of American performing musicians and composers, emerged again as an issue in the halls of Congress. In 1938 Senator Claude Pepper's Subcommittee of the Committee on Education and Labor held hearings on "A Bill to Provide for a Permanent Bureau of Fine Arts." A total of forty-two artists, musicians, actors, authors, and other creative Americans spoke on behalf of the legislation that would have established artistic priorities for the national government. Governor Elmer A. Benson of Minnesota offered a summary to the subcommittee in which he argued that federal assistance to the arts

> through Federal relief programs has provided a kind of "people's patronage" of the arts, to replace vanishing private patronage and to support and expand already existing but limited municipal patronage in a few localities. By means of the Federal Arts Act, a permanent set-up will be provided, to continue in effect the beneficial effects of this new people's patronage of the arts, and at the same time eliminate some of the limitations that accompany a straight relief project.[62]

Roy Harris, representing a group of eighty American composers, spoke on behalf of the legislation. He stressed the potential for developing American music, and he argued that musical progress in this country was hindered by the lack of resources and economic support for composers. Without such support, he noted, fine composers did not create "a new expression, with a different set of time values and a different tempo, and all that sort of thing, which belongs to our people" because they had to concentrate on making a living by teaching, conducting, or performing.[63]

Harris and his organization supported the legislation under consideration, but they also advocated a much broader approach to the problem of supporting American music, calling for full-scale government-sponsored support of American composers. Harris testified that if this country could support

> 100 composers a year at a wage of $2,000 a year an enormous amount would be done for creative music in this country. You see, the composer's problem is not one of having a public personality, it is one of being very still and being able to first learn his language, which is about an 8 years job, just like learning surgery is an 8 years job, then he has to fashion an idiom out of that language to express his time and his people; then he has to have that appraised, and that cannot be appraised until it has been publicly performed and well performed.[64]

Harris also requested that the director of the proposed Bureau of Fine Arts be specifically interested in contemporary artists and modern creative art and music. But the senators were not prepared to adopt Harris's proposal because they regarded his plan to support one hundred composers as "a grand show of talent" rather than a relief measure. In a time of severe economic distress, it would have been difficult indeed to have offered taxpayers' money to support anything other than projects designed specifically to relieve that distress.

Just as "Dr. New Deal" gave way to "Dr. Win the War," the Federal Music Project mobilized its forces in support of the War effort. As long as WPA units performed for USO gatherings, gave concerts at defense plants, for bond drives, and at military installations, and generally offered their instruments and voices to the cause, the Project was able to continue its relief efforts, albeit on a severely limited basis. The official entry of the United States into World War II marked the end of the Federal Music Project/WPA Music Program as anything more than an accompaniment to the larger national support for the war. Congressional support was more difficult to obtain than it had been prior to Pearl Harbor, and one House member, commenting on what he saw as an extravagent expenditure of $940,106 for the New York City Music Project, asked, "Isn't it time to quit fiddling around? The money for this music project would be enough to buy three bombers."[65] For many composers, World War II brought a change from working in WPA projects to working for the government in uniform, and some, like Marc Blitzstein, even wrote music on commission for the Army.

Government support for music prior to 1935 occasionally provided music for presidents and research facilities for scholars, but it provided almost no government-supported musical education or encouragement for composers to create American music. During the Depression, the Federal Music Project made Americans more familiar with the folk music of various parts of the country, provided classes in music, free concerts, and chances to sing for fun, and it also contributed to an enriched debate over the importance of nationalism in concert music through the Composers' Forum-Laboratory concerts. If American composers did not earn much on the government payroll by writing music, they were able to perform valuable functions within the realm of music as copyists, arrangers, performers, teachers, and administrators. When they did serve in a Federal One project as composers, they communicated with an audience on subjects of current interest and were very often conscious that their music bore the label, "Made in America."

6

Lectern and Silver Screen: American Modernism and Its Audience

American composers have long struggled to practice their craft and earn a living in the process. Many have earned regular salaries as professors in colleges, universities, or conservatories, and, more recently, as film composers. Both "alternative careers" for composers place restrictions on the individual creative personality. Academe can be both liberating and stifling: for the composer-in-residence with the freedom to experiment and concentrate on his own work as a composer, the only drawbacks to academic employment might be a relatively low salary or the occasional demand for a commencement piece that is at least vaguely comprehensible to the board of trustees. But for the band director, theory teacher, or professor of music history who was originally trained as a composer, the demands of academic life can easily preclude any creative composition at all. In this respect, the academic composer whose primary activities are in the classroom or committee is in a similar position to that of his colleagues in other departments—he is constantly searching for the time and energy to do the original work for which he was trained.

In contrast, the film composer might be extremely well compensated for his efforts, and there is little question that his job description demands that he compose. But he might ultimately have little control over the shape of his creative product or the use to which it is put. If he was trained in the techniques and outlook of the modern composer, he might have to suspend his commitment to experimentation and his interest in the possibilities of "organized sound" in the interest of providing the right music for a particular scene, thereby keeping his job. Whereas academe was an important locus for the development of the "new" music in the first half of the twentieth century, Hollywood was a place to make money. Both environments welcomed the American composer and utilized his talents, albeit in different ways, and the demands of each realm on the modern composer contributed significantly to the development of modern American music and the careers of American composers.

In a nation of relatively little artistic patronage, the American composer has had to survive economically by means of his other talents. Arthur Farwell, a composer who often directed his pen to the task of commenting on the musial scene in the first two decades of the twentieth century, observed that the American composer,

> on whose eduation *as a composer* much money has been spent, finds himself in a perplexing situatoin; he discovers that his country will accept any pay readily enough for his services as a teacher, performer, etc, but that it apparently has no use for him *as a composer*, the very thing he has been educated to be.[1]

Farwell's remarks in 1912 were echoed thirty-five years later by A. Walter Kramer, a prolific but not well-known modern composer who realized early in his career that his music would probably not yield enough in royalties and performance fees to pay for its creation. He wrote that, because he had financial obligations and did not want "to live in an attic, I went into musical journalism and managed to make a living, even in the depression. My colleagues also did something else, do you realize that everybody is doing something else now but composing?"[2] And Minna Lederman, the editor of *Modern Music* and an active participant in the League of Composers when it provided commissions and first performances (but no cash awards) to composers whose works might not otherwise have been heard at all, remarked that the contemporary American composer, "that is, the composer of 'serious music,' is a Cinderella who never shakes off the garments of poverty. . . . No matter how successful or even fashionable, his music simply will not earn him a living."[3]

Lederman's points were underscored by the pitifully small financial outlay for new commissions of the major American symphony orchestras, of which the New York Philharmonic's expenditure of only .4 percent of its total budget in 1937 provided the most prominent example. And even for the most popular composers whose music reached the programs of major orchestras several times in a season, royalty payments were never sufficient to support the creator. Daniel Gregory Mason, a composer whose Romantic symphonic works were performed often in this country in the early twentieth century, was unable to support himself exclusively as a composer. His popular *Chanticleer* Overture cost $188.65 in materials and copyist fees to compose. The work earned $200 in performance fees and an additional $449.61 in publisher's royalties. Not taking Mason's labor into account, the net profit for this piece was only $460.66. But the picture looks even worse when we consider that Mason's Second Symphony, a composition that he felt was superior to the *Chanticleer* Overture, cost him $395.13 to compose and earned only $175.00, a net loss for the piece of $225.13 and a gain for his combined efforts of only $235.53.[4] It was fortunate that Mason also wrote books of music criticism and taught at Columbia University.

American composer-professors emerged as practitioners of many musical crafts at the end of the nineteenth century, and they have remained the mainstay of college and university music departments and conservatory faculties. In many cases, most notably those of John Knowles Paine at Harvard, Horatio Parker at Yale, and Edward MacDowell at Columbia, a composer respected for his creative output was called upon to organize and administer an academic department, to perform, and to teach. Composing under those circumstances became something less than the primary focus of the work life of the composer-professor, and even the teaching of composition was an activity that often had to be fitted into spare time off campus.

Before academic institutions conferred professional respect and academic credit on the study of musical composition, they had to recognize the importance of music study in general to the academic curriculum. A few varieties of musical study and practice had existed at America's earliest institutions of higher learning. Samuel Eliot Morison found evidence of ballad singing and the playing of instruments at seventeenth-century Harvard College. These activities coexisted with the obviously preferred method of musical expression, psalm singing. In general, however, any secular musical activity met with the disapproval of the leaders of the Harvard community. Leonard Hoar, president of the college in the late seventeenth century, refused his nephew's request for a violin with this remark:

> if you be not excellent at it Its worth nothing at all. And if you be excellent it will take up so much of your mind and time that you will be worth little else: And when all that excellence is attained your acquest will prove little or nothing of real profit unless you intend to take up the trade of fiddling.[5]

There being few opportunities for "fidlers" in colonial Massachusetts, the nephew, Josiah Flynt, returned to his divinity studies after Hoar's admonition. Except for an occasional reference to the theoretical principles of music in a course on mathematics and the appearance of papers on musical topics in the *theses mathematicae* of 1717 and 1723, there was little secular music at Harvard until at least the mid-eighteenth century. In 1757 *Alfred the Great,* a masque composed by the Englishman Thomas Arne, was performed at the College. Musicologist Oscar Sonneck suggested that some new tunes might have been added to the original piece by Francis Hopkinson, who was a student at the time.[6]

Until the end of the nineteenth century, college music was an informal undertaking that was often sponsored by student groups. No consideration was given to the possibility of studying music for academic credit. Students heard music in chapel, at concerts, and in fraternity houses but not in class. Devotional music and concert entertainment that included many a performance of Handel's *Messiah* and various light classical pieces, supplemented by occasional evenings of banjo playing and serenading, constituted neither a music program nor an organized approach to music appreciation for college students. Such light and popular musical entertainments were likely to be denigrated by critics who approved only of European "classical" music, which, they felt, would exert a proper moral and educational influence on its listeners.

In 1837 members of the Pierian Sodality at Harvard University advocated a more formal recognition of music in the college curriculum. In a report that described music as "something which sooner or later would hold its place in every liberal system of education," the members of this highly regarded performing group called for the establishment of a professorship in music, saying that the subject was "as worthy as any other science" of that distinction.[7] It was to be some time, however, before Harvard or any other academic institution in the United States followed the suggestion of the Pierians.

Music, and with it the American composer, moved closer to full recognition in the academic community in 1876 with the appointment of John Knowles Paine as a full professor at Harvard. Paine had begun his teaching career in Harvard Square as an unpaid instructor in 1862. His duties consisted of playing the organ and preparing the choir for participation in religious services. In fact, the 1862–63 Harvard catalogue noted under the heading "Vocal Music," that "Instruction in music, with special reference to devotional services in Chapel is open to all undergraduates. Separate classes for graduates will be formed if desired." In 1863 Paine introduced a series of lectures on musical form that were offered at no cost and with no credit to graduate students, but it was not until 1870 that enrollment was sufficient to keep these University Lectures in Music going. By the 1871–72 academic year,

Paine's success not only as a composer but also as a professor was confirmed by the appearance of a few music courses in the Harvard College catalogue.

Music survived at Harvard in spite of hostility from some members of the Harvard Corporation. According to M. A. DeWolfe Howe, it was the historian Francis Parkman who, following the example of Marcus Porcius Cato (234–148 BC), declared on more than one occasion that"musica delenda est."[8] But music was not destroyed at America's most prestigious university, and Paine's efforts as a professor and a composer facilitated the growth of music study as a serious academic discipline.

Between 1872 and 1877, Paine held a chair in Composition, Musical History, and Aeshetics at Boston University while he continued to build a music program at Harvard. The academic environment provided him with at least a minimal salary and some time to compose between his university obligations and private composition students. Paine wrote neither to please popular tastes not to convey a specifically "American" cultural message. Employment in academe offered him a forum for his pedagogical ideas as well as the opportunity to influence a number of students, including the composers Frederick S. Converse and John Alden Carpenter, and Henry T. Finck, one of New York's prominent music critics in the early decades of the twentieth century. Paine's influence spread even further with the publication in 1885 of the lecture notes for his History of Music Course and the posthumous appearance in 1907 of his text *The History of Music to the Death of Schubert*.

The first generation of American composer-professors did not settle into a regular routine of classes, committee responsibilities, and private teaching with time left over for practicing their own compositional craft. An indication of the versatility and commitment to teaching and performing as well as composing, and the difficulties inherent in making a living from music at the end of the nineteenth century, appears in one student's account of a typical work week for Horatio Parker, the composer and founder of the School of Music at Yale University:

Saturday afternoon	Choir rehearsal in New York.
Sunday	Morning and evening service.
Monday	Afternoon and evening in Philadelphia for rehearsals of Eurydice and Orpheus Clubs. Night train back to New York and New Haven.
Tuesday	Two classes at Yale. Derby, Connecticut Choral Club.

Wednesday	Lecture on History of Music and Composition classes at Yale.
Thursday	Rehearsal of New Haven Symphony.
Friday	Off again for New York.[9]

Even as Parker and his colleagues were working to establish music as a viable part of the academic curriculum, the informal, popular, and largely student-run musical organizations that preceded and then coexisted with academic music departments provided recreation and promoted college pride. College music nights and serenades by the glee club or fraternity choir were part of a school's tradition, valued as much for their sentimental contriution to school spirit as for the quality or educative values of the performance itself. One Yale alumnus recognized the popular nature of such informal music-making and commented that, at least prior to World War I, informal college music found its chief expression

> through the medium of small glee clubs and quartets, with occasional attempts at instrumental ensembles of banjo and mandolin clubs and, in the last few years, jazz orchestras. In order to make up a concert program, it was frequently necessary to draw upon almost any talent of an entertainment nature which presented itself, such as monologues, tap dances, ventriloquism and whistling solos, so that the so-called glee club concert resembled for many years a vaudeville.[10]

Just as informal musical activities at colleges served a variety of social and inspirational purposes, early academic music departments took on several forms and served differing functions. In the early years of the nation's history, Thomas Jefferson hoped to establish music as part of the course of study at the University of Virginia. He advertised for a "gentleman proficient on two instruments who could also teach musical composition." But with no suitable respondents and a chronic shortage of university funds, Jefferson failed to realize his plan to set aside one room in the school's central building solely for musical instruction. Jefferson's idea that music study was important to academic life did not take hold early at the University of Virginia, as there was no organized department of music there until 1919. Grinnell College, a liberal-arts institution in Iowa, required its students to study vocal music by 1874, although this endeavor carried with it no academic credt. The following year the college established a diploma course in music for teachers. The training of teachers in music fundamentals as well as the more formal education of future music teachers was to become a major function of the college music department. And Wellesley College women had to travel to a nearby music school for instruction until the college incorporated the local center of musical instruction as its regular department in 1898. According to the 1882 catalogue, music instruction, which consisted mainly of courses in history and appreciation, was in good company. The bulletin announced that "Music, Drawing, Painting, and Taxidermy are open to Juniors and Seniors."[11]

The period around the end of the nineteenth century was one in which music gained some acceptance in academe. But that acceptance was predicated on the assumption that the study of music could help students to achieve some other desired end. From John Sullivan Dwight's advocacy of the "right" music to cultivate proper civic and community values to the belief in some circles during World War I that the wrong music, specifically that emanating from an enemy culture, would corrupt Americans and undermine their loyalty, music was credited with powers over mind and soul. Music came to college as light entertainment, but it entered the classroom as serious art, the purpose of which transcended the understanding of the C-major triad or sonata form.

By the time Randall Thompson, a composer of choral music who was using his skills as a writer and editor, compiled a study on *College Music* for the Association of American Colleges in 1935, music as art shared space in the university curriculum with music as a theoretical discipline and as a component of the education of young children for which certified professionals required training. Music as a creative end in itself in the form of composition study received less attention. The purpose of employing composers as college professors was not primarily to train the next generation of American composers. Instead they were called upon to teach theory to performers, music history to future musicologists, and music appreciation to science majors. In these instances, the composer-professor utilized his ancillary skills to further the cause of music in the classroom. Like scholars in other fields, he produced his own creative work on his own time outside of the classroom.

That composition study for its own sake has emerged in academe after the establishment of music theory, history, and performance as legitimate parts of the music curriculum may be attributed in part to the problem of "fitting" lessons in composing music into departmental schedules. Composition is studied most effectively on a one-to-one basis with a student bringing his or her work to the teacher for evaluation. A "lesson" may consist of trying out passages at the piano, singing melodies to see how they feel as well as how they sound, discussions of technical devices or theoretical approach, or even long periods of silence. Clearly, it is much easier to organize courses of study in music theory or history than it is to arrange such informal lessons in compositions into neat lesson plans with examinations at appropriate points in the overall course of study. It is also possible to offer courses in other aspects of music to nonmajors who simply wish to learn something about music. In order to "learn something about composing," a student needs an extensive background prior to the first lesson. This factor necessarily limits enrollment in composition classes and makes the professor who spends a class hour teaching twenty-five theory students more "productive" than the one who spends the same period with a class of only two or three composition students. Composition study doesn't pay for itself, except in the less tangible way of preparing a new generation of composers. Prior to World War II, it was still often necessary for the American composer in academe to earn his keep by teaching theory or directing a performing ensemble.

The development of composition study with particular emphasis on the encouragement of young modern composers who sometimes chose to express a national identity in their music was an important aspect of Howard Hanson's long tenure at the Eastman School of Music, the conservatory of the University of Rochester that could well afford, thanks to the support of George Eastman, to devote considerable resources to the training of American composers. Opened in 1921, the Eastman School soon gained a reputation as a supportive environment for American composers under Hanson's directorship from 1924 to 1964. In explaining his personal philosophy regarding the importance of composition study to the development of music in the United States as well as the cultivation of a multifaceted American music, Hanson wrote that his own work as a professor was predicated on the assumption that

> composition is the most important thing in music and that the composer is the hub of the musical world. . . . The corollary to my first theorem is that as the composer is of prime importance in music so is the national composer important in the development of a national musical culture.[12]

In the spring of 1925, Hanson began to realize the goal of supporting the creative work of his colleagues with the first of a series of American Composers' Concerts. New pieces by Bernard Rogers, Quincy Porter, Aaron Copland, George McKay, Mark Silver, Donald Tweedy, and Adolph Weiss were selected from more than fifty works submitted to a jury of Ernest Bloch, Albert Coates, and Hanson for this May 1, 1925, program. Hanson described the impact of this new and unique form of encouragement for American composers provided by an academic institution as extremely important for modern, experimental composers whose music might not otherwise be heard. The public reaction to this annual concert series, he wrote,

> was favorable. Listeners began to discover for themselves the fascinating adventure of hearing new music. Sometimes they suffered, but they came

again and again, and in increasing numbers. It was interesting to hear the new music, to see the composer and, on occasion, to hear him talk about his own work.[13]

Hanson soon discovered that older, more established composers also wished to place their programs on the concerts at Eastman, and by 1931, the annual Festival of American Music featured a broad range of musical styles. Hanson described the series as "very eclectic," with the newest symphonic, choral, and chamber works appearing along with the music of Paine, Chadwick, Gilbert, Stillman Kelley, and MacDowell. Often, the composers appeared and discussed their problems and compositional approaches with eager audiences, thus developing what Hanson called "a sympathetic understanding of one another. They have found that the American composer is trying to do a distinctive piece of work in expressing through music the life of his own country."[14]

Hanson noted that, occasionally, the experimental nature of the Festival and some of the music that appeared on its programs drew criticism, sometimes on economic grounds:

Some felt that this "coddling" of the young composer was a waste of money. After all, was it not the tradition of good composers to starve in the garret and be "discovered" after they were dead? One ultra-conservative critic remarked that the concerts had been going on for five years and he had not observed that we had discovered any Beethovens. George Eastman's answer was characteristic of the man, "If we discover one Beethoven in fifty years I shall consider this venture an enormous success."[15]

Whether or not the series yielded any Beethovens, it presented in its first twenty years more than nine hundred new and old compositions by four hundred American composers, from the best known to the most obscure. These composers expressed the life of their country in a variety of ways, from the symphonic style of American Romanticism to the serialism or jazz explorations of the contemporary avant-garde. As a regular fixture of the spring concert season that was supported by an academic institution, the Festival of American Music provided first hearings of the music of such modern composers as Elliott Carter, Henry Cowell, Paul Creston, David Diamond, Otto Luening, Douglas Moore, Wallingford Riegger, Elie Siegmeister, William Grant Still, and Paul White.

In addition to presenting American music and bringing the nation's composers in direct contact with audiences for new music, the American Composers' Concerts of the 1920s influenced instruction at the Eastman School of Music. Hanson wrote that when he arrived at the school in 1924,

> there was one student majoring in composition. At the present time [1931] there are eighteen students majoring in composition, of which number seven are undergraduate and eleven are graduate students. These students are motivated by the same desire, not only to express themselves, but to add something to the development of American music.[16]

Hanson was quick to point out that Eastman's entire music theory department, "from the first classes in theory and dictation up to the advanced study of orchestration, has been imbued with the creative ideal." Theoretical study at Eastman was more than writing exercises to develop musical discipline, as it was part of a musical environment that encouraged young American composers to write music and also provided ample opportunities for performances of student works. The Eastman director expressed his enthusiasm for the concerts of American music and the milieu in which they flourished. "It is impossible," he wrote, "to live in the midst of such an atmosphere without feeling its stimulus and essential productivity."[17]

Increased opportunity for performance and experimentation in the realm of modern music existed in the United States after World War II. With its symphony orchestras; publishing facilities; colleges, universities, and conservatories; and critical establishment intact after the War, this country could realistically claim to be the locus of the most important musical activity in the Western world. The training of the next generation of composers, performers, conductors, and teachers provided employment for many immigrant and native-born American music professionals, many of whom had been trained as composers. As these men and women took their places in rapidly expanding music departments, the importance of the American university to the advancement of post-War society became clear. In 1963 Daniel Bell called the academic environment the "dominant force in the American cultural world today: many novelists, composers, painters, and critics find their haven in the far-flung universities."[18] And Roger Sessions noted the importance of the university environment to the creativity of the American composer:

> As regards musical composition, perhaps the most striking fact is that the important recent developments have taken place in the universities, at least as much as in the conservatories. The universities, due to their independence, seem more ready to experiment and are therefore less bound by tradition. They are more willing to adapt themselves to changing conditions. Since they are in no way bound to the exigencies of the large-scale music business, they are, as a rule, aware of the character of contemporary culture and especially of its creative aspects.[19]

After World War II, as university enrollments expanded, opportunities to study music in college also grew, and with this growth the tendency to employ composers in the academic community to write music and teach composition also emerged. A few composers were even granted "composer-in-residence" status that allowed them to teach advanced students and to spend most of their time writing music for their own purposes. Observing the growing number of composer-professors whose principal responsibility was to compose, Roger Sessions wrote in 1956, "One finds more or less distinguished names on university faculties all over the country, and of the young composers a characteristically great number are university graduates."[20]

As more students chose to study composition at the college level after World War II, American composers began to discuss their function within the university community. Many had not attained the privileged "composer-in-residence" status, and were still expected by universities to be good composers, good teachers, and active department members. In 1949 the *Composers' News Record* published the comments of several composers who were also teachers, in "Teaching as a Composer's Craft." Ernst Křenek, the experimental composer whose success with the opera *Jonny spielt auf!* in the 1920s had given him the financial independence to write music that was not popular and hardly ever performed, emigrated to the United States in 1938 and taught at Vassar College, Los Angeles City College, Hamline College, and the Chicago Musical College. Křenek commented that composers aren't needed to teach the "craft" of composition, but that "the powers of imagination and vision necessary for original creation of any consequence may be greatly strengthened by a pedagogical influence that aims at more than conveying a set of safe and sound procedures." Křenek emphasized that, all too often, young composers were indoctrinated in their elementary courses with "the narrowmindedness, bigotry and prejudice that are so difficult to correct later on." Composers, he felt, should not attempt to instruct their students in technical details—they should help to inspire students.[21] Křenek's view that exercise and discipline in the teaching of composition had only limited value in inspiring musical creativity stands in marked contrast to that of the theory teachers interviewed for Randall Thompson's 1935 study. Not only does it represent the position of a teacher who was primarily a composer, it also reflects the experimental and adventurous outlook of a modernist.

Edwin Gerschefski, a composer and dean of the Converse College of Music in South Carolina, regarded the university composer as "almost indispensible" because he possessed "knowledge of the intricacies that lie between the analytical theory, or imitative composition, and self expression."[22] He saw the college composer as a guide for the knowledgeable student rather than a tutor for the untrained would-be composer.

The contributors to "Teaching as a Composer's Craft" were all successful composers, often in the modern idiom, who had accepted positions as professors of music or composers-in-residence in order to earn a livelihood. In their comments, many conceded that teaching composition was actually only one component of their academic lives. While these men all expressed the desire for more time to compose, they also recognized the need for good teaching and the encouragement of young composers. Ernst Křenek urged composers to become active teachers, arguing that status as a composer-in-residence, for example, was a mixed blessing. While such a position could be comfortable for a while, Křenek asserted that the creative composer with composer-in-residence status could soon come to feel like "an expensive drone, without real authority to influence the educational program of the institution."[23] And Walter Piston, a distinguished professor of music at Harvard University, noted the danger that universities might regard the composer who does not teach as a man who does not earn his keep. Piston felt that the composer was more independent if he could be paid not only to compose but also to teach. In these comments there is an underlying assumption that if the university pays a composer only to compose, it will necessarily have something to say about what and when and how he may choose to meet this obligation. Even though Křenek and Piston recognized that teaching might not be an endeavor for which composers are specifically trained and that time spent in the classroom was time away from one's own projects, composers were freer to experiment and to create on their own time, just as scholars in other academic disciplines prepared works for publication in addition to their teaching commitments.

American composer-professors after World War II trained their students in the techniques of modern musical composition. In this endeavor, they were preceded by a number of European composers who emigrated to the United States, bringing with them as early as the 1920s new conceptions of how to organize musical sound. The work of European émigré composers as teachers left its mark on the post-World War II generation of American composers. Even if these young Americans did not follow precisely the trails blazed by Edgard Varèse, Béla Bartók, Arnold Schoenberg, Igor Stravinsky, Ernst Křenek, Paul Hindemith, and Darius Milhaud, they did utilize the creative ideas of their teachers as starting points for compositions that employed the serialism, Neoclassicism, and polytonality of earlier modern music and also pressed into service a new generation of sound-producing devices, including synthesizers and electronic instruments.

Edgard Varèse arrived in the United States in 1915. His experiments with rhythmic organization and his ideas on new ways to organize musical sounds and silences provided models for many American composers, even those who did not study with him. Bartók, Schoenberg, and Stravinsky were also important influences on composers in this country, even though they did not count a large number of Americans among their pupils. Bartók arrived here in 1940 and spent the last years of his life composing rather than teaching. Poor health prevented him from taking a university position or accepting many private pupils, but his music remains of special interest to students who are interested in orchestral color, rhythmic organization, and formal musical architecture. Karel Husa, a modernist composer who now teaches at Cornell University, counts Bartók among his important teachers. Stravinsky came to this country in 1939 and settled in Los Angeles, where he composed many new works, some utilizing his own version of serial technique. He also compiled many volumes of his own writings and recollections with the assistance of Robert Craft. It would be difficult to find a contemporary composer who has not learned by example from the music of Igor Stravinsky. Schoenberg, who settled in the United States in 1933, taught at the University of California at Los Angeles from 1936 to 1944 and continued to contribute to the development of modern music with his further refinements of serial technique, an approach to composition that he had introduced in the early decades of the twentieth century. As we have seen, Ernst Křenek taught at a number of American colleges after his arrival here from Germany in 1938. In 1948 he moved to Los Angeles to concentrate on composing and lecturing.

Paul Hindemith was another émigré composer who contributed to the training of young composers through his music and his lectures in addition to formal instruction. He gave the Norton Lectures at Harvard University in 1949–50. Having arrived in this country in 1940, Hindemith spent much of his time teaching at Yale and the Berkshire Summer Music Festival at Tanglewood, where his students included Lukas Foss and Leonard Bernstein, both of whom can be considered among the important American modern musical personalities of the late twentieth century. Hindemith returned to Europe in 1953 to teach in Zurich. Some of his more prominent American students were Samuel Adler, Charles Bestor, Ulysses Kay, Claudio Spies, Francis Thorne, and Yehudi Wyner. Darius Milhaud also counted a large number of American pupils. This iconoclastic and experimental composer left France in 1940 to settle permanently in the United States. He had a long teaching career from 1940 to 1971 at Mills College in Oakland, California, and he also taught at the Aspen, Colorado, Summer Music Festival. His students included Steve Reich, a composer whose "minimalist" style represents one facet of the avant-garde in the 1980s; Seymour Shifrin; Morton Subotnik, an avid experimenter in the 1960s with electronic music; and Robert Washburn.

In recent decades composition students have also been able to find many native-born modern American composers with whom to study at a major university, conservatory, or small college. Roger Sessions and Milton Babbitt attracted many students to Princeton through the 1960s, and the opportunity to experiment in the Columbia-Princeton Electronic Music Center in New York, founded by Otto Luening and Vladimir Ussachevsky of Columbia University, brought many young composers to Morningside Heights. Famous and lesser-known composers-in-residence have also contributed to the development of new music by American student composers. That these emerging American composers and their teachers attached little importance to the national character or identity of their work underscores the importance of the ideas of modern composition to their creative output. University communities have been receptive to modern music that has allowed flexibility and freedom of stylistic expression to the American composer whose music is now respected throughout the world.

But the new and experimental in music that an academic environment can tolerate and even appreciate has not always provided sufficient financial reward by itself in a culture attracted to what will "sell." It is no wonder, then, that some American composers have found a home, whether permanent or temporary, in the realm of more popular and accessible music that has enabled them to exercise their skills in orchestral writing and, at the same time, pay for more than the cost of manuscript paper and the services of a copyist. Recognition and remuneration, two elements of the creative and cultural marketing process that are not always accorded to composers in academe, have been available to some degree to composers of theater and film music. In a few cases, these composers were even able to expose a broad audience to a few seconds of modern music, albeit as an accompaniment to the action on the screen.

In 1938 Irving Kolodin called attention to the fact that "serious" American composers were being heard in the theater. From Virgil Thomson's *Four Saints in Three Acts,* Kurt Weill's score for *Johnny Johnson,* and the music for Sean O'Casey's *Within the Gates* composed by Lehman Engel to Marc Blitzstein's *The Cradle Will Rock,* Aaron Copland's *The Second Hurricane,* and the broad spectrum of Federal Theatre Project productions that included musical scores, American audiences were now able to hear music by composers who had previously been associated only with the modern, difficult, experimental idiom of the 1920s. Previously known only to a small audience of modern music connoisseurs, these composers were able to reach large theater audiences. Kolodin suggested that, in some cases at least, the greatest talent of American composers lay in the writing of music for dramatic productions, especially those in which contemporary issues and even a bit of agit-prop writing was hardly out of order in 1938. Commenting on the advantages of composing for the theater, Kolodin noted that

> it is impossible for an artist to function without an audience. Encountering a mountainous indifference to their works in the concert halls of the land—where a single performance of a concerto or a symphony is considered a triumph by the composer fortunate enough to persuade a conductor to favor his work—these composers are gone elsewhere in quest of an audience, achieving success undoubtedly beyond their most optimistic expectations. Aside from the *réclame* that accrued to him, it is probable that Marc Blitzstein earned more money from the run of "The Cradle Will Rock" than he had in all his previous career as a composer. And, despite the common belief to the contrary, even our American composers like to think they are performing a function in society which entitles them to a wage, however modest.[24]

Kolodin's remarks reflected two major concerns of the American composer of the 1930s, the desire that his music be heard and understood as a contribution to the larger cultural development of the nation and his very real need, especially during the Depression, to earn a living from his craft. He suggested that, perhaps in the theater, the American composer could indeed find a receptive home. His music for political dramatic texts could be appreciated by audiences for whom the daily newspapers provided acceptable material for dramatic production. And he could even gain a hearing for some of his more "modern" musical moments in the theater. Commenting on *The Cradle Will Rock,* Kolodin gave at least grudging recognition to Blitzstein's talent as a modernist and real appreciation for his talents as a musical dramatist:

> Recognizing the deficiencies of Blitzstein's score and the needless ugliness of some of the writing (in those moments when he recalled that he was, after all a "modern" composer), it is also possible to admire wholeheartedly the prevailing vigor of the music and, above all, the surprising gift for characterization that spoke from almost every page. Without departing from a musical idiom that was intelligible to the least sophisticated listener, Blitzstein found apt, concise musical phrases to limn such personages as Editor Daily, Mr. Mister, Junior Mister, Moll and Reverend Salvation, to make the characters apparent even without the affirmation of words. From Mozart to Strauss, the ability to characterize in music has been a distinguishing mark of every successful musical dramatist.[23]

For the American composer, the theater represented one important source of musical and monetary recognition. Like European composers earlier in the twentieth century who had found in the ballet an outlet for modernist expression, the Americans who composed for dramatic productions were fortunate, according to Kolodin, as it was in the theater that their abilities could be recognized. "Compared with the prejudices, traditions, and stagnation of the musical world," he wrote, "the theatre, with all its 'commercialism' and tawdriness, is in an enviable state of health."[26]

The recognition and remuneration, so much desired by American composers, along with the commercialism and tawdriness that the critics were quick to expose, were present to an even greater degree in Hollywood, where a composer at the peak of his career could earn a large income in a commercial medium in which his art was secondary to box office receipts. Film score composers are generally required to write evocative music, whether as background to a dramatic scene or to set a mood before the action begins. Occasionally, the modern film composer is called upon to evoke an "American" scene, although most of the time national considerations do not figure in his creative process as he contributes to a multi-faceted art form by writing music on demand. More importantly, the film score composer can occasionally use his experience and training in modern music to give a film just the mood or effect it requires.

Although his position was a conservative one indeed, the famous conductor Sir Thomas Beecham raised an interesting issue in 1945, when he asked, "Why should we have music in the movies?" Arguing that music for films was unnecessary, Beecham asserted that no great composer

> ever wrote for films. It's only the supreme vanity of film producers that makes them think they can turn fourth rate composers into first rate composers in the movies. The movies are sheer bedlam in a madhouse. God! Now that the silent films are through you can't go anywhere and hear nothing.[27]

Bedlam in a madhouse or serious art, by the 1940s film music was well established, with large studio music departments to provide support for the efforts of the rest of the film industry. Further, Hollywood, the locus of commercial film production since the 1920s, could command the efforts of composers with diverging compositional perspectives, from the romantic to the experimental. Feature and documentary film scores were composed by anonymous lesser composers at the big studios and by some of the United States's best-known and most respected composers for the concert hall.

In his review of Virgil Thomson's score for *Louisiana Story*, Frederick W. Sternfeld defended the contemporary composer as a contributor of film scores, especially for documentary films, arguing that this medium allows the composer's art to reach a broader audience than does the typical concert of contemporary music. In the musical score for director Robert Flaherty's film, Thomson artfully combined Cajun folk songs and hints of twelve-tone compositional technique. Sternfeld argued that the documentary genre was superior to the typical Hollywood product because

> the makers of documentaries have faith in Twentieth Century composers. Flaherty, Lorentz, Rodakiewicz, Van Dyke, all realize that a contemporary film requires a contemporary score. Instead of commissioning paste-and-scissors jobs of Chopin, Tchaikowsky, et al., they have offered opportunities to our foremost composers. They have done so neither with the pretense of altruism nor with despotic arrogance, but with a singleness of purpose that demands the contemporary musician because his idiom fits the job. The time-honored general formula that allows full rein to a master craftsman, once chosen, is the one largely responsible for the superior musical scores of the documentaries.[28]

A documentary film score composer, according to Sternfeld, has the added advantage of being free of the type of director "who seeks to appeal to the lowest common denominator." He can compose his own score, using the techniques and sounds of modern music, when they suit the demands of the story.

The documentary film could even employ a musical idiom that was little understood by most concert audiences. In the fall of 1948, the University of California at Los Angeles sponsored a congress on the theme of "Music in Contemporary Life" at which a session of music for films featured an experimental effort by Hanns Eisler and Paul Adorno entitled *White Floats.* The film was financed by a grant from the Rockefeller Foundation and was produced "with the deliberate purpose of finding out whether atonal music composed on Schoenbergian principles can be used in motion pictures." The score was difficult to comprehend by itself, but it apparently provided the appropriate backdrop to the action on the screen. Alfred Frankenstein reviewed the score and described the interaction of the music and the film's action:

> White floats are icebergs. The picture represented glaciers breaking off into the sea, vast ice fields, snow fields, and frigid, towering black mountains. And the busy, scurrying, scuffling and scrabbling of the music was incredibly perfect for its purpose. Furthermore, as Adorno pointed out, there was an intimate synchronization between music and film possible in no other idiom, thus each aimless creeping wisp of blown snow had its own line of score.[29]

This type of experimental film worked well with the music of the twelve-tone idiom that, to most listeners, was difficult, if not inaccessible. It is likely that the visual and musical elements enhanced each other, as viewers could associate the action on the screen with the sound track.

But the majority of feature films, especially in the decades prior to World War II, did not offer experimentation but entertainment to audiences that would have had little comprehension of modern music if they had heard it in the concert hall. Hollywood was not a primary force for the encouragement of modern music, but a number of highly trained composers created for the silver screen. Sometimes, they were called upon to write music less than worthy of their talents and training, and the existence of studio music departments that turned out what can only be called "hack work" certainly demeaned the talents of many fine composers. But the medium could also produce some extraordinary writing, occasionally even in the modern idiom.

Composing for commercial films is no easy task. The pressures on the creative imagination are considerable, and a composer must be flexible to meet the demands of studio schedules. Further, there is a difference between writing for an orchestra, soloist, or chamber group where the attention is focused on the music and its interpretation and creating music whose purpose is to *underscore* the action on the screen. Film composer Max Steiner, whose principal credits included *Symphony of Six Million* and *Bird of Paradise* (1932), *King Kong* (1933), *The Charge of the Light Brigade* (1936), and *Gone with the Wind* (1939), wrote in his autobiography that there is "an old bromide in this business to the effect that a good film score is one you don't hear. . . . The danger is that music can be so bad, or so good, that it distracts and takes away from the action."[30] A film composer also has to contend with a lack of understanding or appreciation on the part of those who pay his salary. Bronislau Kaper, a European-born and -trained composer who wrote the scores for *I Take This Woman* (1940) and *The Chocolate Soldier* (1941), noted that the first thing a Hollywood composer has to realize is that he is not his own boss. The second thing is that the people for whom he works

> know a lot less about music than he does. Sometimes they know so little it can almost reduce a composer to tears. My boss at MGM for many years was the great Louis B. Mayer, and I use the word "great" with respect because he ran the best film factory in the world, and he ran it beautifully. But his musical taste was limited. Mr. Mayer loved the works of the operetta composers, and that was the kind of music he wanted in his pictures.[31]

A composer under contract to MGM studios was clearly not encouraged to experiment musically. In fact, it was likely that the MGM music library under Mayer's reign was as busy finding examples of his beloved operetta music and buying up the copyrights or paying user fees as the major composers like Kaper were composing original music.

Hanns Eisler, a modernist composer who turned to the music of the class struggle and to social and political criticism of art, also used the factory analogy in describing the workings of the major studio music departments. Writing music for a particular mood or scene on the screen was the job of the journeyman composers who did not populate Hollywood's top ranks. They composed exclusively on assignment, often on the basis of a director's conception in a system that allowed for little real creativity or experimentation with the modern music that producers seldom considered "good box office." Eisler noted that every major studio

> has five or six musical specialists who are permanenty employed and who have to keep punctually to their office hours. Number one is a specialist in military music, number two in sentimental love songs, number three is a better trained composer for symphonic music, for overtures and intermezzi, number four is a specialist in Viennese operetta, five is for jazz. So if music is required for a film, then every composer has to work on a certain section, according to his specialty. The composers have no idea what is happening in the rest of the film or what his fellow musician is composing, everyone merely does his own particular bit.[32]

Fortunately, for many top Hollywood composers, the rationalization process had not proceeded so far in film music production as to deny their creative impulses, as Eisler implies was the case for the members of the lower ranks of studio composers.

When asked if they changed their compositional styles to accommodate the special needs of the film medium, a number of movie composers, most of whom also wrote for the stage and the concert hall, commented that, while their styles did not change, the collective nature of a film effort necessitated certain modifications in approach. Marc Blitzstein agreed with Steiner that "in films music must never occupy the whole concentration of the audience." Paul Bowles, who had collaborated with Virgil Thomson on various stage works, added to his list of compositional "tools" for film writing a stop watch, metronome, and a knowledge of mathematics, all of which wuld become essential to the modernist composer after World War II who utilized synthesized sound and composed in terms of "sound events" of a precise duration rather than traditional measures or musical sections. Aaron Copland strssed the need in music for the movies for simple melodies with basic orchestration, and William Grant Still noted that

> a change in my usual methods of composition was usually necessitated by the two time elements—the matter of having to catch a cue at a certain

time affects the style of the writing; and the excessive speed at which the film compser must work hampers him and makes good work rare.[33]

Commenting on Aaron Copland's score for *The Red Pony,* Lawrence Morton was less convinced that the pressures of writing for Hollywood rendered composer's work less good. He compared music for the concert hall and the movie theater, arguing that

> there are differences in motivation and, consequently in architecture, in expressiveness and in general "philosophical" content. All functional music is necessarily filtered through the medium of another art form—choreography, a libretto, a poem, a film. But it is not, by that token, any less authentic a revelation of a composer's personality and vision.[34]

Copland the modern composer utilized harsh dissonances in selected places in *The Red Pony* score to underscore tension and drama of the story. For the climax of the film, Tom Tiflin's fight with the buzzards over the body of the pony,

> the violence and terror of the materials come from their dissonance, the tortured rhythms, harsh orchestration, high tessitura and abrupt changes of register. . . . One of the musicians who played it, an "old timer" in the profession, told this writer, "It's the most terrific fight music I ever played, and it's *music* too."[35]

For all the effectiveness of his film writing, Copland, in Morton's estimation, never abandoned his commitment to composing modern and accessible music. *The Red Pony* score had its premiere as a concert suite in Houston before an appreciative audience. Morton complimented both the concert suite and the film score by noting that, while the suite needs no special program notes in the concert hall, "there is not a note in the score that doesn't serve the screen. One *can* serve two masters."[36]

Whether he was a newcomer or a veteran in Hollywood, the film composer had to adjust his style to the special nature of film music, writing either music that is precisely keyed to the action on the screen or background or transitional music that is clearly subordinate to the action. Even Roy Webb, a composer best known for his work in comedy films, commented that the composer for the cinema "has to be careful not to be carried away by the musical qualities of his composition."[37] But Hanns Eisler took a more radical position, advocating a film music genre that did not necessarily provide an aural guide to the action but one which serves a more subtle function, not merely "to illustrate the film, but to explain it and comment on it. That may sound abstract, but my experience has shown that large sections of film can be made much more effective by this method."[38] Ironically, the view of film music offered by this modernist composer also described the approach of many film composers trained in nineteenth-century symphonic writing who offered music for the screen that interpreted the broad message of a film rather than each specific scene.

Erich Wolfgang Korngold was a symphonic and operatic composer whose independence as a highly paid studio composer permitted him to work from a vision of the whole film, almost in the manner of a director. In addition to reading the script, he viewed the film, reel by reel, many times, while composing appropriate music without regard to the timing of specific scenes. It was not until the final print was ready for dubbing that Korngold began the process of "fitting" music of the correct length to each scene. His creative process was one in which the music had a life of its own first before it became part of the larger medium of the feature film.

Korngold's stye of film composition was consistent with his Romantic orchestral style that had made him the *wunderkind* of Vienna in the first decades of the twentieth century. His music for the concert hall and opera house was celebrated, as were his film scores for *Robin Hood* and *Anthony Adverse*, both of which received Academy Awards, and *Of Human Bondage*, *The Sea Hawk*, and *Elizabeth and Essex*. Korngold recognized that his fine shadings of orchestral color, counterpoint, and dynamics might well be lost in the final editing process, and he is said to have remarked that a film composer's immortality lasts from the sound stage to the dubbing studio.

After World War II, Korngold returned to Vienna, where he found that musical times had changed and that his style was no longer greeted with enthusiasm. He never adopted the musical ideas or techniques of the avant-garde, and he saw himself as outside the mainstream of current musical events. He lived the last years of his life in North Hollywood, but he did not return to writing film scores, preferring instead to compose such concert pieces as the Symphony in F-sharp (1951–52). This work, an apparent throwback to earlier musical times, was not recorded until 1975, the year that the New York City Opera performed his most famous opera, *Die tote Stadt*, which had received its premiere in Vienna in 1920. Ironically, the City Opera production was sucessful in part because of the superimposition of film segments on to the stage action, a technique that is still somewhat experimental in the opera house. The effect is dramatic, as it uses footage of the city of Bruges to complement the lush romantic evocation of this "Dead City."

Hollywood benefited not only from the services of composers under contract to major studios but also from the contributions of composers who came to the film industry for special projects. Aaron Copland's music was in demand for a number of special films that diverged from the Hollywood norm. Lewis Milestone hired him to compose the score for the film version of *Of Mice and Men* in 1940. Copland used a small orchestra, and he integrated some themes into the score that sounded like folk melodies, although they were newly composed and orchestrated in his modern style of the 1935–45 period. He used a similar light touch to evoke American images in the film version of Thornton Wilder's *Our Town* (1940). The music for *The Heiress* won Copland an Academy Award in 1949. It includes dance tunes to create the atmosphere of New York in the 1850s and attaches a leitmotif to each of the three main characters, a device Copland did not often use.

Writing in the *Musical Quarterly,* critic Frederick W. Sternfeld commented that, as a film composer, Copland possessed "uncanny judgment" with respect to tempo, silence, repetition, spacing, and contrast, all important elements in the synthesis of film and music as well as in modern composition. His writing revealed an "awareness of the public's response to dramatic entertainment without, however, any condescension to that public." A composer with a keen sense of dramatic effect and the flexibility to try studio techniques such as overdubbing that may enhance a film score but do not correspond to the sound an orchestra actually makes in a live performance, Copland communicated to a mass audience without ever losing his ties to 'serious' music for the sake of popularity.[39]

Copland was not alone in his maintenance of ties to the world of modern concert music even as he composed for popular entertainment films. Miklos Rosza, a film composer of considerable success, continued to compose concert music. He conducted the premiere of his own *Concert for String Orchestra* with the Los Angeles Philharmonic in 1944. According to the announcement of this performance in *Film Music Notes,*

> Rosza is chiefly concerned with making music for music's sake. He believes the trend of American composers is pointing in this direction too. The rage is over, he says, for the impressionistic, highly programmatic music of some years back. His compositions are thematic, rhythmic, virile, and sane.[40]

The balance between popularity and writing music that is taken seriously is a preoccupation of many contemporary American film composers. Jerry Goldsmith, who composed the scores for *Seven Days in May* (1964), *A Patch of Blue* (1965), *The Planet of the Apes* (1968), *Patton,* (1970), and *The Omen* (1976), commented on his approach to writing film music and the common perception that film score composers are less skilled and serious than their counterparts who write for smaller audiences:

> I compose music for films, which makes me a film composer. Which is fine except that the tag "film composer" in this country has come to have a kind of second-class ring to it. This is ridiculous. People have never tagged Paul Hindemith or Arnold Schoenberg as "professor composers" with the implication that it was a lesser rank. Some men who write music earn a living by teaching. Still others, like me, make our way by working in films. We are all composers. I tackle every assignment just as seriously as if I were aiming it at the concert hall.[41]

Goldsmith noted that film music has become more sophisticated in recent years, as have film audiences. He said that the public ear is now becoming

> attuned to everything. It's possible to use almost any style in scoring and not shock audiences. A generation ago, "Le Sacre du Printemps" was considered way-out. Now it isn't. Avant-garde music is readily available and so is electronic music, and all these forms can be used in scoring.[42]

To create image an effect, the modern film composer himself is now attuned to trends in modern music. Through the vehicle of commercial films, he can experiment and reach a broad American audience. It is the modern movement, with its experiments in tonal organization and, more recently, the generation of electronic sound, that has provided new and important tools for the film composer. As Goldsmith noted, today's film composer is more fortunate than his predecessor because "he can attempt more than he could two decades ago."[43] It is possible that the prediction of one analyst of film music in the 1940s is being realized. Alice Evans Field suggested that one day, historians might

> look back on the twentieth century as the beginning of a notable departure in music, something truly American, inspired by its union with the motion picture. Certainly the new medium is attracting the attention of the great American composers today.[44]

In the twentieth century, composer-professors and writers of film scores have found solutions to the problem of how to continue their creatve activities and still earn a living. The academic composer has been more likely to explore the technical and technological frontiers of modern music than to write music expressive of a past American frontier. And the film score composer did not always choose the theme of his assignments. He wrote regional or "American" music when the film called for it. For both groups of composers, Americanism in music ceased to be a vital force in their creative efforts. Instead, members of both groups contributed significantly to the exposure of the public to the sounds of modern music. The academic composer might write for a limited audience, but he was almost certain to receive support and commentary from concert-goers who were eager to see what the academic avant-garde was up to. And film score composers could occasionally take advantage of the developments in music in the previous century to provide large audiences with musical materials that were so effectively woven into the texture of the film that most movie-goers would not even realize that they were listening to modern music.

Epilogue

In 1922, composer and critic Deems Taylor commented on the nature and condition of music in the United States for a survey of American civilization. He found little of interest or merit in the writing of composers here, arguing that, if the American composer is not heard more often in the concert halls of the country, "it is because he is not good enough. There is, in the music of even second-rate Continental composers, a surety of touch, a quality of evident confidence in their material and ease in its handling that is rarely present in the work of Americans."[1] Taylor suggested that American composers had little to say because the American nation had little to offer in the realm of culture for its citizens. He noted that

> Wagner wrote "Die Meistersinger" in a deliberate attempt to express the German artistic creed; Verdi wrote consciously as an Italian; Glinka founded an entire school of composers whose sole aim was to express Russia. Such a task is beyond the American. The others were spokesmen for a race: he has no race to speak for, and the moment he pretends that he has, and tries to speak for it, he becomes conscious and futile. To speak of American music, in any ethnic sense, is naive; you might as well speak of Baptist music.[2]

Taylor's prediction in the early 1920s that American composers would not be able to create serious music because the culture of the nation was a heterogeneous one soon proved to be irrelevant, as the debate over the nature of American music changed with the immersion of more and more American composers in the international language of musical modernism.

Nationalism alone as a motivating force for American composers produced neither a unique national music nor many compositions of lasting value. The "nationalists-by-quotation" of the early decades of the twentieth century tended to be nostalgic, anti-modernists who looked to local and regional folk music and the tonal language of Romanticism for the solution of the problem of creating a national music. They tried to "fit" folk melodies into compositions that were Romantic in sound and style, while ignoring the fact that the validity of nineteenth-century Romanticism had been challenged internationally as composers found it increasingly difficult to express their ideas in the Romantic structural context.

American composers were among those who said that the Romanticism of the nineteenth century had played itself out and that new means of musical expression were needed. The emergence of new techniques and approaches to composition, all under the rubric of modernism, provided new opportunities for the American composer. Always the younger, less-experienced sibling in the relationship with his ninteenth-century European musical family, the American composer had found himself perceived as inferior. But in the twentieth-century quest for a modern musical language, the American composer suffered no such disadvantage, and the creative efforts of Antheil, Sessions, Copland, and many others placed American composers in the forefront of the modern movement in the 1920s.

At home the hostility of many nationalist composers to the emerging modern idiom often sparked a discussion of nationalism and modernism in antithetical terms. John Powell, a nationalist who incorporated Anglo-American folk tunes into many of his works, called American modernists "Chaotics," whose compositions were "nothing more or less than cheap replicas of the recent European Bolshevists."[3] Powell denied the validity of musical modernism because it was a response to rather than a natural outgrowth of the Romantic music that had preceded it. He declared that no language "can be artificially manufactured; and if such a thing were possible that language would still be of no value save as a vehicle for a mathematical treatise. This is even more true of music, the language of mood and emotion."[4]

Modernist composers often asserted that the ideas and constraints of Romanticism were no longer for the expression of nationalist or any other musical ideas. Roger Sessions argued in 1941 that musical rules and standards

> retain their validity only as long as they are in the process of development. After this process has stopped, they wither and die, and can be re-created only by a conscious and essentially artificial effort, since they are suited only to the content which has grown with them.[5]

Individuality of expression was not in conflict with the desire to create modern music that celebrated America and was accessible to a large audience. Between 1935 and 1945, the label "modern composer" applied to non-nationalists like Sessions as well as to such composers as Copland, Thomson, and Harris, whose concerns for a time were with the national in music as well as with the modern. It was modern music that liberated the American composer from the constraints of nationalism by quotation and helped him to express the variety of the American experience rather than continue the fruitless search for cultural unity. He could use what he had learned in Europe and what he had discovered on his own to write modern American music that was accepted with interest in Europe and by his colleagues at home. The modern idiom was an international one that American composers had helped to forge.

During the Depression and World War II, American composers and writers on music discussed the importance of nationalism and accessibility in concert music. One of Elliott Carter's first major orchestral works was a ballet score on an American theme, *Pocahontas* (1938). Carter felt at the time that he had to compose in a style "that would be easier to perform and would appeal more directly to what I imagined to be the listening abilities of the average concert-goer, a point of view a number of American composers adopted at the time."[6] Today, these issues do not occupy a central place in musical debate, as the modern idiom offers a variety of ways to express one's ideas, irrespective of their "national" content or presumed acceptance by audiences. As American composers have gained confidence in and acceptance of their work, Virgil Thomson's comment that American music is simply that which is written by American composers is now true.

American composers could rightly feel that the post-World War II world would bring new opportunities for their music to be heard by American and international audiences. The earlier doubts about the validity of American cultual achievement that had long permeated the writings of musical commentators gave way to confident assertions of pride in American music. In 1952 the advisory board of the National Association for American Composers and Conductors surveyed its twenty-nine members on the problems of the American composer. The results indicated a consensus that American audiences could now hear more music by their own composers than in past decades, although there was some concern that a "star system" focused most of the attention, as well as rare fellowship, commission, and performance opportunities, on a small group of Americans who were already well established. On the issue of whether American composers should try to distinguish their music from that composed in Europe, one unnamed board member commented that the best music written in the world

> is being written in the United States, some of it by native composers. In so far as "independence"is concerned, I do not consider it detrimental to our music to depend in some measure upon the music of Western Europe; to speak of an international language rather than a chauvinistic or even regional language. I do not condone imitation, but I consider it not only unwise but impossible to reject all "influence."[7]

The international musical language was and remains a modern idiom that encompases a broad range of styles and techniques. It is the music that European and American composers have been experimenting with, as serialists, Futurists, Dadaists, Neoclassicists, Neoromantics, minimalists, and eclectics since the years immediately following World War I. And for all its claim to international recognition, when composed by Americans, it is *American* music.

Notes

Introduction

1. David Ewen, *Music Comes to America* (New York: Thomas Y. Crowell, 1942), 154–55.

2. With the remark that "the dissonances of to-day are the consonances of tomorrow," Nadia Boulanger noted that the techniques of the new music of the 1920s included the formation of chords with intervals other than the third, the use of unfamiliar scales, such as Church modes and pentatonic scales, and a focus on abstract form rather than literary or pictorial inspiration. See "Modern French Music," a lecture delivered at The Rice Institute on January 27, 1925 and published in *The Rice Institute Pamphlet* XIII/2 (April 1926), 116–17, 147.

3. Composer Edgar Varèse called in the 1920s for the redefinition of music as "organized sound," charting a course away from personal expressiveness of presumably universal emotions. Nadia Boulanger noted a change in music in this decade away from the autobiographical and individual focus of the nineteenth century toward a more classic art "whose movement and life are in the music, not in any qualities of 'expression'." See "Stravinsky," *The Rice Institute Pamphlet* XIII/2 (April 1926), 193.

Chapter 1. Perceptions of Concert Music in the United States

1. W. H. Hadow, *Collected Essays* (London: Oxford University Press, 1928), 3.

2. G. B. S. in *The World* (London, June 13, 1894), reprinted in Eric Bentley, ed., *Shaw on Music* (Garden City, N.Y.: Doubleday and Co., Inc., 1956), 59.

3. *An Addition to the Present Melancholy Circumstances of the Province Considered* (Boston: S. Kneeland, 1719), 7.

4. One important divergence from this pattern occurred in the Moravian settlements in Pennsylvania. The Moravians brought a German cultural heritage to their new environment, where they performed cultivated music in their own churches and communities and contributed a long line of composers to American music, from Jeremias Dencke (1725–95) to Edward W. Leinbach (1823–1901). Generally, however, Moravian music remained outside the mainstream of American cultural development and had little influence on questions of the character and necessity of creating a representative American music.

5. Thomas J. Wertenbaker, *The Golden Age of Colonial Culture* (Ithaca, N.Y.: Great Seal Books, 1949), 38.

6. See the Preface to the *Bay Psalm Book* in William P. Trent and Benjamin H. Wells, eds., *Colonial Prose and Poetry—The Transplanting of Culture, 1607–1650* (New York: Thomas Y. Crowell, 1901), 121.

7. Mark Van Doren, ed., *Samuel Sewall's Diary* (New York: Macy-Masius Publishers, 1927), 104.

8. But Mather did not support all musical innovations, even when they had the potential to improve singing during worship. In Book V of the *Magnalia Christi Americana* (London, T. Parkhurst, 1702, 1702), he addressed the question, "Whether Instrumental Musick may lawfully be introduced into the Worship of God, in the Churches of the New Testament?" He concluded that instruments had no place in the meetinghouse, and congregational churches did not permit the playing of organs until the mid-eighteenth century.

9. Cotton Mather, "The Accomplished Singer" (Boston: B. Green for Samuel Gerrish, 1721), 1.

10. Ibid.

11. Richard L. Bushman, *From Puritan to Yankee* (New York: W. W. Norton and Company, 1967), 21.

12. William Billings, *The New-England Psalm Singer, or American Chorister* (Boston: Edes & Gill, Prtrs., 1770), 20.

13. Billings, *The New-England Psalm Singer*, 2.

14. See Nahum Mitchell, "William Billings," *The Musical Reporter*, No. 7 (Boston, 1841), 350–51.

15. William Billings, *The Singing Master's Assistant* (Boston: Draper & Fulsom, 1778), 102.

16. Ibid.

17. The printer John M'Culloh enhanced Billings's reputation by printing some of his anthems and by including "Jargon" in the *Selection of Sacred Harmony* (1790). Billings's music also sometimes appeared in collections with works by European composers. See David P. McKay and Richard Crawford, *William Billings of Boston* (Princeton: Princeton University Press, 1975), 153–54.

18. *The Columbian Magazine or Musical Miscellany* (Philadelphia, April 1778), 212–13.

19. Hopkinson has often been called America's first published composer, based on the 1759 appearance of his song, *My Days Have Been So Wondrous Free*. But musicologist Irving Lowens found evidence that, although it is not conclusive, points to the composition of an original psalm setting, *100 Psalm Tune New*, by John Tufts in his *A Very Plain and Easy Introduction to the Art of Singing Psalm Tunes* (1721). Lowens suggests that Tufts "may well have a valid claim to be considered the first American composer" in "The First American Music Textbook," *Music and Musicians in Early America* (New York: W. W. Norton and Company, 1964), 53–54.

20. Paul Leicester Ford, ed., *The Writings of Thomas Jefferson* (New York: G. B. Putnam's Sons, 1892–98), Vol. 2, p. 159 (letter dated June 8, 1778).

21. In an undated letter to Peter Franklin, "On the Defects of Modern Music," Franklin noted several "defects and improprieties" in an aria from Handel's "Judas Maccabeus." See Jared Sparks, ed., *The Works of Benjamin Franklin* (Boston: Charles Tappan, 1848), Vol. 6, pp. 269–73. Franklin expressed similar sentiments on the value of simple, unadorned music in a letter to Lord Kames, written from London on June 12, 1765. See Leonard Labaree, ed., *The Papers of Benjamin Franklin* (New Haven: Yale University Press, 1968), Vol. 12, pp. 158–65.

22. Letter to Mary Stevenson, March 25, 1763, in Labaree, ed., *The Papers of Benjamin Franklin*, Vol. 10, p. 233.

23. Some of these spectacles had a revolutionary flavor designed to appeal to the pro-French faction of Jeffersonian democrats. One such entertainment was a re-enactment of

the guillotining of Louis XVI at a Philadelphia tavern. Advertisements described the miraculous climax of the show, "when the head falls in a basket, and the lips, which are first red, turn blue." See Foster Rhea Dulles, *America Learns to Play* (Gloucester, Mass.: P. Smith, 1963), 42.

24. *The Battle of Trenton* portrays "The Army in Motion," "Attack-Cannons-Bombs," "Flight of the Hessians," "General Confusion," "Articles of Capitulation Signed," "Trumpets of Victory," and "General Rejoicing." John Tasker Howard described some of the patriotic music of this period in *The Music of George Washington's Time* (Washington, D.C.: United States George Washington Bicentennial Commission, 1931).

25. Even in the cities, there was some brief interest in the preservation of older musical traditions. One writer in *The American Magazine* objected to the tendency to "consider music merely as a source of pleasure—not attending to its influence on the human mind and its consequent effects on society." Arguing that vocal (presumably religious) music "represented the unity of sounds and sentiments," this writer called for the founding of a school in New York to preserve and teach the traditional styles of psalm singing, a plan that was never realized. "For the American Magazine to the Public," *The American Magazine* (June 1788), 49.

26. Hans Gram, Samuel Holyoke, and Oliver Holden, *Massachusetts Compiler of Theoretical and Practical Elements of Sacred Vocal Music . . . Chiefly selected or adapted from modern European publications* (Boston: Isaiah Thomas & Ebenezer T. Andrews, 1795). The Preface to this volume makes special mention of the importance of "good musical emigrants [who] are daily seeking asylum in this country," a development that the editors considered a positive one for American musical culture.

27. Andrew Law, *Musical Primer* (Cheshire, Conn.: William Law, 1793), 5.

28. John Hubbard, "An Essay on Music, Pronounced before the Middlesex Music Society, Sept. 9, A.D. 1807, at Dunstable, Mass." in John C. Swan, ed., *Music in Boston* (Boston: Trustees of the Public Library of the City of Boston, 1977), 27.

29. Rev. Sydney Smith asked, in his review of Adam Seybert's *Statistical Annals of the United States of America* (Philadelphia, 1818), "In the four quarters of the globe, who reads an American book? or goes to an American play? or looks at an American picture or statue?" *Edinburgh Review*, Vol. XXXIII (January 1820), 79.

30. Anthony Philip Heinrich, *The Dawning of Music in Kentucky*, op. 1 (Philadelphia: Bacon & Hart, 1820), 1.

31. Fry was quoted in "Mr. Fry's "American Ideas' About Music," *Dwight's Journal of Music* II/23 (March 12, 1853), 181.

32. Ibid.

33. "Mr. Bristow's Rip Van Winkle at Niblo's," *New York Musical Review and Choral Advocate* VI/21 (October 6, 1855), 335.

34. "Josef Gungl on Musical Taste in America," *Dwight's Journal of Music* II/2 (December 18, 1852), 83–84. Reprinted from *Neue Berliner Musik-Zeitung* (February 4, 1849).

35. "Musical Review," *The Harbinger* II/6 (January 17, 1846), 88–89.

36. "Musical Review," *The Harbinger* II/7 (January 19, 1846), 109–10.

37. *Euterpiad; or Musical Intelligencer, Devoted to the Diffusion of Musical Intelligence and Belles Lettres*, April 11, 1822. In his remarks on *The Dawning of Music in Kentucky*, Parker praised the "vigor of thought, the variety of ideas, originality of conception, classical correctness, boldness and luxuriance of imagination, displayed throughout."

38. John Sullivan Dwight, "Father Heinrich in Boston, *The Harbinger* III/4 (July 4, 1846), 58–59.

39. "Introductory," *Dwight's Journal of Music* I/1 (April 10, 1852), 4.

40. "Prospects for the Season," *The Harbinger* III/19 (October 17, 1846), 301.

41. "The Boston Academy of Music," *The Harbinger* III/24 (November 21, 1846), 381.

42. "Editorial," *Dwight's Journal of Music* XI/14 (July 4, 1857), 110.

43. Ibid.

44. "The Concerts of the Past Winter," *The Dial* (July 1840). Henry Russell was a popular English entertainer who resided in the United States between 1835 and 1840.

45. Ralph Waldo Emerson, "The American Scholar" (1837) in Mark Van Doren, ed., *The Portable Emerson* (New York: Penguin Books, 1946), 23, 46.

46. "Musical Review," *The Harbinger* II/21 (May 2, 1846) 333.

47. "Gottschalk," *Dwight's Journal of Music* II/20 (February 19, 1853), 158.

48. Irving Lowens, *Music and Musicians in Early America* (New York: W. W. Norton, 1964), 228.

49. John Sullivan Dwight, "Music as a Means of Culture," *The Atlantic Monthly* XXVII/155 (September 1870), 326.

50. "Gottschalk in Boston—Then and Now," *Dwight's Journal of Music* XXII/2 (October 11, 1862), 223.

51. Rupert Hughes, *Contemporary American Composers* (Boston: L. C. Page and Company, 1900), 146.

52. Steven Ledbetter has compiled *A Handlist of Compositions with Orchestra by New England Composers, ca. 1875–1925,* which provides information on the work of seventeen composers, all of whom lived or worked in New England. Given the musical importance of Boston and of Harvard University, this list includes almost all of the important American Romantic composers of the late nineteenth century. Information on the existence and availability of music by these composers on recordings is available in Carol Oja, ed., *American Music Recordings: A Discography of 20th-Century U.S. Composers* (Brooklyn, N.Y.: Institute for Studies in American Music, 1982).

53. See Dr. Heinrich Möller, "Can Women Compose?" *The Musical Observer* XV/5 (May 1917), 9–10 and XV/6 (June 1917), 11–12.

54. Leipzig: Breitopf & Hartel, 1882.

55. "American Composers," *The Musical Courier*, XLVIII (February 17, 1904), 23.

56. Ibid.

57. Philip Hale, "Causerie," *The Boston Home Journal*, cited in Swan, ed., *Music in Boston*, 93.

58. Concert review in *The Portland Transcript* (1861), cited in M. A. DeWolfe Howe, "John Knowles Paine," *The Musical Quarterly* XXV/3 (July 1939), 259.

59. "Music," *The Atlantic Monthly* XXXVII/224 (June 1876), 764.

60. Richard Aldrich, "John Knowles Paine," *Dictionary of American Biography* (New York: Charles Scribner's Sons, 1934), 152.

61. Paul Rosenfeld, "Beginnings of American Music," in Herbert A. Liebowitz, ed., *Musical Impressions: Selections from Paul Rosenfeld's Criticism* (New York: Hill & Wang, 1969), 234.

62. Ibid., 237.

63. Olin Downes, "An American Composer," *Musical Quarterly* IV/1 (January 1918), 35–36.

64. See Edwin Carty Ranck, "The Mark Twain of American Music," *Theatre Magazine* XXVI/19 (September 1917), 172.

65. Henry F. Gilbert, "The American Composer," *Musical Quarterly* I/2 (April 1915), 178.

66. Henry F. Gilbert, "Folk Music in Art-Music—A Discussion and a Theory," *Musical Quarterly* III/4 (October 1917), 599.

67. Quoted in Isaac Goldberg, "An American Composer," *The American Mercury* XX/59 (November 1928), 331.

68. *Comment and Criticism on the Work of Henry F. Gilbert, Composer* (Boston: n.p., 1926). Among Gilbert's more overtly Americanist compositions were the *Comedy Overture on Negro Themes* (1905), *Three American Dances* (1911), the *Negro Rhapsody* (1913), and the score to the ballet, *Dance in the Place Congo* (1918).

69. Henry F. Gilbert, "Nationalism in Music," *The International* VII/2 (December 1913), 369.

70. Arthur Farwell, "The Struggle Toward a National Music," *North American Review* DCXXV (December 1907), 570.

71. Quoted in Edward N. Waters, "The Wa-Wan Press—An Adventure in Musical Idealism," in Gustave Reese, ed., *A Birthday Offering to Carl Engel* (New York: G. Schirmer, 1943), 222.

72. Farwell, "The Struggle Toward a National Music," 566, 567.

73. New York Philharmonic Society *Concert Program*, March 2, 1913.

74. New York Philharmonic Society *Concert Program*, December 6, 1914.

75. Charles Wakefield Cadman, "The Idealization of Indian Music," *Musical Quarterly* I/3 (July 1915), 395, 396.

76. "American Music—What Is It?" *Musical America* IV/9 (July 14, 1906), 7.

77. Angelo M. Read, "Negro Melodies, Not American Music," *Musical America* IV/13 (August 11, 1906), 2.

78. Angelo M. Read, untitled article, *Musical America* IV/20 (September 29, 1906), 13.

79. Daniel Gregory Mason, *The Dilemma of American Music* (New York: Macmillan, 1928), 12–13.

80. "American Composers Who Are Gaining Recognition Abroad," *Musical America* VI/16 (August 31, 1907), 3.

81. John C. Freund, "Popular Music as a Revelation of National Character," *Musical America* VI/20 (September 28, 1907), 7.

82. Charles Edward Ives, *Essays Before a Sonata* (New York: W. W. Norton and Company, 1961), 11, 51.

83. Ibid., 22.

84. Charles Edward Ives, *Memos* (New York: W. W. Norton and Company, 1972), 29 and *passim*.

Chapter 2. Celebrations of National Power

1. Jack Cameron Dierks, *A Leap to Arms—The Cuban Campaign of 1898* (Philadelphia: J. B. Lippincott Company, 1970), x. See also John M. Dobson, *America's Ascent: The United States Becomes a World Power, 1880–1914* (De Kalb, Ill.: Northern Illinois University Press, 1978), 4.

2. These and many other examples of popular sheet music from the Spanish-American War period are part of the Lathrop C. Harper Collection at the New-York Historical Society.

3. Henry Nash Smith, ed., *Popular Culture and Industrialism, 1865–1890* (New York: New York University Press, 1967), ix.

4. *Official Monthly Bulletin of the Great National Peace Jubilee and Music Festival*, No. 1 (February 1869), 5.

5. Ibid., 29.

6. Ibid., 7.

7. Ibid., 7.

8. There is one reference in the February 1869 Prospectus for the Festival to "The Union Pacific Railroad Galop, Respectfully Dedicated to the President and Officers of the Road" by an unknown composer.

9. *Official Monthly Bulletin* (February 1869), 30.

10. "The Jubilee in Retrospect," *Springfield Republican* (June 21, 1869), reprinted in *Dwight's Journal of Music* XXIX/8 (July 3, 1869), 59.

11. Ibid.

12. "Peace Festival and its Results," *New York Sun* (June 23, 1869), reprinted in *Dwight's Journal of Music* XXIX/8 (July 3, 1869), 59.

13. John Sullivan Dwight, "The National Peace Jubilee," *Dwight's Journal of Music* XXIX/8 (July 3, 1869), 60.

14. John Sullivan Dwight, "The Second Gilmore Jubilee," *Dwight's Journal of Music* XXXII/8 (July 13, 1872), 270.

15. William M. Evarts, "Oration," in United States Centennial Commission, *International Exhibition, 1876*, Vol. II, *Reports of the President, Secretary, and Executive Committee* (Washington, D.C.: 1880).

16. Fred A. Shannon, *The Centennial Years* (Garden City, N.Y.: Doubleday and Company, 1967), 2–3.

17. John Brinkerhoff Jackson, *American Space, The Centennial Years, 1865–1890* (New York: W. W. Norton and Company, 1972), 17, 21.

18. Richard R. Nicolai, *Centennial Philadelphia* (Bryn Mawr, Pa.: Bryn Mawr Press, 1976), 42.

19. John Maass, *The Glorious Enterprise: The Centennial Exhibition of 1876 and H. J. Schwartzmann, Architect-in-Chief* (Watkins Glen, N.Y.: American Life Foundation, 1973), 16.

20. Jackson, *American Space*, 235.

21. Ibid., 233.

22. While the exhibiting countries were asked to send representative examples of painting, sculpture, and photography "of a high order of merit," the quality has been described as "indifferent" in most cases. Richard R. Nicolai cited 2,749 examples of American art works and 4,398 from other countries on exhibit. See *Centennial Philadelphia*, 60. According to John Brinkerhoff Jackson, only England sent examples of its best art. He called the American works, with the exception of some groups of photographs, "poorly chosen." See *American Space*, 236.

23. Grant's remarks at the opening of the Philadelphia Centennial Exhibition are cited in Nicolai, *Centennial Philadelphia*, 53.

24. W. S. B. Matthews, *A Hundred Years of Music in America* (Chicago, 1898; reprinted, New York: AMS Press, 1970), 420.

25. Leon Stein, Introduction to George P. Upton, ed., *Theodore Thomas, A Musical Autobiography* (Chicago: A. C. McClurg, 1905; reprinted, New York: DaCapo Press, 1964), A-13 and *passim*.

26. Matthews, *A Hundred Years of Music in America*, 421.

27. *New York Daily Tribune* (September 8, 1875), 4.

28. *New York Daily Tribune* (September 20, 1875), 4.

29. Ibid.

30. Rose Fay Thomas, *Memoirs of Theodore Thomas* (New York: Moffat, Yard, and Company, 1911), 110.

31. Henry T. Finck, *Wagner and His Works* (New York: Scribner, 1893), Vol. II. p. 509.

32. Wagner to Thomas (Berlin, March 25, 1876) in Thomas, *Memoirs of Theodore Thomas*, 116.

33. Ibid., 111.

34. Charles Edward Russell, *The American Orchestra and Theodore Thomas* (Garden City, N.Y.: Doubleday, Page and Company, 1927), 100.

35. Excerpt from *The Tribune* (Philadelphia, May 10, 1876) reprinted in *Dwight's Journal of Music* XXXVI/4 (May 27, 1876), 238.

36. John Sullivan Dwight, "The Centennial Music," ibid., 238.

37. Abram Loft, "Richard Wagner, Theodore Thomas, and the American Centennial," *Musical Quarterly* XXXVII/2 (April 1951), 193.

38. "Amusements," *Public Ledger* (Philadelphia, July 1, 1876), 1.

39. Thomas, *Memoirs of Theodore Thomas*, 119.

40. Russell, *The American Orchestra and Theodore Thomas*, 103.

41. *United States Statutes at Large*, Vol. XXVI, p. 62.

42. Smith, *Popular Culture and Industrialism*, xv.

43. J. Seymour Currey, *Chicago: Its History and Its Builders* (Chicago: S. J. Clarke Publ. Co., 1912), Vol. III, p. 2.

44. Henry Van Brunt, "The Columbian Exposition and American Civilization," *The Atlantic Monthly*, Vol. XLII (May 1893), 579.

45. Van Wyck Brooks, *The Confident Years: 1885–1915* (New York: E. P. Dutton Company, 1952), 163.
46. Smith, *Popular Culture and Industrialism*, xv.
47. Joseph Kirkland, *The Story of Chicago* (Chicago: Dibble Publishing Company, 1892), 136, 214.
48. Russell, *The American Orchestra and Theodore Thomas*, 195–200.
49. "World's Fair Music," *The British Musician* (London, May 1893), 67.
50. See Thomas, *Memoirs of Theodore Thomas*, 377. J. Seymour Currey commented that such harmony did not encourage originality. In general, the designing artists and architects "adopted established architectural traditions and styles, and worked on accepted formulas. None of the designers was to make special features outside of the accepted styles, and there were to be no eccentricities of personal taste." See Currey, *Chicago: Its History and Its Builders*, 37.
51. Currey, *Chicago: Its History and Its Builders*, 30–31.
52. Ibid., 60.
53. See Thomas, *Memoirs of Theodore Thomas*, 382–83 for the entire program.
54. Ibid., 388–89.
55. Ibid., 389.
56. *Music Hall Series Concert Program*, August 4, 1893. *Arthur Mees Program Collection* (privately printed, n.d.).
57. Excerpt from *The Providence Journal* (early June 1893), reprinted in "Music at the Fair," *Music* (July 1893), 305.
58. "Music at the Fair," *Music* (July 1893), 311.
59. Russell, *The American Orchestra and Theodore Thomas*, 225.
60. Ibid., 232.
61. Rupert Hughes, *Contemporary American Music*, (Boston: L.C. Page, 1900), 376.
62. Frank Morton Todd, *The Story of the Exposition* (New York: G. P. Putnam's Sons, 1921), Vol. II, p. 57.
63. Ibid., 405–6.

Chapter 3. World War I and the Challenge of 100% Americanism

1. *Boston Symphony Orchestra Programme*, Special Insert, October 26, 1917.
2. Henry F. Gilbert, "Music After the War," *The New Music Review and Church Music Review*, IX/218 (January 1920): 45.
3. George Creel, *How We Advertised America, The First Telling of the Amazing Story of the Committee on Public Information That Carried the Gospel of Americanism to Every Corner of the Globe* (New York: Harper & Brothers, 1920), 5. See also Stephen Vaughan, *Holding Fast the Inner Lines, Democracy, Nationalism, and the Committee on Public Information* (Chapel Hill: University of North Carolina Press, 1980) and James R. Mock and Cedric Larson, *Words That Won the War, The Committee on Public Information, 1917–1919* (Princeton: Princeton University Press, 1939) for a discussion of the issues of democracy and wartime consensus.
4. Creel, *How We Advertised America*, 3.
5. Ibid.
6. Other familiar songs in the arsenal of the Four Minute Men included *America, The Battle Hymn of the Republic, Dixie, There's a Long, Long Trail, Tramp, Tramp, Tramp, Saving Food, When Johnny Comes Marching Home, Pack Up Your Troubles, When You Come Home,* and *America, the Beautiful*. See Mock and Larson, *Words That Won the War*, 124.
7. Ibid. The Commission on Training Camp Activities expressed the hope that an American song comparable to *It's a Long Way to Tipperary* would be composed for this country's War effort. See May Stanley, "Wanted: Singing Leaders for Army Camps," *Musical America* XXVI/17 (August 14, 1917), 3. John Alden Carpenter and other important American musicians participated in the U.S. Committee on Music for the Army and Navy. See "To Standardize All Music for Army and Navy," *Musical America* XXVI/19

(September 8, 1917), 1 and "Making Singing Sailors for Uncle Sam's Navy," *Musical America* XXVII/13 (January 26, 1918), 3.

8. *School and Society*, Vol. VII (June 22, 1918), 750.

9. State of California, *Third Biennial Report of the State Board of Education* (1918), 31–33.

10. Tour concerts in 1917–18 were played in Detroit, Baltimore, Washington, several cities in Ohio, Toronto, and numerous communities in upstate New York where, no doubt, the performances were major cultural events. Tour concerts usually replicated those presented in Carnegie Hall and at the Brooklyn Academy of Music.

11. New York Philharmonic Society *Concert Program*, December 13 and 14, 1917. Wagner was indeed a revolutionary sympathizer who fled Dresden for Weimar in 1849 after a warrant was issued for his arrest. For a detailed account of this period of the composer's life, see Vol. II of Ernest Newman's *The Life of Richard Wagner* (New York: Alfred A. Knopf, 1937), which covers the period from 1848 to 1864.

12. Howard Shanet, *Philharmonic: A History of New York's Orchestra* (Garden City, N.Y.: Doubleday and Company, 1975), 228.

13. Richard Schickel, *The World of Carnegie Hall* (New York: Julian Messner, 1960), 117 and Shanet, *Philharmonic*, 228.

14. Philip Hale in *The Boston Herald*, cited in M A. DeWolfe Howe, *The Boston Symphony Orchestra, 1881–1931* (Boston: Houghton Mifflin Company, 1931), 131.

15. Editorial in *The Providence Journal*, cited in Howe, *The Boston Symphony, 1881–1931*, 132.

16. "Maj. H. L. Higginson Defends Symphony," *The Boston Globe* (November 1, 1917), 4.

17. "Threat to Disband Boston Symphony," *The New York Times* (November 1, 1917), 10.

18. "Damrosch Would Provide Substitute for Muck," *The Boston Globe* (November 1, 1917), 4.

19. "Threat to Disband Boston Symphony," *The New York Times* (November 1, 1917), 10.

20. Boston Symphony Orchestra Archives, scrapbook collected by Marcus Carroll. This article, "Colonel Would Intern Dr. Muck as Alien," is undated but may come from the *Boston Herald and Journal* of November 3, 1917.

21. "Ex-Governor Warfield Would Mob Muck," *The New York Times* (November 5, 1917), 13.

22. "Declares Muck Must Not Lead in Baltimore," *The Boston Globe* (November 5, 1917), 3.

23. "Baltimore Forbids Dr. Muck's Concert," *The New York Times* (November 6, 1917), 13.

24. "Department of Justice Probing Muck Case," *The Boston Globe* (November 3, 1917), 4.

25. "Boston Symphony Plays Anthem, Dr. Muck Ready to Resign," *The Boston Globe* (November 3, 1917), 1–2.

26. "Renews Dr. Muck Protest," *The New York Times* (March 12, 1918), 12.

27. Mrs. Jay was quoted at length in "Dr. Manning Joins Attack on Dr. Muck," *The New York Times* (March 13, 1918), 9.

28. "Dr. Muck Sent Back to Germany," *The Boston Globe* (August 21, 1919), 1.

29. Boston Symphony Orchestra Archives, Marcus Carroll scrapbook, undated articles from *The Boston Post*.

30. "Maj. Higginson Quits Symphony," *The Sunday Herald* (Boston), April 18, 1918.

31. "Dr. Muck Leaves for Copenhagen," *The Boston Globe* (August 21, 1919), 10.

32. See Irving Lowens, "L'Affaire Mück, A Study in War Hysteria, 1917–1918," *Musicology* I/3 (1947).

33. "Music World Agog Over Question of Mück's Successor," *Musical America* XXVII/26 (April 27, 1918), 1.

34. Ibid., 1.

35. Ibid., 3. *Musical America* even suggested that subscribers to the magazine might want to submit their own choices for the Boston position.

36. "Rabaud, Boston Symphony's New Leader, Arrives: Defers Announcement of His Plans," *Musical America* XXIX/1 and 2 (November 2 and 9, 1918), 3–4.

37. Programs from the Chicago and Cincinnati Symphony Orchestras indicated that these midwestern orchestras were more like Boston than New York. German music never disappeared (although there were no performances of Wagner's works in Cincinnati in 1918–19), but it was never played as frequently after the War as before the conflict. In both cities, traditional German Romantic music was leavened with French and Russian pieces and, in Chicago at least, thanks to the efforts of conductor Frederick Stock, with a larger number of compositions by Americans.

38. See the published Symphony Hall Programs of the Boston Symphony Orchestra and H. Earle Johnson, *Symphony Hall, Boston* (Boston: Little, Brown and Company, 1950).

39. "Musical Alliance Begins Move for Wider Introduction of Music in America's Public Schools," *Musical America* XXVII/20 (March 16, 1918), 5.

40. "Americanism is Keynote of N.Y. Teachers' Sessions," *Musical America* XXVIII/9 (June 29, 1918), 1.

41. "Managers Prepare for Post-Bellum Music Boom," *Musical America* XXVIII/25 (October 18, 1918), 21, 23.

42. "Select American Concertmaster for Boston Symphony," *Musical America* XXVIII/19 (September 7, 1918), 1–2.

43. "Gatti Announces Complete Plans for the Season," *Musical America* XXVI/21 (September 21, 1917), 1.

44. "Halt German Opera at the Metropolitan," *The New York Times* (November 2, 1917), 13.

45. *The New York Evening Post* editorial was quoted at length in "Opera Comes Under the Metropolitan Ban," *Musical America* XXVII/2 (November 10, 1917), 1.

46. "No Ban on German Masters in Either France or England," *Musical America* XXVII/10 (January 5, 1918), 1.

47. "Patriotic Opening for the Met's Operatic Season," *Musical America* XXVII/3 (November 17, 1917), 1.

48. "Pittsburgh Bans Kunwald Concert and German Music," *Musical America* XXVII/5 (December 1, 1917), 1.

49. "May Disband Boston Symphony for Period of War," *Musical America* XXVII/6 (December 8, 1917), 1.

50 Ibid. See also Frances Anne Wister, *Twenty-Five Years of the Philadelphia Orchestra* (Philadelphia: Edward Stern and Company, 1925), 117, 120.

51. When word reached New York that Kreisler had been wounded at the battle of Lemburg, there was much concern for his future playing career. The violinist was not disabled permanently, and his arrival in New York in November of 1914, was warmly noted in the press. See Richard Schickel, *The World of Carnegie Hall*, 166–67.

52. "Kreisler, Goaded by Attacks, Gives Up All Concerts," *Musical America* XXVII/5 (December 1, 1917), 1.

53. Schickel, *The World of Carnegie Hall*, 177.

54. Robert W. Wilkes, "Plan for the Stimulation of American Composition," *Musical America* XXIX/12 (January 18, 1919), 13.

55. "Music's Future Belongs to the Extremists, Declares Alfredo Casella," *Musical America* XXIX/23 (April 15, 1919), 15.

56. Dorothy J. Teall, "Says We Should Not Love Germanism in Music Less But Modernism More," *Musical America* XXX/1 (May 3, 1919), 30–31.

57. Hubert Foss and Noel Goodwin, *London Symphony—Portrait of an Orchestra* (London: The Naldrett Press, 1954), 77.

58. Thomas Russell, *The Proms* (London: Max Parrish, 1949), 49.

Chapter 4. Modernists in Search of an Audience

1. Filippo Tommaso Marinetti, "Futurist Manifesto" (1909), quoted in Carl Van Vechten, *Music and Bad Manners* (New York: Alfred A. Knopf, 1916), 193.

2. James Weldon Johnson, *The Autobiography of an Ex-Colored Man* (New York: Alfred A. Knopf, 1927), 87.

3. Ibid.

4. Darius Milhaud, "The Day After Tomorrow," *Modern Music* III/1 (November–December 1925), 22–23.

5. Ibid., 117–18.

6. Ibid., 147–48.

7. Joseph Machlis, *Introduction to Contemporary Music* (New York: W. W. Norton and Company, 1979), 204.

8. See *Modern Music* VI/4 (May–June 1929), 30 and VII/4 (June–July 1930), 30 for reviews of *Jonny Spielt auf!* in New York.

9. Vernon Duke, *Passport to Paris* (Boston: Little, Brown and Company, 1955), 211.

10. John Alden Carpenter, "Skyscrapers: A Ballet of Modern American Life" (New York: G. Schirmer, 1926), 1.

11. Critical discussion of the importance of this concert appeared in Deems Taylor's review in the *New York Times*, Henry T. Parker's comments on a repeat performance in Boston in the *Evening Transcript*, (January 30, 1924), and Carl Van Vechten, "George Gershwin, An American Composer Who is Writing Notable Music in the Jazz Idiom," *Vanity Fair* XXIV/3 (March 1925), 40, 78.

12. Samuel Chotzinoff, "George Gershwin's 'Rhapsody in Blue'," *Vanity Fair* XXII/6 (August 1924), 28.

13. Leonie Rosensteil, *Nadia Boulanger, A Life in Music* (New York: W. W. Norton and Company, 1982), 153.

14. Virgil Thomson, *Virgil Thomson* (New York: Alfred A. Knopf, 1966), 117.

15. Ibid., 118.

16. Aaron Copland and Vivian Perlis, *Copland, 1900 Through 1942* (New York: St. Martin's/Marek, 1984), 75–76 and Aaron Copland, *Copland on Music* (Garden City, N.Y.: Doubleday and Company, 1960), 87.

17. Thomson, *Virgil Thomson*, 54.

18. Copland and Perlis, *Copland, 1900 Through 1942*, 103.

19. Ibid., 104–6.

20. See Arnold Dobrin, *Aaron Copland, His Life and Times* (New York: Thomas Y. Crowell, 1967), 75. Koussevitzky remained a friend of the modern American composer throughout his tenure as conductor of the Boston Symphony Orchestra from 1924 to 1949. See Hugo Leichentritt, *Serge Koussevitzky, The Boston Symphony Orchestra and the New American Music* (Cambridge: Harvard University Press, 1946).

21. Copland and Perlis, *Copland, 1900 Through 1942*, 119 and Oscar Thompson, *Great Modern Composers* (New York: Dodd, Mead Company, 1941), 46.

22. Samuel Chotzinoff, Review of Aaron Copland's "Concerto for Piano and Orchestra," *New York World* LXVII/23,908 (February 4, 1927), 4–5.

23. Oscar Thompson, Review of George Gershwin's "An American in Paris," *The New York Post*, cited in Nicholas Slonimsky, *Lexicon of Musical Invective, Critical Assaults on Composers Since Beethoven's Time* (New York: Coleman-Ross, 1965), 105.

24. Virgil Thomson, "The Cult of Jazz," *Vanity Fair* XXIV/4 (June 1924), 54, 118.

25. Copland and Perlis, *Copland, 1900 Through 1942*, 165.

26. Aaron Copland, *The New Music* (New York: W. W. Norton and Company, 1941), 71.

27. Roy Harris, "The Crisis in Music 2," *The New Freeman* I/6 (April 19, 1930), 135.

28. Aaron Copland, *Music and Imagination* (Cambridge: Harvard University Press, 1952), 99–100.

29. Richard Aldrich, "Some Judgments on New Music," *The New York Times* (February 11, 1923), X-5.

30. Arthur Farwell, "The Zero Hour in Musical Evolution," *Musical Quarterly* XX/1 (January 1927), 89.

31. Louis Gruenberg, "For an American Gesture," *League of Composers Journal* I/2 (n.d.), 27. Frank Patterson, "Folk Fables," *League of Composers Journal* II/2 (April 1925), 26. A. Walter Kramer, "American Composers III, Louis Gruenberg," *Modern Music* VIII/1 (November–December 1930), 3.

32. Henry F. Gilbert, "Notes on a Trip to Frankfurt in the Summer of 1927, With Some Thoughts on Modern Music," *Musical Quarterly* XVI/1 (January 1930), 26.

33. Maxwell Geismar, "No Man Alone Now," *Virginia Quarterly Review* XVII (September 1942), 530.

34. I am indebted to Arthur Cohn, director of Serious Music at Carl Fischer, Inc., for his observations on music and politics in the 1930s. Mr. Cohn was a contributor to *Music Front*, the journal of the Workers' Music League, an organization affiliated with the Communist Party. Most of his own compositions, however, were abstract and not political at all in content. Interview with Arthur Cohn, February 25, 1982.

35. Mike Gold, "Toward an American Revolutionary Culture," *New Masses* (July 1931), 13.

36. Mike Gold, "What a World," *The Daily Worker* (October 19, 1933), 5.

37. "Workers Music," *New Masses* (July 1931), 13.

38. *Red Song Book* (New York: Workers' Music Library Publishers, 1932), 3.

39. Foreword, *Workers Song Book* (New York: U.S.A. Section of the International Music Bureau, 1934).

40. Aaron Copland, "Workers Sing!" *New Masses* (June 12, 1934), 28.

41. Ibid.

42. Carl Sands, "A Program for Proletarian Composers," *The Daily Worker* (January 16, 1934), 5.

43. Cowell was quoted in "Symposium and Concert at John Reed Club," *The Daily Worker* (December 20, 1934), 5.

44. Mike Gold, "Change the World!" *The Daily Worker* (June 11, 1934), 5.

45. Lan Adomian, "What Songs Should Workers' Choruses Sing?" *The Daily Worker* (February 7, 1934), 5.

46. Charles Louis Seeger, "On Proletarian Music," *Modern Music* XI/3 (March–April 1934), 125.

47. In addition, Cowell was one of fifty-three signatories to a statement in support of the presidential candidacy of William Z. Foster in 1932. This statement was expanded into a broader attack on the two major political parties in *Culture and Crisis: An Open Letter to the Writers, Artists, Teachers, Physicins, Engineers, Scientists, and Other Professional Workers of America* (New York: League of Professional Groups for Foster and Ford, 1932).

48. Henry Cowell, "Useful Music," *New Masses* (October 29, 1935), 26.

49. Marc Blitzstein, "Music Manifesto," *New Masses* (January 23, 1936), 28.

50. Hanns Eisler, "Reflections on the Future of the Composer," *Modern Music* XII/3 (May–June 1935), 183.

51. "Einiges über die Lage des modernen Komponisten," (1935), reprinted in Manfred Grabs, ed., *Hanns Eisler: A Rebel in Music* (New York: International Publishers, 1978), 107, 109, 112.

52. Blitzstein's compositions while he was in the Army Air Force illustrated his belief in the correctness of the war against fascism. He wrote a choral work performed by enlisted black soldiers entitled *Freedom Morning*. He responded to a commission from the Eighth Air Force with the *Airborne Symphony*, a work about the life of a serviceman. It is scored for orchestra, men's chorus, and narrator. He also composed a film score, *The True Glory*, for the Army.

53. Copland, *The New Music*, 144.

54. Michael Gold, "Change the World!" *The Daily Worker* (October 17, 1935), 5.

55. Kathleen Hoover and John Cage, *Virgil Thomson, His Life and Music* (New York: Thomas Yoseloff, 1959), 65.
56. Thomson, *Virgil Thomson*, 264.
57. Thomson, *Virgil Thomson*, 270.
58. Ibid., 275.
59. Copland, *The New Music*, 119–20.
60. Arthur Farwell, "Roy Harris," *Musical Quarterly* XVIII/1 (January 1932), 31–32.
61. Copland, *The New Music*, 119–120.
62. Copland, *The New Music* (rev. ed., 1967), 125.
63. Roger Sessions interview with Vivian Perlis, May 4, 1983, in Copland and Perlis, *Copland, 1900 Through 1942*, p. 149.
64. See *The Musical Experience of Composer, Performer, Listener* (Princeton: Princeton University Press, 1950), "The Composer and His Message," in Augusto Centano, ed., *The Intent of the Artist* (Princeton: Princeton University Press, 1941), and Roger Sessions, "Music in Crisis," *Modern Music* X/2 (January–February 1940), 73.
65. Roger Sessions, "On the American Future," *Modern Music* XVII/2 (January–February 1940), 73.
66. Roger Sessions, *The Musical Experience of Composer, Performer, Listener*, 118.
67. Copland, *The New Music*, 131.
68. Copland and Perlis, *Copland, 1900 Through 1942*, 86.
69. Jack Beeson, "Otto Luening," *The New Grove Dictionary of Music and Musicians*, Vol. II, p. 309.
70. In 1947, correspondence with Copland, Harris, Hanson, and Douglas Moore led Lora Gahimer to conclude that American composers were no longer trying to write specifically "American" music (although Harris continued to compose pieces with American programmatic titles). See her M.A. essay, "Attitudes on Contemporary Composition, As Exemplified by Copland, Hanson, Harris, and Moore" (Eastman School of Music, 1947).
71. Elliott Carter, "The Rhythmic Basis of American Music," *The Score—A Musical Magazine* (London) No. 12 (June 1955), 27.

Chapter 5. The National Government and National Music

1. *History of the Marine Band* (Philadelphia: United States Marine Corps Publicity Bureau, 1937), 7.
2. H M. Kallen, "The Arts and Thomas Jefferson," *Ethics* LIII/4 (July 1943), 237. Kallen called Jefferson the "father" of the modern Marine Corps Band.
3. See Grace Overmeyer, *Government and the Arts* (New York: W. W. Norton and Company, 1939), 151 and *The New Grove Dictionary of Music and Musicians*, Vol. 10, pp. 811–12.
4. National Conservatory of Music, New York, *Concert Program*, January 11, 1868.
5. Merton Robert Aborn, "The Influence on American Musical Culture of Dvořák's Sojourn in America" (Ph.D. diss. Indiana University, 1965), 69, 268, 279.
6. National Conservatory of Music, *Concert Program*, February 19, 1890.
7. Henry T. Finck, *My Adventures in the Golden Age of Music* (New York: Funk & Wagnalls, 1926), 275.
8. Aborn, "The Influence on American Musical Culture of Dvořák's Sojourn in America," 71.
9. Ibid., 76.
10. Aborn cited a 1946 letter from the law firm of Choate, Mitchell, and Ely to Mrs. Thurber's daughter, Mrs. Jay Layng Mills, that indicated that the Conservatory functioned from "1885 to about 1920." Ibid., 315. The Conservatory is listed in *Musical America's Guide* (New York: *Musical America*, 1927), 208, but it is not listed in the 1928 edition. It appears that the Conservatory maintained its 53 W. 74th St. address for some time after the school ceased operation.

11. H. R. 6050, 75th Congress, 2d session (1937).

12. Aborn, "The Influence on American Musical Culture of Dvořák's Sojourn in America," 320.

13. Frank Damrosch, "The American Conservatory, Its Aims and Possibilities," *Music Teachers' National Association Studies in Music Education, History, and Aesthetics*, Vol. I (1906), 15–16.

14. See the following articles, all from the pages of *Musical America*, "Government Conservatory Idea," X/15 (August 14, 1909), 16; "Plan Conservatory on National Lines," XVI/17 (August 31, 1912), 1; "Great National Conservatory America's Need in Music, Declares Eddy Brown," XXIII/15 (February 12, 1916), 17; and "Bill for a National Conservatory Now Ready in House," XXVII/18 (March 12, 1918), 1. In 1910 Manhattan Borough President George McAneny had advocated municipal support for music in "Handsome New Home for New York Institute of Musical Art, *Musical America* XIII/1 (November 12, 1910), 3. Musical entrepreneur Leopold Godowsky called for government and private patronage in "Godowsky Would Create New Musical Headquarters of the World" *Musical America* XVIII/3 (November 23, 1912), 3.

15. Oscar Sonneck in *Musical America* (1909), reprinted in *Suum cuique; Essays in Music* (New York: G. Schirmer, 1916), 107.

16. Committee on Education, House of Representatives, 65th Congress, 2d session, Haering on H.R. 6445 (June 14, 1918), 3.

17. Ibid., 5.

18. Ibid., 9.

19. Hearings on H.R. 6445 (June 17, 1918), 15.

20. Alfred T. Marks, "Bill for National Conservatory Introduced by Senator Fletcher Provides Also for Art Ministry," *Musical America* XXX/6 (June 7, 1919), 1.

21. Alfred T. Marks, "New Bill for National Conservatory Eliminates Evils of Fletcher Measure," *Musical America* XXX/10 (July 5, 1919), 6.

22. Committee on Education, House of Representatives, 68th Congress, 1st session, Hearings on H.R. 7011 (March 25, 1924), 4.

23. Ibid., 5.

24. Ibid.

25. Warren I. Susman, *Culture and Commitment* (New York: George Braziller, 1973), 15. Jane deHart Mathews discussed the art of this period in terms of what she called "cultural democracy," in which the artist is integrated into American life as his work becomes more representative of America and more accessible to an "average" audience. See "Arts of the People: The New Deal Quest for Cultural Democracy," *Journal of American History* XLII/2 (September 1975), 316 and *passim*, and Walter Abell, "Man's Art and Man's Future," *The American Scholar* XII/1 (Winter 1942–43), 79–91.

26. William F. McDonald, *Federal Relief Administration and the Arts* (Columbus: Ohio State University Press, 1969), 587.

27. See Cornelius Baird Canon, "The Federal Music Project of the Works Progress Administration: Music in a Democracy" (Ph.D. diss., University of Minnesota, 1963), and Jannelle Warren Findley, "Of Tears and Need: The Federal Music Project, 1935–1943" (Ph.D. diss., George Washington University, 1973).

28. National Broadcasting Company program, October 11, 1933, cited in McDonald, *Federal Relief Administration and the Arts*, 35.

29. George Foster, "Record of Program Operation and Accomplishments: The Federal Music Project, 1935–1939; The WPA Music Program, 1939–1943"(Washington, D.C.: WPA Music Program, 1943), Record Group 69, Interior Division, National Archives and Records Service (NARS), 6.

30. Proceedings, WPA Staff Conference, June 16, 1935, cited in McDonald, *Federal Relief Administration and the Arts*, 32.

31. WPA, *Bulletin 29, Supplement No. 1* (September 30, 1935), Exhibit 1 in Foster, "Record of Program Operation and Accomplishments."

32. Interview with Arthur Cohn, February 25, 1982.

33. On WPA interference in the Federal Writers Project, see Jerre Mangione, *The Dream and the Deal* (Boston: Little, Brown Company, 1973). Richard D. McKinzie's *The New Deal for Artists* (Princeton: Princeton University Press, 1973) discusses the operation of the Federal Arts Project, and Karal Ann Marling's *Wall-to-Wall America* (Minneapolis: University of Minnesota Press, 1982) analyzes local and federal opposition to some of the work done for Post Office murals throughout the country. Jane deHart Mathews's *The Federal Theatre, 1935–1939: Plays, Relief, and Politics* (Princeton: Princeton University Press, 1967) discusses the extent to which the Project and its director, Hallie Flanagan, were held suspect on political grounds and by those who felt that the use of tax dollars for drama was a tremendous boondoggle.

34. Letter from Nicolai Sokoloff to the administrator of the Denver Music Project, January 20, 1936.

35. Canon, "The Federal Music Project," 71, 73.

36. See McDonald, *Federal Relief Administration and the Arts*, 906 and John Tasker Howard, "Better Days for Music," *Harper's*, Vol. 174 (April 1937), 485.

37. Tony Buttitta and Barry Witham, *Uncle Sam Presents, A Memoir of the Federal Theatre, 1935–1939* (Philadelphia: University of Pennsylvania Press, 1982), 194.

38. Ashley Pettis, "The WPA and the American Composer," *Musical Quarterly* XXVI/1 (January 1940), 110.

39. Composers' Forum Transcripts, Concert of Music by Ruth Crawford (Seeger). Federal Music Project files, Record Group 69, NARS.

40. Olin Downes, "Laboratory for Native Composers," *The New York Times* (January 10, 1937), X-7.

41. "Composers on the Grill," *The New York Times* (February 13, 1938), X-7.

42. Cited in Foster, "Record of Program Operations and Accomplishments," 134.

43. From *Musical Quarterly*, see especially Felix Borowski, "John Alden Carpenter" XVI/4 (October 1930) and Arthur Farwell, "Roy Harris" XVIII/1 (January 1932). Arthur Foote discussed musical Americanism in "A Bostonian Remembers" XXIII/1 (January 1937), and Ashley Pettis analyzed government support for American music in "The WPA and the American Composer" XXVI/1 (January 1940). The most relevant articles from *Modern Music* include the "American Composers" series, which presented portraits of selected American composers, and Irving Weil, "The American Scene Changes" VI/4 (May–June 1929). George Antheil made a case for American music in "Wanted—Opera by and for Americans" VII/4 (June–July 1930). Other articles that argued along the same lines included Aaron Copland, "The Composer in America, 1923–1933" X/2 (January–February 1933); Arthur Farwell, "Pioneering for American Music" XII/3 (March–April 1935); Howard Hanson, "American Procession at Rochester" XIII/3 (March–April 1936); and Charles Seeger, "Grass Roots for American Composers" XVI/3 (March–April 1939). Roger Sessions argued against the need for nationalism in American music in "On the American Future" XVII/2 (January–February 1940).

44. Composers' Forum Transcript, concert of music by Marion Bauer, January 8, 1937.

45. Composers' Forum Transcript, concert of the music of Aaron Copland, February 24, 1937.

46. Composers' Forum Transcript, music of William Schuman, June 15, 1938.

47. Composers' Forum Transcript, concert of music by Roy Harris, October 11, 1938.

48. McDonald, *Federal Relief Administration and the Arts*, 643.

49. Harry L. Hewes, "Indexing America's Composers," *The Christian Science Monitor* (April 5, 1941), 7.

50. Earl Vincent Moore, "Choral Music and the WPA Music Program," *Music Teachers' National Association Studies in Musical Education, History, and Aesthetics* (1939), 336–37.

51. Ibid., 7.

52. George Foster to Earl Vincent Moore, July 12, 1940. Document 211.1, Record Group 69, NARS.

53. Canon, "The Federal Music Project," 174. The results of yearly surveys were printed in the *Bulletin* of the American Composers' Alliance.

54. Jacques Barzun makes this point in *Music in American Life* (Bloomington: Indiana University Press, 1956), 31.

55. "Government Vandalism," *The New Republic* LXXXXI/1180 (July 14, 1937), 266.

56. H.R. 30, "An Act to protect for American actors, vocal musicians, operatic singers, and orchestral conductors the artistic and earning opportunities in the United States, and for other purposes" in "The Problem of the Foreign-Born Artist: Controversial Views of Dickstein Bill," *Musical America* LVII/3 (February 10, 1937), 16.

57. Ibid.

58. Ibid., 17.

59. Ibid., 17, 185.

60. "Musicians Testify on Dickstein Measure," *Musical America* LVII/4 (February 25, 1937), 1.

61. "Dickstein Hearings are Completed in Capital," *Musical America* LVII/5 (March 10, 1937), 3.

62. Subcommittee of the Committee on Education and Labor, United States Senate, 75th Congress, 3d session. Hearings on S. 3296, "A Bill to Provide for a Permanent Bureau of Fine Arts," February 28 and March 1 and 2, 1938, p. 2.

63. Ibid., 20.

64. Ibid., 21.

65. "House Group Votes Against Funds," *The Washington Post* (March 11, 1942), 5.

Chapter 6. Lectern and Silver Screen

1. Farwell's remarks are quoted in Irving L. Sablonsky, *American Music* (Chicago: University of Chicago Press, 1969), 155–56.

2. A. Walter Kramer, "American Creative Art." *Proceedings, National Federal of Music Clubs*, Vol. II (1937), 42.

3. Minna Lederman. "No Money for Music," *North American Review* 243/1 (Spring 1937), 124.

4. Daniel Gregory Mason, *Music in My Time*, cited in Howard Taubman, *Music as a Profession* (New York: Charles Scribner's Sons, 1939), 231.

5. Samuel Eliot Morison, *Harvard College in the Seventeenth Century* (Cambridge: Harvard University Press, 1936), Vol. II, p. 643.

6. Oscar G. Sonneck, *Francis Hopkinson, The First American Poet-Composer, and Our Musical Life in Colonial Times* (Philadelphia: The Pennsylvania Society of the Colonial Dames of America, 1919), 6.

7. Report of the Pierian Sodality, Harvard University (1837), cited in Frederic L. Ritter, *Music in America* (New York: Charles Scribner's Sons, 2nd ed., 1900), 248.

8. M. A. DeWolfe Howe, "John Knowles Paine," *Musical Quarterly* XXV/3 (July 1939), 264.

9. David Stanley Smith, "A Study of Horatio Parker," *Musical Quarterly* XVI/2 (April 1930), 159.

10. Marshall M. Bartholomew in the *Yale Alumni Weekly*, December 19, 1930.

11. Randall Thompson, *College Music, An Investigation for the Association of American Colleges* (New York: Macmillan, 1935), 162, 204, 205.

12. Letter from Howard Hanson to Olin Downes in "American Music at Rochester Festival," *The New York Times* (May 31, 1931), X-8.

13. *Eastman School of Music, University of Rochester Alumni Bulletin*, Vol. 16, Nos. 3–4. (June 1945), 5.

14. "American Music at Rochester Festival," *The New York Times* (May 31, 1931), X-8.

15. *Eastman School of Music, University of Rochester Alumni Bulletin*, Vol. 16, Nos. 3–4 (June 1945), 5.

16."American Music at Rochester Festival," X-8.

17. Ibid.

18. Daniel Bell, "Modernity and Mass Society: On the Varieties of Cultural Experience"

in Morton White and Arthur M. Schlesinger, Jr., eds., *Paths of American Thought* (New York: Houghton Mifflin, 1963), 424.

19. Roger Sessions, *Reflections on the Musical Life of the United States* (New York: Merlin Press, 1956), 115.

20. Ibid., 116.

21. "Teaching as a Composer's Craft—A Symposium," *The Composers' News Record*, No. 9 (Spring 1949), 1.

22. Ibid.

23. Ibid., 2.

24. Irving Kolodin, "Concert Hall Into Theatre," *Theatre Arts Monthly* (October 1938), 729.

25. Ibid., 731.

26. Ibid., 732.

27. Sir Thomas Beecham in *Life*, cited in *Film Music Notes* IV/4 (February 1945), 1.

28. Frederick W. Sternfeld, "Louisiana Story," *Film Music Notes* VII/1 (September–October 1948), 5–6.

29. Alfred Frankenstein, "Musicians Congress," *Film Music Notes* IV/2 (November 1944), 9.

30. Parts of Steiner's unfinished autobiography are included in Tony Thomas, ed., *Film Score, The View from the Podium* (South Brunswick and New York: A. S. Barnes and Company, 1979), 81.

31. Bronislau Kaper in Thomas, ed., *Film Score*, 119–20.

32. Hanns Eisler, "Hollywood Seen from the Left" (1935) in Manfred Grabs, ed., *Hanns Eisler: A Rebel in Music* (New York: International Publishers, 1978), 103.

33. Harriet Johnson, *Your Career in Music* (New York: E. P. Dutton, Incorporated, 1944), 184–85.

34. Lawrence Morton, "The Red Pony," *Film Music Notes* Special Issue (February 1949), 3.

35. Ibid., 8.

36. Ibid.

37. Roy Webb, "Things a Motion Picture Composer Has to Think About," *Film Music Notes* I/1 (October 1941), 2.

38. Hanns Eisler, 'On the Use of Music in Sound Film," (1936), in Grabs, ed., *Hanns Eisler: A Rebel in Music*, 124.

39. Frederick W. Sternfeld, "Copland as a Film Composer," *Musical Quarterly* XXVII/2 (April 1951), 161, 162.

40. *Film Music Notes* IV/4 (January 1945), 2.

41. Jerry Goldsmith in Thomas, ed., *Film Score*, 223.

42. Ibid., 228.

43. Ibid., 229.

44. Alice Evans Field, "Scoring Film Drama," *Film Music Notes* III/8 (May 1944), 6.

Epilogue

1. Deems Taylor, "Music," in Harold E. Stearns, ed., *Civilization in the United States: An Inquiry by Thirty Americans* (New York: Harcourt, Brace & Co., 1922), 200.

2. Ibid., 214.

3. John Powell, "Music and the Nation," *Rice Institute Pamphlets* X/3 (July 1923), 152.

4. Ibid., 151.

5. Roger Sessions, "The Composer and His Message," in Augusto Centano, ed., *The Intent of the Artist* (Princeton: Princeton University Press, 1941), 127–28.

6. Elliott Carter, "The Composer's Choices," in Else and Kurt Stone, eds., *The Writings of Elliott Carter* (Bloomington: Indiana University Press, 1977), 195.

7. "Symposium on the Problems of the American Composer," *National Music Council Bulletin* XII/2 (January 1952), 14.

Bibliography

I. General Historical Sources

Aaron, Daniel. *Writers on the Left*. New York: Oxford University Press, 1961.

Abell, Walter, "Man's Art and Man's Future." *The American Scholar* XII/1 (Winter 1942–43): 79–91.

An Addition to the Present Melancholy Circumstances of the Colony Considered. Boston: S. Kneeland, 1719.

Alexander, Charles C. *Here the Country Lies, Nationalism and the Arts in Twentieth Century America*. Bloomington: Indiana University Press, 1980.

——— *Nationalism in American Thought, 1930-1945*. Chicago: Rand, McNally and Company, 1969.

The American Magazine (New York), 1788.

The American Magazine of Art, 1925–1935.

The American Mercury, 1926–1934.

The Atlantic Monthly, 1870.

The Boston Globe, 1917-1919.

The Boston Herald, 1906.

Brooks, Van Wyck. *The Confident Years: 1885–1915*. New York: E. P. Dutton Company, 1952.

Brown, Rollo Walter, *Lonely Americans*. New York: Coward, McCann, 1929.

Bryce, James. *The American Commonwealth*, Vol. III. New York: Macmillan, 1888.

Bushman, Richard L. *From Puritan to Yankee*. New York: W. W. Norton and Company, 1967.

Buttitta, Tony and Witham, Barry. *Uncle Sam Presents, A Memoir of the Federal Theatre, 1935–1939*. Philadelphia: University of Pennsylvania Press, 1982.

The Chesterian (London).

The Christian Science Monitor, 1941.

Coben, Stanley and Ratner, Lorman, eds. *The Development of an American Culture*. Englewood Cliffs, N.J.: Prentice-Hall, 1970.

Commager, Henry Steele. *The American Mind*. New Haven: Yale University Press, 1950.

Committee on Education, House of Representatives, 65th Congress, 2d session. Hearing on H.R. 6445 "to establish a national conservatory of music art for the education of advanced pupils in all its branches, vocal and instrumental, as well as painting, drawing and etching" (June 17, 1918).

Committee on Education, House of Representatives, 68th Congress, 1st session. Hearing on H.R. 7100 "to create a commission to ascertain the feasibility of establishing a National Conservatory of Music" (March 25, 1924).

Committee on Education and Labor, United States Senate, 75th Congress, 3d session. Hearings on S. 3296 "to provide for a permanent Bureau of Fine Arts" (February 28 and March 1 and 2, 1938).

Creel, George, *How We Advertised America*. New York: Harper & Brothers Publ., 1920.

Cultural Directory II: Federal Funds and Services for the Arts and Humanities. Washington: Smithsonian Institution Press, 1980.

Culture and Crisis: An Open Letter to the Writers, Artists, Teachers, Physicians, Engineers, Scientists, and Other Professional Workers of America. New York: League of Professional Groups for Foster and Ford, 1932.

Currey, J. Seymour. *Chicago: Its History and Its Builders*, Vol. III. Chicago: S. J. Clarke Publ. Co., 1912.

Curti, Merle. *The Growth of American Thought*. New York: Harper & Row, 3d ed., 1964.

Demos, John. "Notes on Life in Plymouth Colony." *William and Mary Quarterly*. 3d Ser., XXII (1965): 264–86.

Department of the Interior, Bureau of Education, Bulletin No. 18, "Americanization as a War Measure (1918).

The Dial (Boston).

Dictionary of American Biography. New York: Charles Scribner's Sons, 1934.

Dierks, Jack Cameron. *A Leap to Arms—The Cuban Campaign of 1898. Philadelphia: J. B. Lippincott Company, 1970.*

Dobson, John M. *America's Ascent: The United States Becomes a World Power, 1880–1914*. DeKalb, Ill.: Northern Illinois University Press, 1978.

Dulles, Foster Rhea. *America Learns to Play*. Gloucester, Mass.: P. Smith, 1963.

Emerson, Ralph Waldo. "The American Scholar," in Mark Van Doren, ed., *The Portable Emerson*. New York: Penguin Books, 1946.

Federal Theatre, Washington, D.C.

Flanagan, Hallie. *Arena*. New York: Duell, Sloan, and Pearce, 1940.

Ford, Paul Leicester, ed. *The Writings of Thomas Jefferson*. New York: G P. Putnam's Sons, 1892-98.

Garnett, Michael. "Nothing to Write About." *Federal Theatre* II/1 (n.d.).

Geismar, Maxwell. "No Man Alone Now." *Virginia Quarterly Review* XVII (September 1941): 515-34.

Ginger, Ray. *Age of Excess—The United States from 1877 to 1914*. New York: Macmillan, 1965.

Gold, Mike. "Toward an American Revolutionary Culture." *New Masses* (July 1931): 13, and other articles in *New Masses* and *The Daily Worker*

"Government Vandalism." *The New Republic* (July 14, 1937), Vol. LXXXXI, No. 1180, pp. 265–66.

Greven, Philip. "Family Structure in Seventeenth Century Andover, Massachusetts." *William and Mary Quarterly*. 3d Ser., XXIII (1966):234–56.

Gross, Robert A. *The Minutemen and Their World*. New York: Hill & Wang, 1976.
Gummere, Richard M. *The American Colonial Mind and the Classic Tradition*. Cambridge: Harvard University Press, 1963.
The Harbinger (Boston).
Harris, Seymour. *A Statistical Portrait of Higher Education*. A Report for the Carnegie Commission. New York: McGraw-Hill, 1972.
The International (New York), 1912–1913.
Jackson, John Brinckerohoff. *American Space, The Centennial Years, 1865–1890*. New York: W. W. Norton and Company, 1972.
Johnson, James Weldon. *The Autobiography of an Ex-Coloured Man*. New York: Alfred A. Knopf, 1927.
Jones, Howard Mumford. *Ideas in America*. Cambridge: Harvard University Press, 1974.
Josephson, Matthew. *Portrait of the Artist as American*. New York: Harcourt, Brace and Company, 1930.
Kallen, H. M. "The Arts and Thomas Jefferson." *Ethics* LIII/4 (July 1934).
The Kenyon Review, Giambier, Ohio, 1937.
Kirkland, Joseph. *The Story of Chicago*. Chicago: Dibble Publ. Co., 1892.
Kohn, Hans. *American Nationalism*. New York: Macmillan, 1957.
Labaree, Leonard, ed. *The Papers of Benjamin Franklin*. New Haven: Yale University Press, 1968.
Lerner, Max. *America As Civilization*. New York: Simon & Schuster, 1957.
———. *A Troubled Feast*. Boston: Little, Brown, rev. ed., 1979.
Leuchtenburg, William E. *Franklin D. Roosevelt and the New Deal, 1932–1940*. New York: Harper & Row, 1963.
McDonald, William F. *Federal Relief Administration and the Arts*. Columbus: Ohio State University Press, 1969.
McKinzie, Richard D. *The New Deal for Artists*. Princeton: Princeton University Press, 1973.
Maass, John. *Tlhe Glorious Enterprise: The Centennial Exhibition of 1876 and H. J. Schwartzmann, Architect-in-Chief*. Watkins Glen, N.Y.: American Life Foundation, 1973.
Mangione, Jerre. *The Dream and the Deal*. Boston: Little, Brown, 1973.
Marling, Karal Ann. *Wall-to-Wall America, A Cultural History of Post-Office Murals in the Great Depression*. Minneapolis: University of Minnesota Press, 1982.
Mather, Cotton. *Magnalia Christi Americana; or The ecclesiastical history of New England, from its first planting in 1620 unto the year of our Lord, 1698*. London: T. Parkhurst, 1702.
Mathews, Jane deHart. "Arts and the People: The New Deal Quest for a Cultural Democracy." *Journal of American History*. LXII/2 (September 1975): 316–39.
———. *The Federal Theatre, 1935–1939: Plays, Relief, and Politics*. Princeton: Princeton University Press, 1967.
Miller, Perry. *Errand Into the Wilderness*. Cambridge: Belknap Press of Harvard University Press, 1956.
———. *Nature's Nation*. Cambridge: Belknap Press of Harvard University Press, 1967.
Mock, James, and Larson, Cedric. *Words That Won the War*. Princeton: Princeton University Press, 1939.

Morrison, Samuel Eliot. *Harvard College in the Seventeenth Century*. Cambridge: Harvard University Press, 1936.
NEA News. Washington, D.C.: National Endowment for the Arts.
The New Freeman. 1930.
New York Daily Tribune. 1917–1919.
The New York Post. 1917–1919.
New York Quarterly. 1850–51.
The New York Times. 1917–1919, 1930–1940.
Nicolai, Richard R. *Centennial Philadelphia*. Bryn Mawr, Pa.: Bryn Mawr Press, 1976.
83/84 New Music Performance and Chamber Music. Washington, D.C.: National Endowment for the Arts, 1982.
Orton, William Alyott. *America in Search of Culture*. Boston: Little, Brown, 1933.
Overmeyer, Grace. *Government and the Arts*. New York: W. W. Norton and Company, 1939.
Public Ledger (Philadelphia), 1876.
Purcell, Ralph. *Government and Art: A Study of the American Experience*. Washington, D.C.: Public Affairs Press, 1956.
Rice Institute Pamphlets. Houston: Rice University.
Rourke, Constance. *The Roots of American Culture*. New York: Harcourt, Brace and Company, 1942.
Santayana, George. *Character and Opinion in the United States*. New York: W. W. Norton and Company, 1967.
School and Society, Vol. VII (June 22, 1918).
Seldes, Gilbert. *The Seven Lively Arts*. New York: Harper and Brothers, 1924.
Shannon, Fred A. *The Centennial Years*. Garden City, N.Y.: Doubleday and Company, 1967.
Shattuck, Roger. *The Banquet Years*. New York: Vintage, 1955.
Smith, Henry Nash, ed. *Popular Culture and Industrialism 1865–1890*. New York: New York University Press, 1967.
Smith, Rev. Sydney. Review of Adam Seybert's *Statistical Annals of the United States of America* in *The Edinburgh Review* XXXIII (January 1820).
Sparks, Jared, ed. *The Works of Benjamin Franklin*. Boston: Charles Tappan, 1848.
Stearns, Harold E., ed. *Civilization in the United States: An Inquiry by Thirty Americans*. New York: Harcourt, Brace and Company, 1922.
Strout, Cushing. *The American Image of the Old World*. New York: Harper & Row, 1963.
Susman, Warren I. *Culture and Commitment*. New York: George Braziller, 1973.
———. *Culture as History, The Transformation of American Society in the Twentieth Century*. New York: Pantheon, 1973, 1984.
Theatre Arts Monthly (New York), 1938.
Todd, Frank Morton. *The Story of the Exposition*. New York: G. P. Putnam's Sons, 1921.
Todd, Lewis Paul. *Wartime Relations of the Federal Government and the Public Schools*. New York: Bureau of Publications, Teachers College, Columbia University, 1945.
Trachtenberg, Alan. *The Incorporation of America, Culture and Society in the Gilded Age*. New York: Hill & Wang, 1982.
Trent, William P., and Wells, Benjamin H., eds., *Colonial Prose and Poetry—The*

Transplanting of Culture, 1607–1650. New York: Thomas Y. Crowell, 1901.
"Unemployed Arts," *Fortune*. XV/5 (May 1937).
United States Centennial Commission. *International Exhibition, 1876*, Vol. II, *Reports of the President, Secretary, and Executive Committee*. Washington, D.C.: U.S. Centennial Commission, 1880.
United States Office of Education. *Biennial Survey of American Education, 1936–1938*. Washington, D.C.: U.S. Office of Education.
United States Office of Education, *Digest of Educational Statistics, 1982*. Washington, D.C.: U.S. Office of Education, 1982.
Van Brunt, Henry. "The Columbian Exposition and American Civilization," *The Atlantic Monthly*, Vol. LXXI (May 1893): 577–88.
Van Doren, Mark, ed. *Samuel Sewall's Diary*. New York: Macy-Masius Publishers, 1927.
Webster, Noah. *Dissertations on the English Language*. Boston: Isaiah Thomas & Company, 1789.
Weightman, John. *The Concept of the Avant-Garde*. LaSalle, Ill. Library Press Incorporated, 1973.
Wertenbaker, Thomas J. *The Golden Age of Colonial Culture*. Ithaca, N.Y.: Great Seal Books, 1949.
White, Morton, and Schlesinger, Arthur M., eds., *Paths of American Thought*. New York: Houghton Mifflin, 1963.
Wiebe, Robert. *The Search for Order, 1877-1920*. New York: Hill & Wang, 1967.
Wittler, Clarence J. "Some Social Trends in WPA Drama." Ph.D. diss., Catholic University, 1939.
Ziff, Larzer. *The American 1890s*. New York: Viking Press, 1966.
Zuckerman, Michael, "The Social Context of Democracy in Massachusetts," *William and Mary Quarterly*. 3d Ser., XXV (1968): 523–44.

II. Music Sources: Books, Documents, Scores, and Unpublished Works

Aborn, Merton Robert. "The Influence on American Musical Culture of Dvořák's Sojourn in America." Ph.D. diss., Indiana University, 1965.
Aird. *Selection of Scotch, English, Irish, and Foreign Airs for the Fife, Violin, or German Flute*. Glasgow: 1775.
Aldrich, Richard. *Concert Life in New York, 1902–1923*. New York: G P. Putnam's Sons, 1941.
American Society of University Composers. *Proceedings*. (1976–77).
Anderson. E. Ruth. *Contemporary American Composers: A Biographical Dictionary*. Boston: G. K. Hall and Company, 1976.
Antheil, George. *Bad Boy of Music*. Garden City, N.Y.: Doubleday, Doran, 1945.
Baker, Theodor. "Uber die Musik der nordamerikanischen Wilden." Leipzig: Breitkopf & Hartel, 1882.
Barnes, Edwin C. *Near Immortals? Stephen Foster, Edward MacDowell, Victor Herbert*. Washington, D.C.: Music Education Publications, 1940.
Barzun, Jacques. *Music in American Life*. Bloomington: Indiana University Press, 1956.
Baskerville, David Ross. "Jazz Influence on Art Music to Mid-Century." Ph.D. diss., UCLA, 1965.

Billings, William. *The New-England Psalm Singer, or American Chorister*. Boston: Edes & Gill, 1770.

———. *The Singing Master's Assistant*. Boston: Draper & Folsom, 1778.

Blitzstein, Marc. "Marc Blitzstein Discusses His Theater Compositions." *Spoken Arts Records*, No. 717.

Boston Symphony Orchestra Programmes, 1900–1920.

Calvocoressi, Michel Dimitri. *Musicians Gallery*. London: Faber & Faber, Limited, 1933.

Canon, Cornelius Baird. "The Federal Music Project of the Works Progress Administration: Music in a Democracy." Ph.D. diss., University of Minnesota, 1963.

Carpenter, John Alden. *Skyscrapers: A Ballet of Modern American Life*. New York: G. Schirmer, 1926.

Centano, Augusto, ed. *The Intent of the Artist*. Princeton: Princeton University Press, 1941.

Chadwick, George W. *Horatio Parker*. New Haven: Yale University Press, 1921.

Chase, Gilbert. *America's Music*. New York: McGraw-Hill, 1955, rev. ed. 1966.

The Columbian Magazine or Musical Miscellany. Philadelphia, 1778.

Comment and Criticism on the Work of Henry F. Gilbert, Composer. Boston, 1926.

Composers' Forum-Laboratory Concert Transcripts.

Cooke, George Willis. *John Sullivan Dwight, Brook-Farmer, Editor, and Critic*. Boston: Small, Maynard and Company, 1898; reprint, New York: Da Capo Press, 1969.

Copland, Aaron. *Copland on Music*. Garden City, N.Y.: Doubleday and Company, 1960.

———. *Music and Imagination*. Cambridge: Harvard University Press, 1952.

———. *The New Music*. New York: W. W. Norton and Company, 1941.

Copland, Aaron, and Perlis, Vivian. *Copland, 1900 Through 1942*. New York: St. Martin's/Marek, 1984.

Cotton, John. *Singing of Psalmes a Gospel Ordinance*. London, 1647.

Cowell, Henry, and Cowell, Sidney Robertson. *Charles Ives and His Music*. New York: Oxford University Press, 1955.

Crawford, Richard. *American Studies and American Musicology, A Point of View and a Case in Point*. New York: International Society for American Music, 1975.

Crawford, Richard, and Hitchcock, H. Wiley. *Andrew Law—Tunesmith*. Ann Arbor: William L. Clements Library, 1961.

Dobrin, Arnold. *Aaron Copland, His Life and Times*. New York: Thomas Y. Crowell, 1967.

Duke, Vernon. *Passport to Paris*. Boston: Little, Brown and Company, 1955.

Eastman School of Music, University of Rochester Alumni Bulletin. Vol. 16, Nos. 3–4 (June 1945).

Edwards, Allen. *Flawed Words and Stubborn Sounds, A Conversation with Elliott Carter*. New York: W. W. Norton, 1971.

Elson, Louis C. *The History of American Music*. New York: Lenox Hill Publishing Co., 1901.

Ewen, David. *Music Comes to America*. New York: Thomas Y. Crowell, 1942.

Faulkner, Robert R. *Music on Demand, Composers and Careers in the Hollywood Film Industry*. New Brunswick: Transaction Books, 1983.

Finck, Henry T. *My Adventures in the Golden Age of Music.* New York: Funk & Wagnalls, 1926.

———. *Wagner and His Works.* New York: Charles Scribner, 1893.

Findley, Jannelle Warren. "Of Tears and Need: The Federal Music Project, 1935–1943." Ph.D. diss., George Washington University, 1973.

Foote, Arthur. *An Autobiography.* Norwood, Mass.: Plimpton Press, 1946.

Fortnightly Musical Review (New York), 1928.

Foss, Hubert, and Noel Goodwin, *London Symphony—Portrait of an Orchestra* (London: The Naldrett Press, 1954), 77.

Foster, George. "A Record of Program Operation and Accomplishments: The Federal Music Project, 1935–1939; the WPA Music Program, 1939–1943." Washington, D.C.: WPA Music Program, 1943. Record Group 69, Interior Division, National Archives and Record Service.

French, Richard T., ed. *Music and Criticism, A Symposium.* Cambridge: Harvard University Press, 1948.

Gahimer, Lora. "Attitudes on Contemporary Composition, As Exemplified by Copland, Hanson, Harris and Moore." M.A. essay, Eastman School of Music, 1947.

Gottschalk, Louis Moreau. *Notes of a Pianist.* New York: Alfred A. Knopf, 1964.

Grabs, Manfred, ed. *Hanns Eisler: A Rebel in Music.* New York: International Publishers, 1978.

Gram, Hans; Holyoke, Samuel; and Holden, Oliver. *Massachusetts Compiler of Theoretical and Practical Elements of Sacred Vocal Music . . . Chiefly selected or adapted from modern European publications.* Boston: Isaiah Thomas and Ebenezer T. Andrews, 1795.

Hadow, Sir William H. *Collected Essays.* London: Oxford University Press, 1928.

Heinrich, Anthony Philip. *The Dawning of Music in Kentucky.* Philadelphia: Bacon & Hart: 1820.

History of the Marine Band. Philadelphia: United States Corps Publicity Bureau, 1937.

Hitchcock. H. Wiley. *Music in the United States: A Historical Introduction.* Englewood Cliffs, N.J.: Prentice-Hall, 1969.

Hoover, Kathleen, and Cage, John. *Virgil Thomson, His Life and Music.* New York: Thomas Yoseloff, 1959.

Howard, John Tasker. *Our American Music.* New York: Thomas Y. Crowell, 1936.

———. *The Music of George Washington's Time.* Washington, D.C.: United States George Washington Bicentennial Commission, 1931.

Howe, M. A. DeWolfe. *The Boston Symphony Orchestra, 1881–1931.* Boston: Houghton Mifflin Company, 1931.

Hubbard. John. "An Essay on Music, Pronounced before the Middlesex Musical Society, Sept. 9, A.D. 1807 at Dunstable, Massachusetts."

Hubbard. W. L., ed. *History of American Music.* Toledo, Ohio: I. Squire, 1908.

Hughes, Rupert. *Contemporary American Composers.* Boston: L. C. Page and Company, 1900.

Ives, Charles Edward. *Essays Before a Sonata.* New York: W. W. Norton and Company, 1961.

Johnson, Ellis A. "The Chicago Symphony Orchestra, 1891–1942—A Study in American Cultural History." Ph.D. diss., University of Chicago, 1955.

Johnson, Harriett. *Your Career in Music*. New York: E. P. Dutton, Incorporated, 1944.

Kendall, Alan. *The Tender Tyrant, Nadia Boulanger, A Life Devoted to Music*. Wilton, Conn.: Lyceum Books, 1977.

Kennedy, Michael, ed. *The Concise Oxford Dictionary of Music*. New York: Oxford University Press, 1980.

Lang, Paul Henry. *One Hundred Years of Music in America*. New York: G. Schirmer, 1961.

Law, Andrew. *Musical Primer*. Cheshire, Conn.: William Law, 1793.

Leichentritt, Hugo. *Serge Koussevitzky, The Boston Symphony Orchestra, and the New American Music*. Cambridge: Harvard University Press, 1946.

Levy, Alan Howard. *Musical Nationalism—American Composers' Search for Identity*. Westport, Conn.: Greenwood Press, 1983.

Liebowitz, Herbert A., ed. *Musical Impressions: Selections from Paul Rosenfeld's Criticism*. New York: Hill & Wang, 1969.

Lowens, Irving. *Music and Musicians in Early America*. New York: W. W. Norton and Company, 1964.

———. *Music in America and American Music*. New York: International Society for American Music, 1978.

McKay, David P. and Crawford, Richard. *William Billings of Boston*. Princeton: Princeton University Press, 1975.

Machlis, Joseph. *American Composers of Our Time*. New York: Thomas Y. Crowell, 1963.

———. *Introduction to Contemporary Music*. New York: W. W. Norton and Company, 1979.

Martens, Frederick. *Leo Ornstein, The Man, His Ideas, His Work*. New York: Breitkopf & Harter, 1918; reprint, New York: Arno Press, 1975.

Mason, Daniel Gregory, ed. *The Art of Music*, Vol. IV, *Music In America*. New York: The National Society of Music, 1915.

———. *The Dilemma of American Music*. New York: Macmillan, 1928.

Mason, Lowell. *The Boston Handel and Haydn Society Collection of Church Music*. Boston: Richardson & Lord, 1823.

Mather, Cotton. *The Accomplished Singer*. Boston: B. Green for Samuel Gerrish, 1721.

Matthews, W. S. B., ed. *A Hundred Years of Music in America*. Chicago, 1898; reprint, New York: AMS Press, 1970.

Mees, Arthur. *Program Collection*, Chicago World's Columbian Exposition, May-October 1893. Chicago: Privately printed, 1983.

Milhaud, Darius. *Notes Without Music*. London: Denis Dobson, 1952.

Morgenstern, Sam, ed. *Composers on Music*. New York: Pantheon, 1956.

Musical America's Guide. New York: Musical America, 1926–28.

National Conservatory of Music (New York) *Concert Programs*, 1868.

New York Philharmonic Society *Concert Programs*, 1842–1926.

Newman, Ernest. *More Essays from the World of Music*. London: John Calder, 1958.

———. *A Musical Critic's Holiday*. New York: Alfred A. Knopf, 1925.

———. *Testament of Music*. New York: Alfred A. Knopf, 1963.

Official Monthly Bulletin of the Great National Peace Jubilee and Music Festival, No. 1, February, 1869.

Parker, John R. *Musical Biography; or, Sketches of the Lives and Writings of Eminent Musical Characters*. Boston: Stone & Fovell, 1824.

Peace Jubilee Programs (1872), Boston.

Perry, Rosalie Sandra. *Charles Ives and the American Mind*. Kent, Ohio: Kent State University Press, 1974.

Red Song Book. New York: Workers' Music Library Publishers, 1932.

Reese, Gustave, ed. *A Birthday Offering to Carl Engel*. New York: G. Schirmer, 1943.

Reis, Claire R. *Composers, Conductors, and Critics*. New York: Oxford University Press, 1955.

Reuss, Richard A. "American Folklore and Left-Wing Politics, 1929–1957." Ph.D. diss., Indiana University, 1971.

Rosenfeld, Paul. *Musical Portraits, Interpretations of Twenty Modern Composers*. New York: Harcourt, Brace & Howe, 1920.

Rosensteil, Leonie. *Nadia Boulanger, A Life in Music*. New York: W. W. Norton and Company, 1982.

Rossiter, Frank. *Charles Ives and His America*. New York: Liveright, 1975.

Russell, Charles Edward. *The American Orchestra and Theodore Thomas*. Garden City, N.Y.: Doubleday, Page and Company, 1927.

Russell, Thomas, *The Proms* (London: Max Parrish, 1949), 49

Sablonsky, Irving L. *American Music*. Chicago: University of Chicago Press, 1969.

Sadie, Stanley, ed. *The New Grove Dictionary of Music and Musicians*. New York: Macmillan, 1980.

Schauffler, Robert Haven, and Spaeth, Sigmund. *Music as a Social Force in America*. New York: The Caxton Institute, 1927.

Schickel, Richard. *The World of Carnegie Hall*. New York: Julian Messner, 1960.

Schwartz, Charles. *George Gershwin, His Life and Music*. Indianapolis: Bobbs-Merrill Company, Incorporated, 1973.

Seeger, Charles Louis. "Music as Recreation." Community Service Circular No. 1 (May 1940).

———. *Studies in Musicology, 1935–1975*. Berkeley and Los Angeles: University of California Press, 1977.

Sessions, Roger. *The Musical Experience of Composer, Performer, Listener*. Princeton: Princeton University Press, 1950.

———. *Reflections on the Musical Life of the United States*. New York: Merlin Press, 1956.

Shanet, Howard. *Philharmonic: A History of New York's Orchestra*. Garden City, N.Y.: Doubleday and Company, 1975.

Shaw, George Bernard. *Shaw on Music*. Garden City: Doubleday and Company, Incorporated, 1956.

Shead, Richard. *Music in the Twenties*. New York: St. Martin's Press, 1976.

Slonimsky, Nicholas. *Lexicon of Musical Invective, Critical Assaults on Composers Since Beethoven's Time*. New York: Coleman-Ross, 1965.

Smith, Julia. *Aaron Copland—His Work and Contribution to American Music*. New York: E. P. Dutton & Co., 1955.

Stone, Else and Kurt, eds. *The Writings of Elliott Carter*. Bloomington: Indiana University Press, 1971.

Stravinsky, Igor, and Craft, Robert. *Exposition and Developments*. Garden City: Doubleday and Company, 1962.

Swan, John C., ed. *Music in Boston, Readings from the First Three Centuries*. Boston: Trustees of the Public Library of the City of Boston, 1977.

Symmes, Thomas. *The Reasonableness of Regular Singing, or, Singing by Note*. Boston: B. Green for Samuel Gerrish, 1720.

———. *Utile Dulci, Or, A Joco-Serious Dialogue Concerning Regular Singing*. Boston: B. Green for Samuel Gerrish, 1723.

Tawa, Nicholas E. *Serenading the Reluctant Eagle, American Musical Life, 1925–1945*. New York: Schirmer Books, 1984.

Thomas, Rose Fay. *Memoirs of Theodore Thomas*. New York: Moffat, Yard and Company, 1911.

Thomas, Tony, ed. *Film Score, The View from the Podium*. South Brunswick, N.J.: A. S. Barnes and Company, 1979.

Thompson, Oscar. *Great Modern Composers*. New York: Dodd, Mead, 1941.

———. *Practical Musical Criticism*. New York: M. Whitmark & Sons, 1934.

Thompson, Randall. *College Music, An Investigation for the Association of American Colleges*. New York: Macmillan, 1935.

Thomson, Virgil. *American Music Since 1910*. New York: Holt, Rinehart & Winston, 1970.

———. *The State of Music*. New York: Vintage, 1939.

———. *Virgil Thomson*. New York: Alfred A. Knopf, 1966.

Upton, George, ed. *Theodore Thomas, A Musical Biography*. Chicago: A. C. McClurg, 1905. Reprinted, New York: DaCapo Press, 1964.

Upton, William Treat. *Anthony Philip Heinrich*. New York: Columbia University Press, 1967.

———. *William Henry Fry*. New York: Thomas Y. Crowell, 1954.

Van Vechten, Carl. *Music and Bad Manners*. New York: Alfred A. Knopf, 1916.

Walker, Alan. *An Anatomy of Musical Criticism*. Philadelphia: Chilton Book Company, 1968.

Willis, Wayne Carr. "A Fanfare for the Common Man: Nationalism and Democracy in the Arts of the American 1930s." Ph.D. diss., Brandeis University, 1977.

Wister, Frances Anne. *Twenty-five Years of the Philadelphia Orchestra*. Philadelphia: Edward Stern and Company, 1925.

Workers Song Book. New York: Workers' Music League, U.S.A. Section of the International Music Bureau, 1934.

Workers Song Book 2. New York: Workers' Music League U.S.A. Section of the International Music Bureau, 1935.

Zanzig, Augustus Delafield. *Music in American Life, Present and Future*. New York: Oxford University Press, 1932.

Zuck, Barbara Ann. *A History of Musical Americanism*. Ann Arbor: UMI Research Press, 1980.

III. Music Sources: Articles and Periodicals

American Composers' Alliance *Bulletin*, 1938, 1952.

American Musicological Society, *Papers*.

Barzun, Jacques. "Music: For Money or Love?" *Harper's* (May 1956): 40–46.

Blitzstein, Marc. "Music Manifestto." *New Masses* (January 23, 1936).
Borowski, Felix. "John Alden Carpenter, American Craftsman." *Musical Quarterly* XVI/4 (October 1930): 443–48.
Boulanger, Nadia. "Lectures on Modern Music," delivered January 27–29, 1925. *The Rice Institute Pamphlets.* Vol. XIII, No. 2 (April 1926).
The British Musician (London), 1893–1908.
Broder, Nathan. "The Music of William Schuman." *Musical Quarterly* XXXI/1 (January 1945): 17–28.
Bukofzer, Manfred. "The New Nationalism." *Modern Music* XXIV/4 (Fall 1946):243–47.
Cadman, Charles Wakefield. "The Idealization of Indian Music." *Musical Quarterly* I/3 (July 1915): 387–96.
Carter, Elliott. "The Rhythmic Basis of American Music." *The Score—A Musical Magazine* (London) No. 12 (June 1955).
Chotzinoff, Samuel. "George Gershwin's 'Rhapsody in Blue'." *Vanity Fair* XXII/6 (August 1924): 28, 82.
Composers' News Record (New York).
Copland, Aaron. "America's Young Men of Promise." *Modern Music* III/3 (March–April 1926): 13–20.
———. "Music Since 1920." *Modern Music* V/3 (March-April 1928): 16–20.
———. "Workers Sing!" *New Masses.* (June 12, 1934).
Cowell, Henry. "Useful Music." *New Masses.* (October 29, 1935).
Crawford, Richard. "A Historical Introduction to Early American Music." *American Antiquarian Society Papers* (1979).
Damrosch, Frank. "The American Conservatory, Its Aims and Possibilities." *Music Teachers' National Association Studies in Musical Education, History, and Aesthetics* (1906): 13–20.
DeKoven, Reginald. "Opera in English and its Bearing on the American Composer and Music in America." *Proceedings of the American Academy of Arts and Letters.* Vol. VII (1914).
Dietz, Robert J. "Marc Blitzstein and the 'Agit Prop' Theatre of the 1930s." *Yearbook of the Inter-American Institute for Musical Research* (Tulane University, 1970): 51–67.
Downes, Olin. "American Music at the Rochester Festival." *The New York Times* (May 3, 1931): X-8.
———. "An American Composer." *Musical Quarterly* IV/1 (January 1918): 23–36.
Dwight, John Sullivan. "Father Heinrich in Boston." *The Harbinger* III/4 (July 4, 1846).
Dwight's Journal of Music (1852-81), Boston.
Einstein, Alfred. "The Composer, the State and Today." *Modern Music* XIII/1 (November-December 1935): 3–12.
Eisler, Hanns. "Reflections on the Future of the Composer." *Modern Music* XII/3 (May–June 1935): 178–86.
Engel, Carl. "George W. Chadwick." *Musical Quarterly* X/3 (July 1924): 438–57.
Erb, J. Lawrence. "The Movement for a National Conservatory of Music and for a Secretary of Fine Arts in the President's Cabinet." *Music Teachers' National Association Studies* (1921): 30–36.

———. "Music in the Education of the Common Man." *Musical Quarterly* V/3 (July 1919): 308–15.

Erskine, John. "MacDowell at Columbia: Some Reflections." *Musical Quarterly* XXVII/4 (October 1942): 395–405.

Euterpiad, or Musical Intelligencer (1822), Boston.

Farwell, Arthur. "Roy Harris." *Musical Quarterly* XVIII/1 (January 1932): 18–32.

———. "The Struggle Toward a National Music." *North American Review* DCXXV (December 1907).

———. "The Zero Hour in Musical Evolution." *Musical Quarterly* XX/1 (January 1927): 85–99.

Gilbert, Henry F. "The American Composer." *Musical Quarterly* I/2 (April 1915): 169–80.

———. "Folk Music in Art-Music—A Discussion and a Theory." *Musical Quarterly* III/4 (October 1917): 577–601.

———. "Music After the War." *The New Music Review and Church Music Review* XIX/218 (January 1920), 45–46.

———. "Nationalism in Music," *The International* VII/2 (December 1913).

———. "Notes on a Trip to Frankfurt in the Summer of 1927, With Some Thoughts on Modern Music." *Musical Quarterly* XVI/1 (January 1930): 21–37.

Goldberg, Isaac. "An American Composer." *The American Mercury* XX/59 (November 1928): 330–35.

Hadow, W. H. "Some Aspects of Modern Music." *Musical Quarterly* I/1 (January 1915): 57–68.

Hamilton, Iain. "The University and the Composing Profession: Prospects and Problems." *Proceedings of the American Society of University Composers* (1966).

Hanson, Howard. "Creation of an American Music." *Music Teachers' National Association Studies* (1926), 229–41.

———. "American Procession at Rochester." *Modern Music* XIII/3 (March–April 1936): 22–28.

———. "Some Suggestions Concerning Graduate Study in Music in the United States." *Music Teachers' National Association Studies* (1933): 99–104.

———. "Twenty Years' Growth in America." *Modern Music* XX/2 (January-February 1943): 95–101.

Harris, Henry J. "The Occupation of Musician in the United States." *Musical Quarterly* I/2 (April 1915): 299–311

Harris, Roy. "The Crisis in Music 2." *The New Freeman* I/6 (April 19, 1930): 134–37.

Henderson, W. H. "Why No Great American Music?" *The American Mercury* XXXII/127 (July 1934): 295–304.

Hewes, Harry L. "Indexing America's Composers." *The Christian Science Monitor*. (April 5, 1941): 7, 12.

Hill, Edward Burlingame. "Jazz." *Harvard Graduates' Magazine* XXXIV 135 (March 1926).

Howard, John Tasker. "The American Composer: Victim of his Friends." *Musical Quarterly* VIII/3 (July 1922): 313–18.

———. "Creative Music in America." *American Magazine of Art* XXII/6 (June 1931): 475–78.

Howe, M. A. DeWolfe. "John Knowles Paine." *Musical Quarterly* XXV/3 (July 1939): 257–67.

Hunter, John O. "Marc Blitzstein's 'The Cradle Will Rock' as a Document of America, 1937." *American Quarterly* XVII/2 (Summer 1966): 227–33.

Jacobi, Frederick. "Homage to Arthur Foote." *Modern Music* XIV/4 (May–June 1937): 198–99.

Kolodin, Irving. "Concert Hall into Theatre. *Theatre Arts Monthly* (October 1938): 727–32.

Kramer, A. Walter. "American Creative Art." *Proceedings, National Federation of Music Clubs* (1937), 39–46.

Kramer, Jonathan D. "Teaching Music to the Amateur Through Composition." *Proceedings, American Society of University Composers* (1976–77).

Lederman, Minna. "No Money for Music." *North American Review* 243/1 (Spring 1937): 124–36.

Leonard, Neil. "Edward MacDowell and the Realists." *American Quarterly* XVII/2 (Summer 1966): 175–82.

Loft, Abram. "Richard Wagner, Theodore Thomas, and the American Centennial." *Musical Quarterly* XXXVII/2 (April 1951): 184–202.

Lowens, Irving. "Writings About Music in the Periodicals of American Transcendentalism." *Journal of the American Musicological Society* X/2 (Summer 1957).

Luening, Otto. "Music." *Proceedings of the Americal Philosophical Society* XXXIII/4 (September 1940): 569–72.

McConathy, Osbourne. "A Musical America." *Music Teachers' National Association Studies* (1921), 11–22.

Mason, Daniel Gregory. "The Depreciation of Music." *Musical Quarterly* XV/1 (January 1929): 6–15.

———. "Sensationalism and Indifference." *Virginia Quarterly Review* I/1 (April 1925): 88–93.

———. "What Can We Do for American Music? *American Magazine of Art* XXIII/2 (August 1931): 138–42.

Mellers, Wilfred. "Language and Function in American Music." *Scrutiny* (Cambridge) X/4 (April 1942): 346–57.

Mitchell, Nahum. "William Billings." *The Musical Reporter*, No. 7 (1841).

Moller, Heinrich. "Can Women Compose?" *The Musical Observer* XV/5 (May 1917): 9–10 and XV/6 (June 1917): 11–12.

Moore, Earl Vincent. "Choral Music and the WPA Music Program." *Music Teachers' National Association Studies, in Musical Education, History, and Aesthetics* (1939): 334–38.

Morin, Raymond. "William Billings—Pioneer in American Music." *The New England Quarterly* XIV/1 (march 1941): 25–33.

Morris, Harold. "American Composers and Critics." *National Music Council Bulletin* V/3 (May 1945): 7–8.

Music Supervisors Bulletin (National Council of Music Supervisors), 1915–1918.

Music Teachers National Association, *Papers and Proceedings* (Hartford, Conn.), 1906–1949.

Musical America (New York), 1905–1945.

The Musical Courier (New York), 1932–1934.

Musical Facts (New York), 1940–1941.

Musical Observer (New York), 1916–1930.

Musical Standard (London), 1921–1928.

Overmeyer, Grace. "The Musician Starves." *The American Mercury* XXXII/126 (June 1934): 224–31.

Pettis, Ashley. "Music Of, By and For the People." *New Masses* (June 26, 1934).

———. "Second Workers' Music Olympiad." *New Masses* (May 22, 1934).

———. "The WPA and the American Composer." *Musical Quarterly* XXVI/1 (January 1940): 101–12.

"The Problem of the Foreign-Born Artist: Controversial Views of the Dickstein Bill." *Musical America* LVII/3 (February 10, 1937): 16–17, 185.

Ranck, Edwin Carty. "The Mark Twain of American Music." *Theatre Magazine* XXVI/9 (September 1917).

Rosenfeld, Paul. "The Advent of American Music." *The Kenyon Review*, Vol. I (Winter 1939): 46–56.

Seeger, Charles Louis. "Grass Roots for American Composers." *Modern Music* XVI/3 (March-April 1939): 143–49.

———. "On Proletarian Music." *Modern Music* XI/3 (March–April 1934): 121–27.

Seldes, Gilbert. "American Noises: How to Make Them—And Why." *Vanity Fair* XXII/4 (June 1924): 59, 86.

Sessions, Roger. "America Moves to the Avant Scene." *Music Teachers' National Association Studies* (1937): 9–20.

———. "Music in Crisis." *Modern Music* X/2 (January–February 1933): 63–78.

———. "On the American Future." *Modern Music* XVII/2 (January–February 1940): 71–75.

Siegmeister, Elie. "Social Influences in Modern Music." *The Modern Monthly* VII/8 (September 1933): 472–79.

Sinclair, Upton. "MacDowell." *The American Mercury* VII/25 (January 1926): 50–54.

Slonimsky. Nicholas. "Composers of New England." *Modern Music* VII/2 (February–March 1930): 24–27.

Smith, David Stanley. "A Study of Horatio Parker." *Musical Quarterly* XVI/2 (April 1930): 153–69.

Sokoloff, Nicholai. "The Federal Music Project." *Music Teachers' National Association Studies* (19346), 56–62.

Sonneck, Oscar G. "The American Composers and the American Publisher." *Music Teachers' National Association Studies* (1922).

———. "To Be or Not To Be—A Critic." *The Musician* VII (September 1903): 321.

Spalding, Walter R. "The War in Relation to American Music." *Musical Quarterly* IV/1 (January 1918): 1–11.

Stein, Leon. "The Materials of Contemporary Music." *The Journal of Musicology* IV/2 (December 1954): 51–88.

Sternfeld, Frederick W. "Copland as a Film Composer." *Musical Quarterly* XXXVII/2 (April 1951): 161–75.

Stock, Frederick A. "Bringing Music to the Nation: Some Recipes." *The Craftsman* XXIX (March 1916), 648-55,658.

"Teaching as a Composer's Craft—A Symposium." *Composers' News Record*, No. 9 (Spring 1949): 1–2.

Thompson, Randall. "The Contemporary Scene in American Music." *Musical Quarterly* XVIII/1 (January 1932): 9–17.

Thomson, Virgil. "The Cult of Jazz." *Vanity Fair* XXIV/4 (June 1925): 54, 118.

Upton, William Treat. "Secular Music in the United States One Hundred Fifty Years Ago." *American Musicological Society Papers* (1941).

Van Vechten, Carl. "George Gershwin, An American Composer Who is Writing Notable Music in the Jazz Idiom." *Vanity Fair* XXIV/3 (March 1925): 40, 78, 84.

von Sternberg, Constantin. "Against Modern'ism'." *Musical Quarterly* VII/1 (January 1921): 1–7.

Waters, Edward N. "The Wa-Wan Press—An Adventure in Musical Idealism" in Gustave Reese, ed., *A Birthday Offering to Carl Engel*. New York: G. Schirmer, 1943.

Weil, Irving. "The Noise Makers." *Modern Music* V/2 (January-February 1928): 24–28.

White, Elsie Fellows. "Music versus Nationalism." *Musical Quarterly* VIII/1 (January 1922): 38–43.

Winter, Marian Hannah. "The Function of Music in Sound Film." *Musical Quarterly* XXVIII/2 (April 1941): 146–64.

Index